LEGAL NEGOTIATION

THEORY AND PRACTICE

Second Edition

By

Donald G. Gifford

Edward M. Robertson Research Professor of Law
University of Maryland

AMERICAN CASEBOOK SERIES®

WEST

Mat # 40335765

American Casebook Series and West Group are trademarks
registered in the U.S. Patent and Trademark Office.

COPYRIGHT © 1989 WEST PUBLISHING CO.
© 2007 Thomson/West
    610 Opperman Drive
    P.O. Box 64526
    St. Paul, MN 55164–0526
    1–800–328–9352

ISBN: 978–0–314–15912–0

TEXT IS PRINTED ON 10% POST
CONSUMER RECYCLED PAPER

For Nancy, Rebecca and Jonathan, and Caroline

*

Preface

This book presents a comprehensive overview of legal negotiation for law students and lawyers studying their negotiating behavior. The analysis presented often is derived from the research of social scientists, but the book is specifically designed to teach the reader how to negotiate more effectively in the actual practice of law. Examples of specific negotiation techniques are included throughout the text, and theoretical models of social scientists are discussed only when the conclusions derived from them are directly relevant to legal negotiation. At the same time, the book avoids the mundane mechanics of both local negotiation practice and "pop-psychology."

Included within this single book are analyses of both competitive negotiation tactics and more collaborative approaches, such as problem-solving and cooperative tactics. No single negotiation strategy works best in all negotiations. Accordingly, the lawyer should be able to employ a variety of approaches and know when each tactic is most appropriate.

Most lawyers not only change their tactics from one negotiation to another, but also use a combination of varying tactics—for example, problem-solving and competitive tactics—within a single negotiation. For this reason, this text divides the negotiation process into six components or subprocesses: negotiation planning, initial orientation, initial proposals, information bargaining, narrowing of differences, and closure. This organization allows discussion in a single chapter of how the different approaches to negotiation—competitive, cooperative and problem solving—address each of these components of the negotiation process.

When the first edition of this book was published in 1989, the idea that the negotiator might employ both problem-solving and competitive tactics within a single negotiation was new within the legal literature. Today the recognition that both "value creation" and "value claiming" are inherent within the negotiation process is widely accepted. In this regard, as well as in many others, this new edition draws upon the excellent recent scholarship about bargaining from our colleagues in the business school world.

At the same time, legal negotiation is a form of client representation. The lawyer's role as an advocate changes the negotiation process in a number of ways that often are not considered in general negotiation texts written by social scientists or business school professors. This book includes separate chapters on Negotiation Planning and Negotiation Counseling, and the impact of the client on the bargaining process is stressed throughout the text.

It also includes a chapter addressing alternative dispute resolution, a topic that at last is deservedly receiving far more attention than it has in the past in the law school curriculum. Yet the centrality of the negotiation process to ADR is not always appreciated. Most forms of ADR serve as means of facilitating bargaining. To understand ADR processes and how they work, the student first must have a firm grounding in the negotiation process itself and appreciate why bargaining sometimes fails in the absence of mediation and other ADR processes.

This second edition has been enriched by the years I spent as Dean of the University of Maryland School of Law and earlier at the West Virginia University College of Law. Most of what I did as a dean was to negotiate with one constituency or another. When I returned to the classroom teaching of Negotiation, Steven Schwinn, my former colleague and team-teacher, taught me important lessons about how to teach negotiation to students more effectively. My colleague Rena Steinzor generously has contributed a superb environmental enforcement negotiation simulation that enriches the Teacher's Manual.

I also want to express my appreciation to Dean Karen H. Rothenberg of the University of Maryland School of Law, who generously has supported my scholarly endeavors, and to Professor Barbara Gontrum, who directs the Thurgood Marshall Law Library. Research librarian Maxine Grosshans was particularly helpful in locating new publications about negotiation, regardless of whether they were from the legal, social science, or business literature. I also thank my diligent and superbly capable student research assistants, Leslie Harrelson (Class of 2009), Jennifer BenEliyahu (Class of 2009), Rachel Hirsch (J.D., 2006) and, particularly, Tom Prevas (Class of 2008), for their wonderful help with research, editing, and proofreading, as well as my daughter Caroline Gifford for her assistance with proofreading. Finally, I express my gratitude to Marie Schwartz who assisted me with document preparation.

DONALD G. GIFFORD

Columbia, Maryland
August 2007

Summary of Contents

*

Table of Contents

*

LEGAL NEGOTIATION

THEORY AND PRACTICE

Second Edition

*

Chapter One

NEGOTIATION STRATEGY FOR LAWYERS

A. INTRODUCTION

1. LEARNING NEGOTIATION SKILLS

Early in the practice of law, the lawyer is sure to be asked, "Do you think we could settle this thing?" or "Could our clients work out a deal here?" Away from judicial chambers and the courtroom, the lawyer is thus initiated into the negotiation process, the single most prevalent and important legal decision-making system.

How can you prepare yourself for this moment? Certainly, knowledge of the substantive law affecting your client's situation will be important, as will be your ability to analyze the legal issues. And nothing is more important to your success as a negotiator than preparation—your understanding of the relevant facts and law and of your client's interests. Additional factors—your personality or your past relationship with the other lawyer—also play a role.

How well you serve your client's interests when you respond to that inquiry depends upon at least one other factor. Practicing attorneys know that a few among them are always able to get a good deal for their clients through skillful negotiation. They also know that skilled negotiators are not born. The ability to negotiate competently is not a trait like blue eyes, quick reflexes or the ability to roll one's tongue. All individuals "learn" to negotiate from infancy as they develop their abilities to influence Mom or Dad, classmates or teachers, to do what they want them to do. Beginning lawyers learn about "legal" negotiation by watching more experienced attorneys negotiate with them or against them. Eventually negotiating techniques are acquired—but often slowly and erratically. Some novice lawyers are fortunate enough to be working with capable negotiators; others are not.

This book provides both the necessary theoretical background and the specific techniques to make you a better negotiator. The prospect of *learning* to become a more effective negotiator should not be a startling one. Few law students and lawyers today would quarrel with the assertion that trial practice courses and texts can teach effective cross-examination skills, however novel that idea may have been a generation or two ago. Part of what is taught as the "art" of cross-examination depends upon the law of evidence, but the most important underpinnings of cross-examination skills lie in the behavioral reactions of the witness and the jurors to the type (leading!) and the pacing of questions. The art and science of negotiation similarly depend upon predictions as to how the other lawyer will respond to your strategic moves as a negotiator—your demands or proposals, arguments and questions. While the interactions of negotiators are less stylized than those of attorney and witness in the courtroom, they can be analyzed and understood in a manner that enables you to become a more capable negotiator.

This is a practical text, designed to assist the law student or lawyer in becoming a better negotiator. It is not merely a theoretical overview of the social psychology of negotiation or of game theory. On the other hand, it is not a cookbook or a mechanic's manual. To be sure, it describes a number of specific negotiating techniques, but the effective legal negotiator cannot be programmed in advance like a computer or trained like a seal. For the lawyer to know when to choose a particular technique, when to extrapolate from a described tactic or when to improvise totally, she[1] needs a fuller understanding of the psychology of legal negotiation. Therefore, the knowledge and theories of social psychologists and others who have studied negotiation will be described and analyzed when they provide helpful insights for the negotiating lawyer.

2. WHAT IS NEGOTIATION?

Everyone knows what negotiation is. Two parties face each other and haggle, whether over the price of an automobile, the terms of a commercial lease, or the control of a corporation. Adjudication, on the other hand, appears to be its polar opposite. Opposing advocates present evidence and arguments to a third party, either judge or jury, and await a binding decision.

The demarcation between these two processes, however, sometimes is obscure. If the prosecutor, in plea bargaining, makes the defendant a "take it or leave it offer" in a case in which the defendant otherwise faces certain conviction on higher charges, is that negotiation or is the prosecutor in reality functioning as a judge? If the parties in a complicated business dispute agree to participate in a "mini-trial,"[2] a formalized presentation of evidence to a third party, and they ask the third party to render a decision but stipulate that it is non-binding, is that an adjudication, a part of the negotiation process, or both?

---

1. Anyone writing about negotiation or other multiple-party human interactions in a modern context realizes the difficulty of pronoun selection. I refer to the principal negotiator as "she" throughout this text; her client and her negotiating counterpart typically are referred to as "he."

2. For a discussion of mini-trials, *see infra* Chapter 12, "Alternative Dispute Resolution and Negotiation," at 234–35.

For the purposes of this book, *negotiation* can be defined as a process in which two or more participants attempt to reach a joint decision on matters of common concern in situations where they are in actual or potential disagreement or conflict.[3] The factor distinguishing negotiation from adjudication is that the parties themselves—not someone else—determine the result, and they must consent to the outcome for it to be operative. Even when the prosecutor possesses overwhelming bargaining power, the plea bargain still requires the defendant's consent. Plea bargaining, therefore, remains negotiation. The "mini-trial" too is a negotiation technique. Although it looks like adjudication, the parties remain free to accept or reject the results of the "mini-trial" and decide the outcome.

Throughout this book the term "bargaining" will be used interchangeably with "negotiation," although many social scientists use it in a more restrictive sense to refer to the presentation and exchange of proposals for the terms of agreement on specific issues.[4]

3. THE CLIENT AND NEGOTIATION

If everyone negotiates constantly, what makes legal negotiation different? The most important distinction is that while the lawyer sometimes negotiates on her own behalf, such as when she negotiates her own salary or her office lease, the essence of legal negotiation is the lawyer's role as a representative of her client. Legal negotiations involve not only a relationship between the two negotiating attorneys, but also relationships between each lawyer and her respective client. The interactions between lawyer and client as a part of the negotiation process will be explored in a comprehensive manner in Chapter 10, "Negotiation Counseling," and the effects of the client on the negotiation process will be considered throughout this book. For now, three differences between legal negotiation and other negotiation are highlighted.

First, the client, and not the negotiator herself, should make the important substantive decisions in negotiation, such as whether to make or accept specific offers. The American Bar Association's *Model Rule of Professional Conduct 1.2* provides that "a lawyer shall abide by a client's decision whether to settle a matter."[5] The rule requires that the lawyer "abide by a client's decisions concerning the objectives of representation" and "consult with the client as to the means by which they are to be pursued."[6] Caselaw[7] and commentators[8] frequently refer explicitly to the lawyer as "an agent" for the client in negotiations.

---

3. *See* Peter H. Gulliver, Disputes and Negotiations: A Cross-Cultural Perspective xiii (1979).

4. *E.g., id.* at 71.

5. Model Rules of Prof'l Conduct R. 1.2(a) (2006).

6. *Id.*

7. *See, e.g.*, Sarkes Tarzian, Inc. v. U.S. Trust Co. of Fla. Sav. Bank, 397 F.3d 577, 587 (7th Cir. 2005) (using agency principles to conclude that attorney lacked authority to bind client in contract negotiations); Panzino v. City of Phoenix, 999 P.2d 198, 203 (Ariz. 2000) (stating that "the attorney-client relationship is governed by principles of agency law"); *In re* Silicone Breast Implant Litig., 761 N.Y.S.2d 640, 643 (N.Y. App. Div. 2003) (upholding settlement agreement entered into by attorney on the

The quality of a negotiated agreement is measured by the extent to which it meets the client's interests, both long term and short term. If the lawyer is to achieve better negotiation results, therefore, she must be able to ascertain the client's true interests and priorities and to counsel the client effectively regarding the alternatives available to him and the consequences of each option.

A negotiated agreement is never any better than the extent to which it serves the client's interests. The lawyer may believe that if she continues her hard-nosed, aggressive bargaining she will be able to extract a better compensation package for her client—a physician hoping to join an existing medical practice. Only her client can decide, however, if the additional compensation is sufficiently important to him to risk the potential jealousy and resentment of his new partners. Similarly, a plaintiff's personal injury attorney may believe that her client has an excellent chance of receiving a verdict in excess of $1.6 million if the case proceeds to trial. But only the paraplegic client can choose between a certain settlement offer of $600,000 and the riskier, albeit more lucrative, prospects at trial. Some of us play the lottery; some of us do not. Because each individual has his own level of risk-tolerance, the client should decide for himself whether the settlement is a "good deal."

On the other hand, the client's decision to accept or reject a negotiated agreement should be a fully informed one. *Model Rule of Professional Conduct 1.4(a)* requires the lawyer to "keep the client reasonably informed about the status of a matter."[9] Thus, the lawyer should continually update the client as the negotiations progress. Further, *Model Rule 1.4(b)* specifically directs the lawyer to "explain a matter to the extent reasonably necessary to permit the client to make informed decisions."[10] The comment to the rule indicates that the lawyer shall promptly inform her client of settlement offers, inform the client of communications from the other attorney during negotiation, and provide the facts relevant to the matter being negotiated.[11]

The lawyer's proper professional role as counselor involves more than merely keeping the client informed, however. *Model Rule of Professional Conduct 2.1* requires the lawyer to "exercise independent profes-

basis of apparent authority in the absence of actual authority).

8. *See, e.g.*, Ronald J. Gilson & Robert H. Mnookin, *Disputing through Agents: Cooperation and Conflict between Lawyers in Litigation*, 94 Colum. L. Rev. 509, 513 (1994) (discussing the tension between game theory and agency theory in legal negotiations by noting that the client-principal's desires, and those of his lawyer-agent, often diverge, discouraging the use of efficient problem-solving tactics); Michael L. Katz, *Game-Playing Agents: Unobservable Contracts as Precommitments*, 22 Rand J. Econ. 307, 311

(1991) (considering the lawyer-agent's effect on game theory).

9. Model Rules of Prof'l Conduct R. 1.4(a) (2006); Restatement (Third) of the Law Governing Lawyers § 20(1) (2000); *see* Susan Martyn, *Informed Consent in the Practice of Law*, 48 Geo. Wash. L. Rev. 307, 310 (1980) (arguing that lawyers have a duty to inform clients of all relevant facts and possible consequences of proposed legal solutions).

10. Model Rules of Prof'l Conduct R. 1.4(b) (2006).

11. *Id.* R. 1.4 cmt. 2.

sional judgment and render candid advice."[12] The rule further suggests that the lawyer's advice include not only legal factors, but also "other considerations such as moral, economic, social and political factors."[13] The paraplegic client ultimately may decide to accept the $600,000 settlement, but his lawyer has the responsibility to assure that he understands that there is a good chance of an even larger verdict at trial and that he appreciates the other consequences of accepting such a settlement. Is he fully aware of how his injury will affect his life and his finances, or is he reacting impulsively to what seems to him a previously unheard of sum of money?

A second difference between the legal negotiation process and other negotiations is the lawyer's role as an intermediary or buffer between her client's interests and the interests of the other party and his attorney. The lawyer's undivided loyalty to her client's interests often conflicts with the pressures she experiences as a negotiator. On one hand, she is professionally obligated to obtain the most favorable settlement possible during negotiation, while on the other, she is subject to professional pressure to pursue settlements that are just and fair to both parties.

The responsiveness of the negotiator to both her client and to the other negotiator, and her position as an intermediary between these competing influences, exemplify what social scientists call *boundary-role conflict*.[14] When negotiating, opposing lawyers attempt to achieve an agreement, at the same time they maintain valuable continuing professional relationships with each other. The lawyers' lack of substantial emotional stakes in the dispute, and the traditions of courtesy and fair play among members of the bar, enable them to reach mutually satisfactory solutions in many cases when the parties themselves cannot. Often, however, there is only a fine distinction between the lawyer legitimately seeking to reconcile conflicting interests and the lawyer wrongfully yielding to peer pressure to accommodate. In extreme cases, the lawyer "sells-out" the interests of the client in order to achieve settlement.

A third difference between legal negotiations and other negotiations also relates to the client's effect on them. Repeated counseling sessions between clients and their lawyers alternate with bargaining sessions between the lawyers representing the parties. Each lawyer meets with her own client to update him on the negotiations and to seek his input.

This interspersing of counseling sessions and bargaining sessions contributes to the extended length of many legal negotiations. Of course, the time period it takes to reach agreement varies greatly with the type and importance of the transaction or case being negotiated. A routine misdemeanor plea bargaining conference may take as little as twenty or thirty seconds; a sophisticated corporate merger or divestiture might go

---

12. *Id.* R. 2.1.

13. *Id.*

14. *See* Dean Pruitt, Negotiation Behavior 41–44 (1981); Richard E. Walton & Robert B. McKersie, A Behavioral Theory of Labor Negotiations: An Analysis of a Social Interaction System 282–302 (1965).

on for months or even years. It took six years to negotiate a bankruptcy reorganization plan for Johns Manville, formerly the largest producer of asbestos products, and twelve years to negotiate a consent decree in civil rights litigation alleging unequal educational opportunities for children of color in Hartford, Connecticut.[15]

Too often law school negotiation teaching leads students to believe that negotiations typically occur in a single face-to-face bargaining session between the two sides. The real-world reality is much different. Negotiating proposals and counter-offers are exchanged through the mail, over the telephone, and by e-mail. In the litigation context, even the amount of the plaintiff's demand in the complaint is a negotiating proposal. In some complex negotiations, the attorneys never meet face to face. In others, many "in person" negotiating sessions occur. The interactions between the negotiators, regardless of whether they are in person, written, telephonic, or electronic, usually are punctuated with each negotiator's interactions with her own client.

This aspect of the legal negotiation process thus resembles the *cyclical process* of negotiation described by social anthropologist Peter Gulliver who studied dispute resolution in two native African cultures.[16] According to Gulliver, the *cyclical process* is one of two separate processes that occur simultaneously during negotiation. It consists of the recurrent cycle of exchange of information between parties, its assessment by the parties, and their adjustments of expectations and preferences as a result of the new knowledge. Gulliver's *cyclical process* accurately reflects the interplay between client counseling and bargaining sessions in the negotiation process. When the lawyer initially discusses with the client the possibility of pursuing a negotiation alternative, the information available to her is usually incomplete. If the client is involved in actual or potential litigation, the lawyer frequently cannot predict with accuracy the eventual trial outcome. In other contexts, if the client's matter does not involve litigation, but instead a sale of assets or a merger of two businesses, the lawyer can offer at best only an educated guess regarding the other party's response to specific negotiation proposals.

Initially, the client is often unable to articulate fully his own goals and preferences. Typically, the client "wants it all" before the negotiations, and unrealistically assesses the likely outcomes of pursuing any of the available alternatives. The client has not decided how much risk he is willing to assume and which of his multiple objectives is his primary goal. Only the negotiation can give him the information necessary to decide these issues.

15. *See, e.g.,* Elaine Jones, *Luck Was Not a Factor: The Importance of a Strategic Approach to Civil Rights Litigation,* 11 ASIAN L.J. 290, 300 (2004) (discussing the role of strategy in the twelve-year negotiation that led to an agreement with the city of Hartford to desegregate forty percent of its public school students).

16. GULLIVER, *supra* note 3, at xv–xvi, 82–89.

In most cases, the lawyer learns much about the problem being negotiated from the other lawyer. Often the negotiation itself is a primary source of information about the underlying subject matter of the negotiation. The discovery process is available only in litigation matters; even there, neither discovery nor independent investigation may be feasible because of the expense they require and the time necessary to complete them. In addition, the negotiation process usually is the lawyer's best source of information regarding the other party's view of the dispute or transaction. Finally, the negotiation is the lawyer's only means of learning what the other party is willing to offer her client.

The client's expectations and the emphasis he places on a particular issue, when compared with other issues, are not fixed and static, but are continuously subject to change during the negotiation. As he learns more about the facts of the situation and how the other party views the issues, his own evaluation of the case often changes. In some cases, the client actually changes his "bottom line," or what I will refer to as his "reservation price"[17]—the least advantageous settlement he is willing to accept—rather than to terminate the negotiation. In some cases, of course, the "bottom line" is fixed and unchangeable. A parent may be unwilling to change his position on the custody of his minor children regardless of what new information he learns during the course of the negotiation; the criminal defendant may be unwilling to accept any plea bargain that includes a jail sentence. Even when the client's "bottom line" does not change, however, his expectations about the other party's posture in the negotiation, or about what will happen if agreement is not reached, often do change.

Thus, negotiation is an *information-gathering* process.[18] Much of the new information gained during negotiation—particularly how the other party views the matter being negotiated—usually cannot be obtained any other way. The nature of the negotiation process confirms the importance of the communication requirements contained in *Model Rule 1.4.* The client reacts to the new information gained during negotiation, often changes his expectations and preferences, and decides, with his lawyer, how together they will respond in the next round of bargaining. The negotiation cycle described by Gulliver begins again.

B. COMPONENTS OF THE NEGOTIATION PROCESS

Most negotiations are characterized by a series of components or "sub-processes" of the larger negotiation whole. In other words, although every negotiation is unique, lawyers face certain inherent elements of the bargaining interaction in most negotiations. As analyzed in this text, negotiation is divided into six component parts:

17. *See* HOWARD RAIFFA, NEGOTIATION ANALYSIS: THE SCIENCE AND ART OF COLLABORATIVE DECISION MAKING 110 (2002) (defining "reservation price" as the minimum value for which a client is willing to settle).

18. The importance of information-gathering from the other party during the negotiating process is the subject of Chapter 5, "Information Bargaining."

(1) negotiation planning and preparation;

(2) establishing a beginning orientation in the negotiation and an initial relationship with the other negotiator;

(3) information exchange;

(4) initial proposals;

(5) narrowing of differences; and

(6) closure.

These negotiation sub-processes do not constitute a rigid sequential model of the negotiation process, even though some scholars identify specific negotiation stages or phases.[19] Sometimes the sequence varies; for example, in many business negotiations, the parties frequently exchange information for a substantial period of time before either negotiator makes a bargaining proposal. On the other hand, in other situations, such as many personal injury lawsuits, the plaintiff's attorney initiates the negotiation process by either filing the lawsuit or sending a demand letter. Information exchange and narrowing of the differences between the parties almost always overlap and occur simultaneously.

Further, most negotiations are multiple issue negotiations. Negotiators often consider distinct issues simultaneously. The negotiators may be nearing resolution of some issues at the same time they exchange initial proposals on other issues. Consider the sale of a business. The parties achieve closure on the form that the transaction will take—for example, whether it is to be a purchase of corporate assets or a purchase of the corporate stock. Simultaneously, consideration of the issue of how much is to be paid by the purchaser is characterized by arguments and threats—tactics typically occurring during the narrowing of differences process. Finally, the negotiators have not begun to discuss initial proposals, or even to exchange information, regarding which key employees will continue with the firm following the purchase. In short, the sequence of these six negotiation "sub-processes" varies from one negotiation to another and even may occur simultaneously on different issues within a single negotiation. Nevertheless, these six sub-processes are present, if only fleetingly, in most legal negotiations.

C. GAME THEORY AND OTHER PERSPECTIVES ON NEGOTIATION THEORY

1. GAME THEORY

During the past half-century, negotiation has become the center of research and study from a number of perspectives. Perhaps the best-known approach begins with "game theory," a field you either may have encountered in your earlier studies or may remember from the 2001 Oscar-award winning movie *A Beautiful Mind*[20] featuring Princeton mathematician John Nash, one of its founding theorists.

---

19. *See, e.g.,* PRUITT, *supra* note 14, at 131–33; GULLIVER, *supra* note 3, at 121–75.

20. © Universal Studios and Dream-Works LLC, 2001.

Game theory is but a beginning point for the study of negotiating behavior in the real world. It "is concerned with situations—games of 'strategy,' in contrast to games of skill or games of chance—in which the best course of action for each participant depends on what he expects the other participants to do."[21] In the simplest examples, the game begins with two players, each of whom has only two specified choices.[22] Each player's payoff depends on both the choice she makes and the choice the other designated player makes. Each player knows what choices the other *could* make, but neither player knows what choices the other player *will* make. For each set of choices made by the two players, there is a specified outcome, and each player knows what these specified outcomes would be if she and the other negotiator make certain combinations of choices.

One of the best-known and simplest games explored by game theorists is the so-called "Prisoner's Dilemma." In its original form, the Prisoner's Dilemma Game is based upon a hypothetical incident in which two suspects, let's call them "Smith" and "Jones," have been taken into custody by the police.[23] The district attorney interviews them separately, encouraging each to confess and turn state's witness against the other suspect in exchange for a lighter sentence. Each prisoner's decision whether or not to confess, like negotiation behavior, must take into account his own actions as well as those of the other suspect. Both prisoners know that if neither confesses, the district attorney does not have enough evidence to convict them on a serious offense and both will receive only relatively light sentences for lesser offenses such as vagrancy. If one confesses and the other does not, the one who confesses will be shown leniency and given perhaps an even lighter sentence, while the other party will be severely punished for the more serious crime. Finally, if both sides confess, each will be punished with a moderate rather than a severe sentence. Each prisoner thus has two possible choices—to confess or not to confess—and a variety of possible outcomes depending not only upon his decision, but also upon the other suspect's decision to confess or not to confess. A matrix illustrating the respective parties' pay-offs therefore looks like this:

FIGURE 1–1

| | | Prisoner Jones | |
		Does not confess	Confesses
Prisoner Smith	Does not confess	1 year for Smith 1 year for Jones	15 years for Smith 6 months for Jones
	Confesses	6 months for Smith 15 years for Jones	7 years for Smith 7 years for Jones

The prisoner's decision matrix is analogous to the negotiator's. If Prisoner Smith cooperates with Prisoner Jones by *not confessing*, he is

21. Thomas C. Schelling, The Strategy of Conflict 9–10 (1960).

22. *See* Raiffa, *supra* note 17, at 54–55.

23. Elliott McGinnies, Social Behavior: A Functional Analysis 417–18, 423–24 (1970).

banking on his trust that Jones will reciprocate the cooperation and also not confess. The risk, however, is that Jones will view Smith's possible cooperation as an opportunity to exploit Smith by engaging in the competitive tactic of confessing, yielding only a short prison term for Jones at Smith's expense.

The Prisoner's Dilemma is inherently a game to be played once (unless Jones and Smith are inept recidivists). Assume that a similar game, with the same specified payoffs, is played again and again, but without any opportunity for the players to communicate with each other between or during the rounds.[24] In each round, Jones and Smith have the opportunity to either trust and *cooperate* with the other (analogous to not confessing) or to *defect* from a trusting commitment to the other (analogous to confessing). What should Smith do? If he thinks Jones will cooperate with him (not confess), his own interests are best served by not cooperating (confessing), which would yield only a six-month sentence for Smith, but a fifteen-year sentence for Jones. On the other hand, if Smith thinks Jones will engage in a competitive move vis-à-vis Smith—by defecting from a trusting relationship (confessing)—he also is better off behaving competitively by defecting (confessing and receiving seven years), than he is cooperating with Jones (not confessing and receiving fifteen years). If Smith begins with a cooperative move (not confessing) and Jones has made the same choice, what happens in the second round? After completion of the first round, have they established a trusting relationship so that Smith can reliably predict that Jones will continue to cooperate? Or does Smith suspect that Jones—who has learned that Smith was inclined to cooperate in the first round—will now act competitively by defecting and try and take advantage of Smith's own cooperation? Or does Smith himself want to behave competitively, by defecting and confessing, taking advantage of Jones' trust in him? If the game is repeated a number of times, sophisticated players often will learn to cooperate with each other, achieving better outcomes for each over the long term, rather than seeking a better payoff, but an unstable one, in the short term.[25]

2. THE LIMITS OF GAME THEORY AND RATIONALITY IN NEGOTIATION

Game theory, as we will see in the sections and chapters that follow, sometimes can offer insights into real world negotiation strategy. But real world negotiation is far more interesting and complex than game theory. For starters, the simplifying assumptions of game theory do not apply in most negotiations. A negotiator's decision need not be made blindly of the other negotiator's decision.[26] The negotiators may communicate with each other: sometimes fully and openly, and sometimes deceitfully. One or more of the alternatives available to the negotiator often do not have a liquidated or specified value. For example, when the

---

24. RAIFFA, *supra* note 17, at 69–70.   **26.** *Id.* at 81.
25. *Id.* at 79–80.

alternative to a negotiated agreement is a trial, the negotiator knows that outcome of that alternative only as a matter of probabilities, not as a certainty. Most important, negotiators are not restricted to only two specified choices. They may respond with a variety of counter-proposals and invent or create new alternatives.

Further, human beings, even when they negotiate, act in ways that deviate from rationality, sometimes in predictable ways. For example, it probably comes as no surprise that lawyers tend to be overly confident and overly optimistic in predicting trial results and other outcomes that favor their clients.[27]

Another pattern of decision-making that departs from rational maximization of results for the client is known as "anchoring."[28] Assume members of a first group of research subjects are asked, "Do you think the distance between San Francisco and Paris is greater or less than 9,000 miles?" and most answer "less." Members of a second group are first asked whether the distance between San Francisco and Paris is greater or less than 4,000 miles. When subjects from both groups are then asked how far the distance actually is, the distances guessed by members of the first group typically are much greater than the distances proffered by members of the second group. The distance in the initial question "anchors" the subsequent answers of the respondents in the first group.[29] Obviously, this finding has implications for how a negotiator might want to pitch her first offer or demand.[30] Similarly, how a proposal is "framed" to the other negotiator may affect how he perceives it, and whether or not he accepts it.[31] In short, you cannot assume that the other negotiator will act strictly in rational ways that maximize his client's gains. Nor, for that matter, can you assume that your own first intuitions as a negotiator are necessarily accurate and rational.

3.   EMOTIONS AND SELF–AWARENESS IN NEGOTIATIONS

As much as anything, learning to negotiate as a lawyer requires you to develop a capacity for both self-awareness and the capacity to "read" the persons with whom you negotiate. Neither you nor those with whom you negotiate are computers. Negotiations, particularly among novice lawyers, sometimes spawn intense emotions, and such feelings can affect both the negotiation process and the negotiation outcome. Before I started to study negotiation as a law student, I perceived myself (accurately, I think) as an intuitively terrible negotiator. (No, I will not

---

27. *See* Richard Birke & Craig R. Fox, *Psychological Principles in Negotiating Civil Settlements*, 4 HARV. NEGOT. L. REV. 1, 1–4 (1999) (arguing that psychological biases in judgment and decision-making act as barriers to beneficial settlements); Dwight Golann, *Cognitive Barriers to Effective Negotiation*, 6 ADR CURRENTS 6 (2001).

28. *See* Gary Goodpaster, *A Primer on Competitive Bargaining*, 1996 J. DISP. RESOL. 325, 351–52 (1996).

29. *See* Amos Tversky & Daniel Kahneman, *Judgment Under Uncertainty: Heuristics and Biases*, 185 SCIENCE 1124, 1128–30 (1974).

30. *See infra* Chapter 6, "Initial Proposals," at pages 124–26.

31. *See* Goodpaster, *supra* note 28, at 351–52.

negotiate a book refund at this point!) With the weight of my client's situation on my shoulders, I experienced anxiety or fear that I would not achieve a desirable outcome for my client; in other words, that I would "fail" as a negotiator. When the other negotiator did not see the situation as I saw it, I became angry and frustrated. Both the fear and the anger impeded my abilities as a successful negotiator.

In teaching negotiation over the course of several decades, I have found that students bring to their negotiation simulations very different levels of natural assertiveness, fear of failure, ability to be empathetic, calmness under pressure, and emotional capacity to think "outside the box." Frequently, the student misdiagnoses the behavior of the person with whom she is negotiating because she assumes that the other person understands the problem the way she does and necessarily shares her own intuitions and emotions about the situation at hand.

This chapter began with the comment, which might have appeared off-handed at the time you first read it, that your earliest negotiations were with Mom or Dad. Yet psychiatrists and analysts tell us that those earliest interactions have had considerable influence both on how we as adults interact with others and on our feelings regarding fear of failure and aggressiveness in dealing with other people.

I am not a psychiatrist, an analyst, or other mental health professional, and chances are, neither is your negotiation teacher. But perhaps the most important thing we can teach you about negotiation is to encourage you to be deliberately introspective about your negotiation behavior. Learn to be conscious of both your natural habits in interacting with others and about how your feelings affect your own negotiation behavior and sometimes get in the way of achieving the best possible result for your client. At the same time, learn to observe carefully the lawyer with whom you are negotiating. Try to evaluate, at least somewhat accurately, what he is honestly feeling and how those emotions may cause him to depart from the choices that you otherwise might expect from someone who always reacts rationally, that is, as the game theorist or the human computer would act.

While the study of negotiation benefits from insights gained from the logical analysis of game theory, it also benefits from an understanding of how social psychology and other disciplines suggest that people react in real negotiation situations. Even more importantly, while this text can teach you something about how negotiators typically interact with each other, negotiation remains an intensely human encounter. Negotiation theory—like theory in any discipline involving human behavior, and unlike mathematics or physics—is not everything. But neither is it nothing. "Judgment"—not algorithms—guides us through most of life's demanding situations.

D. A BASIC TYPOLOGY OF NEGOTIATION TACTICS

The negotiator's goal can be defined as an attempt to reach a joint decision with the other party that provides the greatest possible benefit to her client. How can you and the other negotiator find solutions that maximize your client's interests, as well as those of the other party? When that is not possible, how can the other party and his negotiator be convinced, persuaded, enticed or threatened into agreeing to a negotiated settlement desirable from your client's perspective?

The lawyer's behavior during negotiation can be broken down into discrete tactics or strategic moves. A *tactic,* as the term is used here, is a specific negotiating behavior the lawyer uses when initiating the negotiating exchange with the other attorney or in responding to the other negotiator's negotiation behavior.[32] A *negotiation strategy* is a series of tactics or specific negotiating behaviors that the lawyer uses to facilitate a resolution to the negotiation process that is favorable to her client's interests. The lawyer's negotiation strategy includes decisions made regarding the first proposal, or opening bid, in the negotiation, and the subsequent modifications of that initial proposal.

The lawyer's negotiation strategy is a separate and distinct concept from the lawyer's negotiation *style.* This book will not alter your personal style in interacting with other negotiators or anyone else for the matter. If your basic nature is to be courteous, friendly, tactful and trustful, it probably is not possible or desirable for you to seek a metamorphosis that will turn you into a "raging tiger." On the other hand, if you are naturally inclined to be forceful and aggressive in your relationships with other people, that also will probably not change. To a limited extent, it is possible for negotiators to feign or mimic personal styles. For the most part, however, it is negotiation tactics or techniques that can be consciously analyzed and learned. Specific examples illustrating the distinction between strategy and style will be provided below, but first it is necessary to briefly define the three basic varieties of tactics that will be described in this book.

Unfortunately, no consistent nomenclature of negotiation tactics or strategies exists in either the legal or social scientific literature.[33] In this text, "competitive," "cooperative," and "problem-solving" are defined

---

32. The meaning of "tactic" in this text is devoid of any military or necessarily competitive connotation.

33. For example, as compared with the three basic negotiation strategies described here, Harnett, Cummings, and Hamner identify four separate strategies. *See* Donald L. Harnett, Larry L. Cummings & W. Clay Hamner, *Personality, Bargaining Style and Payoff in Bilateral Monopoly Bargain-*

ing Among European Managers, 36 SOCIOMETRY 325, 328 (1973). Similarly, Horowitz and Willging identify five distinct strategies, *see* IRVING HOROWITZ & THOMAS WILLGING, THE PSYCHOLOGY OF LAW: INTEGRATIONS AND APPLICATIONS 284 (1984), as does Pruitt. *See* Dean Pruitt, *Strategic Choice in Negotiation*, 27 AM. BEHAVIORAL SCIENTIST 167, 167 (1983).

functionally, as organizing concepts designed to help you better understand negotiation behavior.

Previously, we described negotiation "strategy" as the mixture of competitive, cooperative, and problem-solving tactics that you elect to use and combine in any single negotiation. It also has a second meaning. A "pure" negotiation strategy consists of all the tactics categorized in this book as being (1) competitive, (2) cooperative, or (3) problem-solving. *Competitive* tactics, such as high demands, threats or arguments, are those negotiating behaviors designed to undermine the other negotiator's confidence in his bargaining position, and to induce him to enter into an agreement less advantageous to his client than he would have agreed to prior to the negotiation. *Cooperative* tactics include reasonable opening offers, arguments based on what is fair and just, and making concessions to encourage the other negotiator to reciprocate. The use of cooperative tactics is premised on the notion that when one party displays behavior which is fair, reasonable and accommodative, the other party is likely to respond in kind. Finally, *problem-solving* techniques are those negotiating behaviors designed to identify and exploit opportunities for joint gain in negotiations.

How, then, are negotiation tactics classified into one of these three "pure" negotiation strategies? Two factors are involved in this categorizing process:

(1) Does the negotiation tactic focus on garnering a portion of the proceeds of the negotiation for the lawyer's client (*value claiming*) or does it seek to benefit the client by increasing the joint level of satisfaction of both parties (*value creation*)? and

(2) Does the tactic facilitate a *collaborative* working relationship with the other negotiator, or is it designed to foster a relationship in which the negotiator regards the other negotiator as an *opponent* or *antagonist*?

1. VALUE CREATION AND VALUE CLAIMING

In seeking to maximize the interests of her client, the lawyer may work with the other attorney to create a "larger pie" that will benefit both parties by "*value creation.*"[34] She also may use *value-claiming* tactics in order to have her client receive the largest possible share of the available resources. In most negotiations, the lawyer engages in both value-creation and value-claiming tactics.

A value-creation tactic works only if the bargaining situation allows for such joint gains. Negotiation theorists refer to situations in which such gains are possible as *integrative* bargaining contexts and to those in which they are not feasible as *distributive* bargaining situations. A surprising number of negotiations include opportunities for value creation on at least some issues. An *integrative* bargaining situation exists when the parties' interests are not directly in conflict, mutually benefi-

---

34. *See* RAIFFA, *supra* note 17, at 85–86.

cial agreements are possible, and one party's level of satisfaction is not necessarily inversely related to that of the other. Instead of dividing a fixed quantity of resources between them, an integrative bargaining context allows the parties to "problem-solve," i.e., devise mutually satisfying solutions. An obvious example of an integrative context is a profit-sharing agreement between management and labor which will both increase the workers' satisfaction with the negotiated agreement by providing higher compensation and heighten management's enthusiasm by augmenting worker productivity.

Distributive bargaining situations, on the other hand, are those in which there is a pure conflict of interest between the parties; most often, the parties are deciding how to divide a fixed quantity of resources between them. In this context, one party's gain is necessarily the other's loss. This type of bargaining problem has been referred to as a "fixed pie," a "zero-sum game," or "share bargaining." Examples of zero-sum negotiations include the bargaining between the buyer and the seller about the cash price to be paid immediately for anything—a used car, a sophisticated piece of manufacturing equipment or a block of capital stock in a corporation—or the negotiation between the prosecutor and a defense attorney about the length of a recommended criminal sentence.

Whether a bargaining situation is an entirely distributive one or includes integrative possibilities is determined as much by how the negotiator approaches the situation as it is by the inherent nature of the bargaining context. Most negotiations include integrative potential if the lawyer is attuned to possibilities for value creation by being open-minded, creative, and inventive. One critical measure of a lawyer's negotiating ability is how often she can identify integrative potential in an issue being negotiated. The manner in which the negotiator initially defines the problem, the possible resolutions she can identify, and the facts that she regards as important, help to determine whether a bargaining context is distributive or integrative. In this book, I refer to tactics that attempt to create value for both parties as "problem-solving" tactics.

2. THE RELATIONSHIP WITH THE OTHER NEGOTIATOR

The other factor I use to categorize negotiation tactics is whether the tactic results in an *oppositional* or a *collaborative* relationship with the other negotiator. Inherent in the use of problem-solving or value-creation tactics is the notion of a collaborative or accommodative working relationship between the negotiators.

When negotiators employ value-claiming tactics, however, they have a choice. In any given negotiation, or even any particular stage of the negotiation, will each view her relationship with the other negotiator as strictly *oppositional*, or will she seek to foster a *collaborative* or accommodative working relationship even when engaged in value claiming? The competitive strategy or competitive tactics views the relationship with the other negotiator as inherently oppositional, while the cooperative strategy or cooperative tactics seek to foster a collaborative working relationship with the other negotiator.

As previously mentioned, the *competitive strategy* consists of tactics intended to undermine the other negotiator's confidence in his bargaining position. These tactics are designed to induce the other negotiator to enter into an agreement with terms less advantageous to his client than those he would have accepted prior to the negotiation. The competitive negotiator focuses on the distributive aspects of the problem being negotiated and tends to see little advantage to her client that does not come at the expense of the other party. Therefore, the other party to a negotiation is perceived as "the opponent." She seeks to manipulate her opponent's perception regarding the strength of his party's bargaining position so that the opponent accedes to a deal that is more advantageous to her own client. Competitive tactics include extreme initial demands, hiding information from the other party, threats, arguments and conceding reluctantly.

The *cooperative strategy*, on the other hand, while it is a value-claiming strategy and not a value-creation strategy like problem-solving, stresses a more accommodative approach with the other negotiator. The negotiator's tactics are cooperative tactics when she both seeks an accommodative relationship with the other party, but also recognizes that she is operating in a distributive bargaining situation in which gains for her client must come at the expense of the other party and vice versa. Cooperative negotiation behaviors are those tactics which the negotiator uses when she believes that her client's best interests will be served by seeking an agreement which is fair and just to both parties, and by developing a relationship with the other party that is based upon trust and good will. The use of cooperative tactics rests on the notion that "bargainers usually rely on socially constructed norms of reaching agreement that are based implicitly on notions of fair dealing."[35]

What negotiation tactics are included within the cooperative strategy? A cooperative opening bid in a negotiation is a proposal that is favorable to the lawyer's client, but moderate. The cooperative negotiator often initiates the concession-granting process, assuming that the other negotiator will feel bound to reciprocate. Cooperative strategy arguments address what is "fair and just," and do not disparage the other negotiator's alternatives to a negotiated agreement. Thus, cooperative arguments frequently suggest objective criteria as a standard for resolving a disagreement.

Among the three principal negotiation strategies, the use of the cooperative strategy in the actual practice of law is perhaps most difficult to visualize. Why—in a distributive bargaining situation where every widget gained by a party comes at the expense of a widget lost by

---

35. Russell Korobkin, *A Positive Theory*   1817 (2000).
of Legal Negotiation, 88 Geo. L.J. 1789,

the other side—would an attorney strive for an agreement which is "fair and just" to both parties?

The reasons why cooperative negotiation tactics might be preferred over competitive ones will be considered in Chapter Two, "Choosing Effective Negotiation Tactics." The questions raised in the previous paragraph, however, are more troubling in the abstract than they are in the "real world." In contexts other than legal practice, when most individuals interact with friends, acquaintances or family members, cooperative tactics are used frequently. Consider the proverbial tale of the neighbor seeking to borrow a cup of sugar. Most individuals yield to the request because they recognize that at some indeterminate point in the future, they may be asking for an unspecified return favor (or they may be motivated by altruism). It is unheard of for the borrowing neighbor to couple his request with a competitive tactic, such as a threat—"If you do not let me borrow the sugar, I will play 'heavy metal' rock music until the wee hours of the morning and disrupt your family's sleep."

But neighbors are not lawyers with clients who have adverse interests, a skeptic would respond. A survey of the negotiating tactics of practicing lawyers has shown the prevalence of cooperative tactics, however.[36] Attorneys who plan a variety of business deals with each other over a period of decades do not use exclusively competitive tactics when bargaining with each other, even on distributive issues. Even in personal injury negotiations, among the most typically competitive of all negotiations, there often comes a time when two wizened veteran trial lawyers, after days of depositions and motion hearings, sit down together to determine a "just value" for the claim. Prosecutors and public defenders in plea bargaining discuss what constitutes a "fair" deal.[37] At a more theoretical level, Professor Robert Axelrod, in his notable book, *The Evolution of Cooperation,* concludes that "cooperation can indeed emerge in a world of egoists without central authority."[38]

In summary, both competitive and cooperative tactics are value-claiming tactics, affecting how the negotiators will divide the spoils of the negotiation. Among the three strategies, only problem-solving tactics are value-creating tactics. Both problem-solving tactics and cooperative tactics are ones designed to foster a collaborative working relationship

36. *See* GERALD R. WILLIAMS, LEGAL NEGOTIATION AND SETTLEMENT 15–24 (1983); *infra* Chapter Two, "Choosing Effective Negotiation Tactics," at 31–32.

37. *See* MILTON HEUMANN, PLEA BARGAINING: THE EXPERIENCE OF PROSECUTORS, JUDGES AND DEFENSE ATTORNEYS 103–10 (1978); DONALD J. NEWMAN, CONVICTION: THE DETERMINATION OF GUILT OR INNOCENCE WITHOUT TRIAL 114–30 (1966); PAMELA J. UTZ, SETTLING THE FACTS: DISCRETION AND NEGOTIATION IN CRIMINAL COURT 134–36 (1978).

38. Robert Axelrod, THE EVOLUTION OF COOPERATION 20 (1984). According to Axelrod, the main results of cooperation theory "show that cooperation can get started by even a small cluster of individuals who are prepared to reciprocate cooperation, even in a world where no one else will cooperate." *Id.* at 173. Cooperation will be viable, Axelrod argues, when the cooperation is reciprocal and the parties involved are adequately concerned with the future as well as the immediate consequences of their actions. *Id.* Axelrod believes that "once cooperation based on reciprocity is established in a population, it can protect itself from invasion by uncooperative strategies." *Id.*

with the other party; competitive tactics are the outliers in this context, because they result in an oppositional relationship.

E. DISTINGUISHING STYLE FROM STRATEGY

With a basic understanding of the characteristics that define the three pure negotiating strategies, it is now possible to provide specific examples of the difference between a negotiator's personal style and her negotiation strategy. *Style* consists of the lawyer's personal characteristics in interacting with other people; *strategy,* on the other hand, is a set of specific negotiating behaviors.

Differences between *adversarial style* and *friendly style* are somewhat difficult to describe in print because style often is demonstrated most vividly by the negotiator's tone of voice, non-verbal communications and similar nuances. Consider, however, a negotiation between Michelle Chang, a recent law school graduate, and Patrick Quinn, an insurance defense attorney in his sixties. Michelle represents Tamiqua Lewis, the mother of a lead-poisoned child Malik, both in Tamiqua's own right and as natural guardian of her son in litigation, filed against Piccolo Property Management, LLC, a property-holding and management company. Michelle asserts that Piccolo Property Management failed to properly maintain surfaces painted with lead paint within the apartment where the Lewises resided during Tamiqua's pregnancy and during the first four years of Malik's life until his lead poisoning was diagnosed.[39] Piccolo's negligence, asserts Michelle, caused Malik's lead poisoning. Patrick Quinn represents Statewide Equitable Insurance, the insurer who sold Piccolo Property Management a landlord's policy that appears to cover liability to third-persons such as Malik and his family. Michelle filed her complaint three months ago, and Patrick responded with the usual answer denying everything and with a motion to dismiss for failure to state a claim. Patrick has a well-earned reputation as a hard-nosed litigator. What follows are two alternative ways that the first meeting between the lawyers might proceed. What types of tactics does Patrick use in each negotiation? But more importantly, what is very different in the two conversations?

39. This hypothetical negotiation is used as an example in a number of places throughout this book. By way of background, as of 2005, approximately 310,000 American children less than six-years old had elevated blood lead levels in a range that poses a variety of health risks. A major source of lead exposure among these children is lead paint and the dust generated when it deteriorates. Exposure to poorly maintained and deteriorated lead paint can cause young children to develop various health problems, including impaired cogni-tive function, behavioral difficulties, impaired hearing, reduced stature, and, in extreme but now rare cases, even death. Most cases of childhood lead poisoning arise in a small percentage of poorly maintained rental properties. Children from low-income families, often children of color, are disproportionately affected by lead poisoning. Some landlords' liability insurance policies cover childhood lead poisoning, but at least in some jurisdictions, insurers can and do exclude such coverage.

Scenario 1

Patrick and Michelle have never met, but Patrick told his assistant to return Michelle's call requesting an appointment and schedule something for yesterday at 4 p.m. Michelle arrived a few minutes earlier, and waited for twenty-five minutes in the well-appointed reception area of Patrick's medium-sized law firm on the twenty-third floor. Patrick's assistant has just walked Michelle back to Patrick's office with a large walnut desk and a seating area, complete with a coffee table, leather chairs and a sofa.

1—Michelle:	Mr. Quinn, I'm Michelle Chang, representing—
2—Patrick (interrupting):	Michelle, you're a student intern with somebody, right?
3—Michelle:	No, no. I was admitted to the bar last year.
4—Patrick:	We've got too many lawyers already. You practice by yourself?
5—Michelle:	No, I'm with the Public Justice Project.
6—Patrick:	I assume you went to City University?
7—Michelle:	No, I actually attended Elite Law School.
8—Patrick:	Well, I'm sure they didn't teach you anything there. So, I have a meeting with the bar committee that I chair in a few minutes, so we need to get down to business.
9–Michelle:	I represent the Lewis boy that your insured poisoned in its slums.
10–Patrick:	We both know that's bullshit. Why I grew up in a house with lead paint and it didn't do me any harm. It has much more to do with genetics and parenting. I know you're just starting, and they're giving you the cases that are dogs. I could probably convince my client, because of our long-standing relationship, to pay your filing fees and maybe a few bucks so that you could show your supervisor that you're a good

> lawyer. Otherwise, you'll never get a penny, and for that matter, you shouldn't for filing these frivolous cases.

In this first scenario, the *style* of both negotiators, particularly Patrick, is very *adversarial*. He belittles Michelle's inexperience, her legal education, and the merits of her case. He rudely interrupts her and calls her by her first name after she has addressed him as "mister." She responds, when she can get a word in edgewise, in an adversarial style. Compare the following:

Scenario 2

Patrick's assistant returns Michelle's call and suggests that Patrick could meet with Michelle at the Public Justice Project's office in a rundown urban neighborhood. Patrick arrives just a minute or two after the scheduled appointment, and Michelle comes out to the dingy waiting room to greet him.

11—Michelle: Mr. Quinn, it's really nice of you to stop out here. Most attorneys don't venture out to this neighborhood.

12—Patrick: Please, call me Patrick. I'm afraid I don't get out here often, but this office does really good work. May I call you Michelle?

13—Michelle: Sure.

14—Patrick: So you just joined Public Justice? Where were you previously?

15—Michelle: I just graduated from Elite Law School.

16—Patrick: Wow. We're lucky to have you here.

17—Michelle: Thank you. I've heard so much about your reputation as a trial lawyer. But shall we get to business? I wanted to talk with you about the Lewis case. I've prepared a portfolio outlining the testimony we expect from the lead-hazard abatement expert, the treating physician, the economist, and the mother.

18—Patrick: Michelle, I've seen a zillion cases like this one before. The landlord was never cited for a lead violation in these premises and under our Supreme Court's holdings in this area, that's fatal to your case. Plus, we both know that growing up in that neighborhood with a single mother, the young man unfortunately did not have a great future anyway and damages would be low.

> My heart goes out to the Lewises. It's the paint
> companies' fault anyway. But we would not lose
> this case, and unfortunately we cannot pay any-
> thing in settlement, because it would just en-
> courage more cases. I am sorry, but that is
> where my client stands.

The substance or strategy communicated by Patrick in the second scenario is similar to that in the first negotiation—if anything, Patrick's negotiation tactics here are more competitive—he offers nothing. In the first scenario, he at least expressed a willingness to pay filing fees and a few thousand dollars. That would put Michelle ahead substantively compared with where she would be in the second scenario. What is different, however, is the style of the two negotiators, particularly Patrick. Gone are the direct and indirect attacks on Michelle and her clients. Both lawyers express their respect for each other in a variety of ways. When Patrick cannot concede liability, he blames it on his client and explains his basis.

It is important for the lawyer to distinguish style from strategy in a real negotiation for two reasons. First, many of the disadvantages of *competitive tactics*—the possibilities of deadlock and a premature break-down of negotiation, and of generating ill-will and distrust with the other negotiator—can be mitigated if the *style* of the negotiator is *friendly*. Even when the substance being communicated to the other negotiator is very demanding and competitive, friendliness, courtesy and politeness help to preserve a positive working relationship.

Conversely, the beginning lawyer needs to be able to identify *competitive tactics* even when the style of the negotiator is *friendly*. Often, lawyers will be misled by the polite and friendly style of the other lawyer and assume that he is using *cooperative tactics*, i.e., that his goals include a fair and just agreement and a positive, trusting working relationship between the parties. To the extent that the negotiator confuses friendly style for cooperative substance, she may be inclined to reciprocate, and the resulting agreement will disadvantage her client.

Admittedly, the personal style of the negotiator often is intertwined with the negotiation strategy she is using in a specific negotiation or that she prefers to use. A negotiator who has an aggressive and forceful personal style frequently will succeed in causing the other negotiator to lose confidence in himself or his case, thereby inducing him to settle for less than he initially expected—a goal of the competitive strategy. In another instance, however, a negotiator who is courteous, personable and friendly may, through competitive strategic moves such as extreme opening demands and infrequent concessions, be even more successful in destroying the other party's confidence in his case and inducing unilateral concessions from him. Although a negotiator's personal style of interaction positively correlates with her preferred negotiating strategy, separating personal style from negotiation strategies and techniques yields new flexibility for the negotiator. It is possible for the negotiator with a *friendly* personal *style* to adopt *competitive tactics* when it is advantageous, and naturally *adversarial* individuals can adopt *cooperative tactics.*

F. THE STRATEGIC CHOICE MODEL

Lawyers are not born as competitive negotiators, cooperative negotiators or problem-solving negotiators. Specific negotiation behaviors are learned, and as such, they may be selectively employed. The same lawyer who uses competitive tactics in one bargaining session will find her client's interests better served by employing problem-solving methods on another occasion.

Claims that any particular negotiation strategy is superior to the others all of the time, or even most of the time, promise too much. It is the thesis of this book that the answer to which negotiation *tactic* is most effective is: *it depends.*[40] Chapter Two will explore how the negotiator should proceed when deciding which negotiation tactic is likely to succeed at a given point in a negotiation.

The effective negotiating attorney is not only able to use different negotiation strategies in different negotiations, she is also able to use tactics or negotiation behaviors from more than one pure negotiation strategy during the course of a single negotiation. Most negotiations, for instance, include both *value-creating* and *value-claiming* aspects. In collective bargaining, there are predominantly *distributive* issues, such as the hourly rate of wages, as well as issues with significant *integrative* potential, such as the possibility of a contract that yields both job security for the worker and reduced re-training costs for the employer. Even in the largely distributive context of personal injury negotiations, the insurance company frequently is interested in the timing, as well as the amount, of payments to the claimant, and the possibility of a structured settlement thus yields integrative potential. Under these circumstances, the effective negotiator may elect to use problem-solving

---

40. Other scholars of legal negotiation are more confident that a single approach to legal negotiation is superior to other possibilities. In their seminal book *Getting to Yes: Negotiating Agreement Without Giving In*, Fisher, Ury and Patton outline a predominantly *problem-solving* approach to negotiation, and claim that they have found "an all purpose strategy" that can be used in any negotiation. *See* ROGER FISHER, WILLIAM URY & BRUCE PATTON, GETTING TO YES: NEGOTIATING AGREEMENT WITHOUT GIVING IN xix (2d ed. 1991). Students sometimes have referred to the approach outlined in this text as "getting to maybe." Even Fisher, Ury and Patton's *principled negotiation* theory, however, although based predominantly on *problem-solving* tactics, is not a

"pure" strategy and also includes both *cooperative* tactics and *competitive* tactics. For example, Fisher, Ury and Patton recognize that the negotiator "will almost always face the harsh reality of interests that conflict," that is, a *distributive bargaining context*, on at least some issues and that when this occurs, the negotiators should resolve the dispute through the use of "objective criteria," a *cooperative* tactic. *Id.* at 81. Finally, if the other party continues to use competitive tactics, Fisher, Ury and Patton recognize that the negotiator may be forced to present the other party with a "take it or leave it" choice, or even walk away from the negotiation. *Id.* These are *competitive* tactics.

tactics on the issues with integrative potential at the same time that she uses either competitive or cooperative tactics on distributive issues.

The negotiator's preferred approach to a single issue also may change as the negotiation proceeds. Frequently, as will be discussed below, negotiation proceeds from an early phase where both negotiators use predominantly competitive tactics through subsequent stages where problem-solving or cooperative tactics, or both, predominate. It is to be anticipated, therefore, that a negotiator may begin with competitive tactics such as an extreme opening bid and communication of an unwillingness to concede. Later the negotiator may employ cooperative tactics such as expressing a willingness to make concessions if the other negotiator reciprocates, or problem-solving techniques such as proposing that the parties together try to find a solution that will satisfy both of the parties' underlying interests.

The effective negotiator does not decide in advance that she will use only competitive or problem-solving tactics. Instead, the negotiator realizes that at each point in the negotiation, when she has the opportunity to respond to the latest message from the other party, she has three choices. First, she can use a competitive tactic such as a high demand, a refusal to concede, a threat or an argument. Second, she can respond with a cooperative tactic such as making a concession with the expectation that the other side will reciprocate, or referring to objective criteria suggesting how the case should be resolved. Finally, the lawyer can use a problem-solving approach and propose a solution to the parties' problems, suggest an exchange of concessions on different issues or in some other manner initiate a problem-solving process. Once she has made her strategic negotiation move, the lawyer awaits a response from the other negotiator. When it comes, the lawyer evaluates the other party's response and once again decides whether to continue with the same type of negotiation behavior or to switch to another set of tactics.

The idea that the negotiator has the freedom to switch and choose between three very different kinds of behaviors at different points in the negotiation was first advanced by social psychologist Dean Pruitt as the *strategic choice model*.[41] There are, however, practical limits to the lawyer's ability to change strategies during the course of a single negotiation. Assume Patrick uses competitive negotiation tactics, such as an extremely low offer and threats, at the beginning of his negotiation with Michelle regarding compensation for her lead-poisoned client. These tactics may jeopardize the positive working relationship between the two attorneys that is necessary for cooperative and problem-solving tactics to succeed.

Two factors may help Patrick, however, if he decides to shift from competitive tactics early in the bargaining to the later use of cooperative or problem-solving tactics. First, if he maintains a friendly style in his interactions with Michelle, even while using competitive tactics, it is easier to switch to cooperative or problem-solving tactics at a later point.

---

41. PRUITT, *supra* note 14, at 15–16.

He does not generate the same mistrust and ill will that results from a combination of competitive tactics coupled with an adversarial personal style. Second, the length of time that it takes to complete most legal negotiations, and the frequent breaks and interruptions in these negotiations, allow tempers and emotions to cool, and facilitate changes from competitive to more cooperative or problem-solving tactics.

To review, the strategic choice model calls for the lawyer to choose a negotiating tactic from one of the three pure negotiation strategies described in this chapter at each point in the negotiation. Chapter 2 analyzes the factors that the lawyer should use in making her choices. She will need to choose the best possible negotiation tactics during each of the component sub-processes described in the previous section. Accordingly, the core of this book is organized into chapters reflecting the components of the negotiation process: negotiation planning, the initial orientation toward the other party, information bargaining, and initial proposals. Each of these chapters describes competitive, cooperative and problem-solving tactics that the negotiator can employ when engaged in these aspects of the negotiation process. Chapters 8 and 9 then depart somewhat from this organizational structure. Chapter 8 analyzes both the "narrowing of differences" and "closure" sub-processes when the negotiator treats the bargaining context as a predominantly distributive one, that is, she uses competitive and/or cooperative tactics. Chapter 9 then describes the narrowing of differences and closure sub-processes when the negotiator is seeking any possible integrative potential, in other words, she employs problem-solving tactics. These chapters depart from the organizational scheme of the previous four chapters because, even though the narrowing of differences and closure sub-processes are analytically distinct, they tend to blur in practice.

An overview of the negotiation tactics described in this book is provided by Tables 1–1 and 1–2, displayed on the next two pages. Each of the three rows in each of the tables lists the tactics included within a particular "pure" negotiation strategy—the *competitive, cooperative,* or *problem-solving* strategy. The columns in the table identify the six components of the negotiation process just described. Using the table, you can determine the tactics each negotiation strategy would prescribe for each aspect of negotiations. For example, to identify the manner in which a negotiator using competitive tactics would approach initial negotiation proposals, locate the third column on Table 1–1 identified as "IV. INITIAL PROPOSALS." Then move down the column to the row identified as "A. COMPETITIVE." This block in the matrix lists competitive initial proposal tactics:

(1) High initial demand;

(2) Firm demand;

(3) Justification of initial proposal;

(4) False demand;

(5) Demand as a pre-condition to bargaining;

(6) Inflexible first offer (Boulwarism);

(7) Outrage as response to other party's first offer.

Tables 1–1 and 1–2 thus serve as a road map of the tactics to be presented in Chapters Three through Eight of this text. Some of the brief references in the tables probably have little meaning to you now. As you study the remainder of this book, however, return to these tables to review how the specific negotiating tactic described fits into both the ongoing negotiation process and into one of the three basic negotiation strategies. Be aware, however, that most of the tactics listed in Tables 1–1 and 1–2 are presented only in cursory form and that some techniques discussed in the text are deleted from the table because of space limitations.

TABLE 1–1

HOW EACH STRATEGY ADDRESSES COMPONENTS
OF THE NEGOTIATION PROCESS

STRATEGY	I. PLANNING CHAPTER THREE	II. INITIAL ORIENTATION CHAPTER FOUR	III. INFORMATION- BARGAINING CHAPTER FIVE
A. COMPETITIVE	Discuss with client: 1. Reservation points. 2. Sources of power and leverage. 3. Advantages and disadvantages of competitive tactics. 4. Negotiator's restricted authority.	1. Agenda issues. 2. Location of negotiation. 3. Deadlines. 4. Outnumbering other party's negotiators. 5. Bargaining with credentials.	1. Information gathering suggesting other party's reservation points. 2. Concealment of information suggesting client's reservation points or reducing. bargaining leverage. 3. Revealing information increasing bargaining power.
B. COOPERATIVE	Discuss with client: 1. Reservation points. 2. Objective criteria. 3. Advantages and disadvantages of cooperative tactics. 4. Negotiator's flexible authority.	1. Cooperation facilitators. 2. Answering competitive tactics. 3. Initiating trusting behaviors. 4. Discussing bargaining relationship. 5. Active listening.	1. Both information gathering and revealing.
C. PROBLEM-SOLVING	Discuss with client: 1. Underlying interests. 2. "Best alternative to a negotiated agreement." 3. Bridging solutions. 4. Relative priorities among issues. 5. Negotiator's flexible authority.	1. Cooperation facilitators described in (B) above. 2. Identification of other party's interests. 3. Communication of client's interests.	1. Exchanging of information about parties' respective interests.

TABLE 1–2

HOW EACH STRATEGY ADDRESSES COMPONENTS
OF THE NEGOTIATION PROCESS

STRATEGY	IV. INITIAL PROPOSALS CHAPTER SIX	V. NARROWING OF DIFFERENCES CHAPTER SEVEN	VI. CLOSURE CHAPTER EIGHT
A. COMPETITIVE	1. High initial demand. 2. Firm demand. 3. Justification of initial proposal. 4. False demand. 5. Demand as a precondition to bargaining. 6. Inflexible first offer (Boulwarism). 7. Outrage as response to other party's first offer.	1. Convincing other party to concede by using: (a) Arguments, (b) Threats, (c) Breaking-off negotiations. 2. Limitation of concessions. 3. Justification of concessions.	1. Use of deadlines and ultimatum. 2. Drafting agreement where possible.
B. COOPERATIVE	1. Reasonable and moderate demand. 2. Justification with objective criteria. 3. Varied responses to other party's extreme first demand.	1. Initiating exchange of concessions. 2. Promises to induce concessions. 3. Arguments based upon objective criteria. 4. Limiting risks of unreciprocated concessions.	1. Making final concession and inviting reciprocation. 2. Splitting the difference. 3. Constructive ambiguities. 4. Interpreting "Final Offer" as firm, but not final. 5. Re-opening dead-locked negotiations.
C. PROBLEM-SOLVING	1. Information exchange preceding initial proposals. 2. Probing for underlying interests by responding to other party's opening "positions." 3. Establishing "search model." 4. Presentation of bridging proposals conceived with client. 5. Developing solutions with other negotiator.	1. Evaluation of proposed bridging solutions. 2. Refinement of bridging solutions through incorporation. 3. Heuristic trial and error.	1. Agreement on bridging solution. 2. Logrolling. 3. Cost-cutting. 4. Compensation.

TACTICS

A. AN OVERVIEW

To a great extent the negotiator's final success depends upon her ability at each point in the negotiation to make the most effective choice among competitive, cooperative or problem-solving tactics. The optimal choice of tactics usually changes continuously throughout a negotiation. It is a rare negotiation when either of the negotiators employs solely a pure competitive, cooperative or problem-solving strategy throughout the bargaining. Indeed, it frequently is the case that negotiation on various separate and distinct issues progresses at uneven rates, and that the most effective negotiation strategy may consist of employing differing tactics on distinct issues at the same time. For example, an attorney representing a commercial tenant in lease negotiations might use competitive tactics in negotiating over the amount of monthly rent to be charged, at roughly the same time that she is either making a concession on a separate issue by agreeing to pay increased utility costs (a cooperative tactic) or engaging in problem-solving bargaining with the other negotiator to determine the store location.

The choice of whether the negotiation tactic most likely to be effective on a particular issue and at a specific time in the negotiation is a competitive, cooperative or problem-solving one requires a balancing of the factors to be considered in this chapter. Most of the factors discussed affect the negotiator's decision to use a tactic from one of the collaborative strategies—either the problem-solving or the cooperative—or a competitive tactic. In this discussion, the two pure negotiation strategies that foster a positive and accommodative working relationship between the parties, the cooperative and problem-solving strategies, are referred to as *"collaborative strategies."* The other factor analyzed, of course, is whether the negotiation presents sufficient value-creation or integrative opportunities to allow effective use of problem-solving bargaining tactics.

28

The first factor discussed is the other negotiator's probable bargaining strategy. It is the single most important factor to be considered by the negotiator when she chooses her own negotiating tactics. The second factor to be discussed is the question of whether the bargaining context has integrative potential. The chapter then describes the other significant factors to be considered in choosing between competitive tactics and collaborative (either cooperative or problem-solving) tactics:

(1) the stage of the negotiation;

(2) the relative bargaining power of the parties;

(3) the prospects for an ongoing relationship between the parties and concerns about honoring negotiation norms within the bargaining community;

(4) the attitude of the negotiator's client; and

(5) the negotiator's own personality.

B. THE OTHER PARTY'S NEGOTIATION STRATEGY

The purpose of any negotiating tactic is to affect the other negotiator's bargaining behavior in a way that will facilitate an agreement that is advantageous to the negotiator's client. The collaborative strategies attempt to accomplish this by encouraging the other party to reciprocate the negotiator's own cooperative or problem-solving tactics. To be successful, cooperative and integrative tactics require that both negotiators adopt similar tactics.

The whole purpose underlying the negotiator's use of cooperative tactics is the notion that if she concedes and adopts other cooperative tactics, the other negotiator will reciprocate. The major weakness of these cooperative tactics is their vulnerability to exploitation by a negotiator who does not reciprocate. Instead of matching the negotiator's cooperative tactics, the competitively-inclined other negotiator interprets the concessions as a sign of weakness and grants fewer, not more, concessions. Thus, cooperative tactics succeed only if the other lawyer reciprocates and makes concessions. Although problem-solving tactics are somewhat less vulnerable to exploitation by a competitive negotiator than cooperative ones, they also require an exchange of information and responsiveness to the other negotiator's interests and needs. These cooperative tactics may be exploited by the competitive negotiator who refuses to exchange information or to acknowledge the other party's needs.[1]

The Prisoner's Dilemma Game, described in the last chapter,[2] illustrated the risk that a negotiator faces when she employs cooperative

---

1. *See* Dean Pruitt, *Strategic Choice in Negotiation*, 27 AM. BEHAV. SCIENTIST 167, 168 (1983).

2. *See supra* pages 9–10.

tactics. You will recall that in that simulation, each of two co-conspirators had to choose between confessing to his crime or remaining silent. The decision to remain silent was a cooperative move viewed from the perspective of the two prisoners. If neither confessed, both would receive a prison term of moderate length. Such a move required each prisoner to trust the other. On the other hand, if Jones confessed, this was a competitive move from his colleague Smith's perspective. If Smith remained trusting and behaved cooperatively toward Jones by not confessing, then Smith was exploited and received a long prison sentence. If both parties confessed, that is, both behaved competitively toward one another, each would receive a bad result, but Jones would be better off than if he had behaved cooperatively and his move had been exploited by Smith.

The prisoner's decision matrix is analogous to the negotiator's. If Prisoner Smith *cooperates* with Prisoner Jones by *not confessing,* he is banking on his trust that Jones will reciprocate the cooperation and also not confess. The risk, however, is that Jones will view Smith's cooperation as an opportunity to exploit Smith by engaging in the competitive tactic of confessing and realizing a short prison term at Smith's expense.

In short, the best possible result for a negotiator in a single negotiation exists when she makes competitive moves and the other party engages in cooperative behavior. When both parties cooperate, a reasonable, but unspectacular, result is likely for both parties. If both criminal suspects in the Prisoner's Dilemma compete by confessing, then both prisoners receive a substantial prison sentence of seven years. Analogously, if both negotiators engage in competitive tactics, a fairly undesirable result—usually a negotiation stalemate or deadlock—is likely to occur. Finally, however, the worst possible single negotiation payoff for the negotiator occurs when she trusts the other negotiator and engages in cooperative tactics and the other party does not reciprocate, but instead pursues competitive tactics. She receives the negotiator's version of a 15–year prison sentence.

The Prisoner's Dilemma Game thus suggests that use of cooperative or problem-solving tactics is dangerous if the other negotiator is pursuing competitive tactics and cannot be induced to switch to cooperative or problem-solving tactics. The game also suggests that the negotiator may be able to use competitive tactics to take advantage of the other negotiator when he is using cooperative or problem-solving tactics.

This lesson should not be over-learned, however. Unlike the negotiating lawyer, the research subject in the Prisoner's Dilemma Game need not be concerned about the prospect of future negotiations or what other lawyers in the bargaining community think about her negotiating behavior. Other factors considered below, particularly the importance of ongoing relationships with the other party, often suggest that the negotiator use cooperative or problem-solving tactics even when a more competitive approach might achieve better quantifiable results in a single negotiation. Too often, new lawyers have the false impression that competitive

ethos
pathos
logos

tactics best serve their clients' interests and that cooperative tactics are hopelessly naive and vulnerable to exploitation by opposing negotiators. It takes months or years of prematurely terminated negotiations at their clients' expense before they realize that relationships between negotiators and parties "in the real world" are more important determinants of ideal bargaining behavior than outcomes achieved in research settings.

The Prisoner's Dilemma illustrates the importance of the other negotiator's behavior in your choice of effective tactics. A key issue, therefore, is to predict the other negotiator's tactics. Recognizing that you are not a prophet, and may even be a poor poker player, how can you intelligently speculate about the other negotiator's choice of competitive or collaborative tactics?

First, it is helpful to know something about the negotiation behavior of lawyers generally. Are negotiating lawyers *always* raging, sneering, sarcastic antagonists ready to devour the recently graduated lawyer? Although there is considerable variation from one geographical area to another, and among the various substantive law specialties, the available data suggests that negotiating attorneys are considerably more cooperative than might be expected. Gerald Williams has surveyed the actual negotiating behavior of a representative sampling of lawyers in Denver, Colorado and Phoenix, Arizona.[3] Each attorney surveyed was asked to complete a questionnaire describing the characteristics of the attorney with whom she had most recently negotiated and to rate his effectiveness. Williams found that sixty-five percent of the attorneys exhibited a pattern of negotiating traits that he described as the cooperative approach, and that twenty-four percent of the negotiating attorneys displayed a set of characteristics which he designated the competitive approach. The criteria used to divide the sample into these two groups included both characteristics of what has been referred to previously as *style,* and specific negotiating behaviors which are categorized in this text as *tactics.*[4] What is illuminating from the Williams study, however, is the pervasiveness of both a *friendly style* and *cooperative tactics* among the lawyers surveyed.

The extent of the use of cooperative tactics varies dramatically from one geographical area to another, and among various legal specialties. It is widely perceived that negotiators in large urban areas are far more competitive than those in rural areas. The novice negotiator who expects

---

3. GERALD R. WILLIAMS, LEGAL NEGOTIATION AND SETTLEMENT 15–24 (1983).

4. For example, the traits Williams uses to describe his "effective/cooperative" negotiator include both attributes of *style,* such as "courteous," "personable," "friendly," "tactful," and "sincere," and descriptions of *negotiation tactics,* such as "willing to share information," "willing to move from original position," "objective," and "reasonable." *Id.* at 31–34, 35 & 34–35. Conversely, Williams's description of

the *competitive approach* also includes *style* elements, such as "tough," "dominant," "forceful," "aggressive," "attacking," "ambitious," "egoist," and "arrogant," and terms roughly describing *negotiation tactics,* including "made a high opening demand," "used take-it-or-leave-it approach," "rigid," "revealed information gradually," and "used threats." *Id.* at 23–24, 32, 33 & 37–39. Obviously, Williams's survey did not identify the dichotomy between negotiating *style* and negotiation *tactics* previously described in Chapter One.

to find a prevalence of cooperative tactics in the big city probably will be disillusioned quickly. Similarly, negotiation norms vary dramatically depending upon the substance of what is being negotiated. Williams's survey of Phoenix lawyers suggests that the mere threat of filing a lawsuit in a commercial or real property dispute is regarded as a "heavy-handed tactic, likely to incur the wrath of the opponent and be counter-productive."[5] On the other hand, according to Williams, personal injury specialists typically regard a desire to settle a case either prior to filing a lawsuit, or perhaps even more than a few months before trial, as a dangerously naive tactic likely to lead to exploitation by the predominantly competitive negotiators in that environment.

A description of the negotiating behavior of lawyers generally is the crudest possible tool to use to predict how a specific negotiator will react in a specific negotiation to a specific negotiating tactic. What more refined data may be available to assist the negotiator in predicting what negotiating tactics the other lawyer will use?

1. THE OTHER NEGOTIATOR'S BEGINNING TACTICS

The other negotiator's early moves in a negotiation, such as his initial proposals and subsequent modifications of these proposals, often indicate whether he is using predominantly competitive, cooperative or problem-solving tactics. Determining which tactics the other party is using often is more difficult than it sounds. It is possible that the negotiator will misinterpret an extreme demand cloaked in a cooperative style as being a reasonable demand, a cooperative tactic. If this happens, she may enter into an agreement unnecessarily disadvantageous to her client. The negotiator's ability to detect the tactics being used depends heavily upon her level of preparation and her understanding of the substance of the negotiation. If she knows what constitutes a fair and reasonable agreement in advance of the negotiation, she will not mistake a competitive initial proposal, camouflaged in a friendly style, as a fair and reasonable proposal.

The other negotiator's early collaborative (cooperative or problem-solving) tactics that expose him to actual risks or costs are more likely to be true indicators of his intention to continue to pursue collaborative approaches than are less risky opening moves. For example, by openly sharing information with the negotiator, the other lawyer risks the negotiator's use of this information to his client's detriment. This approach, therefore, is a strong signal that the other negotiator is prepared to risk a genuinely cooperative strategy. Conversely, if there are alternative explanations for the other negotiator's initial moves in a negotiation, or if the other party's initial cooperative tactics are dictated by his weak bargaining position, this early cooperation is a less reliable indicator of continued cooperative tactics.

5. *Id.* at 81–82.

2. THE OTHER NEGOTIATOR'S TACTICS IN PRIOR NEGOTIATIONS

The other negotiator's past negotiation history, bargaining with either the negotiator personally or with others, may indicate which tactics he is likely to employ in the present negotiation. Insurance defense attorneys who practice regularly with a plaintiff's personal injury attorney soon come to appreciate whether an initial opening demand of $200,000 from him means that the probable value of the case is $120,000 or only $30,000. If the negotiator has not negotiated with the other attorney previously, she should talk with those who have.

Knowledge of the other negotiator's personality, for example whether he is argumentative or amiable, may also tell the negotiator something about his negotiating tactics. When American presidents negotiate with important foreign leaders they are provided with complete psychological profiles of the other heads of state. Unfortunately, such information is seldom, if ever, available to the practicing attorney. When considering the other negotiator's personality traits, however, it also is important to remember the distinction between style and tactics. Although there is often a correlation between personality traits and negotiation tactics, dominant personality traits more closely mirror negotiating style than tactics. Thus, an amiable personality usually correlates with a *friendly style*, but it might mask *competitive tactics* that the negotiator consciously employs.

3. THE STRATEGY OF SIMILARLY SITUATED NEGOTIATORS

If the negotiator has no information about the past negotiating behavior of her counterpart, less reliable information must be used to make educated guesses about the other negotiator's likely tactics. She may, for example, have information about the past performance of similarly situated negotiators. All claims adjusters working for a particular insurance company may tend to use competitive tactics; all labor lawyers representing a specific union may be competitive in the opening rounds of negotiation; most prosecutors working in a congested urban office may be cooperative. In any of these instances, the socialization of the specific negotiator on the other side of the table probably has been influenced by these patterns.

4. DETERMINING STRATEGY THROUGH ROLE REVERSAL

Perhaps no form of analysis is more useful in determining how the other negotiator will behave in a negotiation than engaging in role reversal. You may be able to anticipate the other party's negotiating tactics by placing yourself in the other's position and determining what tactics she would use if confronted with the pressures and the incentives facing her. You must be aware, however, that although you probably can understand the external factors influencing the other negotiator's behavior, it is more difficult to predict her motivations and internal personality needs as they influence the negotiation. It is dangerous, for example, to assume that the other party necessarily has the same degree of risk tolerance as do you.

C. INTEGRATIVE OPPORTUNITIES

From the perspective of a negotiator trying to decide between *problem-solving* tactics and other approaches, no single issue is more important than deciding whether the matter to be negotiated is a *distributive* or an *integrative* one, or more likely, a mixture of both. Problem-solving negotiation techniques work only in those situations in which at least some integrative (value-creating) potential exists. In a purely distributive bargaining context, the negotiator who wishes to use collaborative tactics is limited to cooperative ones. These cooperative tactics require the negotiator to accept a proposal less satisfying to her client with the hope that the other party will reciprocate.

The most important development in legal negotiation theory in recent years has been the recognition that most negotiable problems include value-creating opportunities. Negotiators make value-creating opportunities possible when both sides are sufficiently skilled and motivated to explore chances for joint gains.[6] Advocates of problem-solving bargaining suggest that most negotiators err when they assume that in order to obtain greater satisfaction for their clients, other parties must suffer lower satisfaction with the agreement. However, even proponents of problem-solving bargaining admit that some negotiations pose purely distributive problems (one-time deals where the only significant issue is price, for example) and that many more negotiations have at least some issues that are predominantly distributive.[7]

Locating value-creating potential is an important aspect of preparing for negotiation. The process of identifying these opportunities for joint gain is considered fully in the next chapter, "Negotiation Planning." For now, it is sufficient to recognize that the two most important types of problem-solving solutions are:

(1) "bridging proposals," which satisfy both parties' underlying interests; and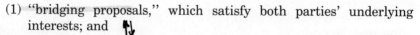

(2) "logrolling agreements," in which the parties trade concessions on different issues on which they place differing priorities so that both parties are more satisfied than if they merely conceded equivalent amounts on each issue.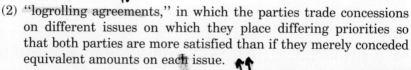

The number of disputed issues in a negotiation therefore is a factor to be considered when choosing negotiation tactics. When the subject matter

6. *See* ROGER FISHER, WILLIAM URY & BRUCE PATTON, GETTING TO YES: NEGOTIATING AGREEMENT WITHOUT GIVING IN 56–80 (2d ed. 1991); Carrie Menkel–Meadow, *Toward Another View of Legal Negotiation: The Structure of Problem Solving*, 31 UCLA L. REV. 754, 794–29 (1984).

7. *See* Roger Fisher, Comment, 34 J. LEGAL EDUC. 120, 123 (1984) (printed as response to White, *The Pros and Cons of Getting to Yes*, 34 J. LEGAL EDUC. 115 (1984) (reviewing ROGER FISHER & WILLIAM URY, GETTING TO YES: NEGOTIATING AGREEMENT WITHOUT GIVING IN (1981))).

No point in mediation if sides are on diff. planets — too expensive.

of the bargaining involves a large number of separate ⸱ ⸱ greater opportunity for value creation. Problem-solving fore, are more likely to be effective. The next chapter al other types of problem-solving solutions that create opportunities for joint gains.

D. STAGES OF A NEGOTIATION

Many social scientists[8] and legal scholars[9] studying negotiation have noted that the negotiation process appears to progress through a series of developmental stages. Although it probably is impossible to impose a rigid structural model on negotiation, the beginning lawyer should be careful that her negotiating behavior is appropriate for the specific phase of the negotiation. In particular, it is important to acknowledge that negotiation often progresses from phases dominated by competitive tactics to stages dominated by cooperative and problem-solving tactics.

In some negotiations, a lawyer's attempts to use problem-solving or cooperative tactics early in a negotiation, and to encourage the other negotiator to reciprocate, will be successful. In other cases, however, the use of cooperative or problem-solving tactics is effective only after the negotiators become frustrated with their earlier lack of success using competitive tactics. An amusing example of the premature use of cooperative tactics is recounted in the folklore of labor relations.[10] During a strike, union leaders reportedly had demanded a wage increase of 8 cents per hour (oh, for the days before inflation!). Management, interested in returning immediately to production, magnanimously offered 10 cents per hour. The union leaders refused to settle and made additional demands, whereupon a costly and lengthy strike followed. How can such seemingly irrational behavior on the part of the union be explained? The early cooperative bargaining behavior of management apparently communicated to the union that if the company was willing to accede and indeed surpass the union's wage demands, then the union was entitled to receive more than it had originally demanded. If the union had received 8 cents an hour after lengthy negotiations, it presumably would

---

8. *See, e.g.,* DEAN PRUITT, NEGOTIATION BEHAVIOR 131–33 (1981); PHILIP GULLIVER, DISPUTES AND NEGOTIATIONS: A CROSS-CULTURAL PERSPECTIVE 121–75 (1975). · ·⸱

9. *See, e.g.,* GERALD R. W‑‑‑‑‑‑ ‑‑‑‑ NEGOTIATION AND SETTLEMEN⸀ Williams identifies four stag⸀ tiation: (1) orientation and argumentation, (3) emerge and (4) agreement or final at 70–85. Menkel–Meadow stages of negotiation which "adversarial" literature as f

(1) prenegotiation strat ning to determine target

points, location and timing of negotiations;

(2) offers and responses (expressions of differences and issue definitions);

(3) information exchange (positions,

have been satisfied. A quick victory, however, would have left the union negotiators with the difficult task of explaining to their constituents their apparent lack of vigor in representing the workers.

Although some commentators claim that an identifiable pattern of progression through the negotiation process exists, it is important to recognize that every single negotiation is unique and that a rigid model cannot be imposed on the negotiation process. Sometimes a negotiation stage will occur very quickly; on other occasions, it will take years. The phases of a negotiation often overlap, and the negotiators may return to an earlier phase, either intentionally or not. Most negotiations are multiple-issue negotiations, and the various issues often are in different phases of maturation at any given time. Nevertheless, if the lawyer is able to recognize how far the bargaining process surrounding any particular issue has progressed, she is more likely to be able to identify effective negotiation tactics at that point in the negotiation.

The social scientists and legal scholars who claim to have defined negotiation stages use different labels, but a significant amount of consistency is apparent in their descriptions of the negotiation process. According to those who study the negotiation process, bargaining typically begins with an *orientation and positioning* phase during which the negotiators usually set the "tone" for the negotiations. Initial encounters between the negotiators are likely to be indicative of both the negotiators' styles and the tactics that will follow. For example, if the attorneys share competitive styles at this stage, the negotiation is likely to be a nasty one. As a part of this orientation and positioning process, the negotiators also make initial presentations to each other about how they view the merits of the transaction or case being negotiated. This often is followed by initial proposals for resolving the disputes between the parties; these early proposals usually are not to be taken as serious attempts to resolve the issues in dispute.

Negotiation then progresses through a phase which many negotiation theorists refer to as *exploration of the issues*. Both lawyers present arguments and selectively disclose information supporting their proposals. At the same time, each negotiator engages in an important information-gathering process concerning the other side's interests and attitudes towards the issues being negotiated. She also learns about facts previously known only by the other side. This stage of the negotiation may include the initial narrowing of differences between the parties as the two negotiators begin to make concessions from their initially extreme positions and drop their arguments on behalf of issues or positions in which their clients are not genuinely interested.

These two phases, *orientation and positioning* and *exploration of the issues*, often are contentious and time-consuming. It is typical in personal injury negotiations, for example, for these stages to go on for many months—and frequently for several years—and then to have the remaining stages of the negotiation take place in weeks, days or even hours. In these cases, it is important for the beginning negotiator not to mistake anything that happens early in the bargaining as a serious effort to resolve the case. These two early phases are also typically more competitive, particularly in negotiations involving fields such as personal injury cases and labor negotiations, than are the later stages.

It is not until a subsequent stage, variously referred to as *"bargaining"* or *"convergence"*[11] that most serious attempts to resolve the differences between the parties occur. Realizing that deadlock is near, one of the parties typically makes a realistic proposal on one or more of the issues—an offer that is intended to be the basis for a final agreement as opposed to a strategic move. Realistic proposals, involving considerable modifications of earlier unrealistic proposals, flow back and forth. Both sides typically make concessions or suggest problem-solving alternatives. This is not to say that all is sweetness and light. Threats and arguments continue and each negotiator still hides her minimal or "bottom line" settlement requirements. The negotiators distinguish those issues which are genuinely disputed from those issues on which compromise or other agreement can be more easily achieved. Then the negotiators move on to trading concessions on issues that the clients would rather not concede, or to deciding that they would rather give up something than have the negotiation stalemate.

Eventually, the negotiation reaches a final stage in which the parties either reach agreement or terminate the negotiation. If the parties successfully negotiate an agreement, the final stage often includes resolving a number of details that have been ignored pending closure on the major issues in dispute.

For someone approaching legal negotiation as a practitioner, and not predominantly as a scholarly observer, two points are critical. First, many—but certainly not all—negotiations follow a pattern of proceeding from *competitive* phases to more *cooperative* or *problem-solving* stages.[12] Second, legal negotiations are often lengthy, and *cooperative* and *problem-solving* techniques sometimes can be risky early in the negotiation unless the negotiator can be sure that such techniques will not lead to exploitation by a *competitive* negotiator.

Competitive tactics early in the negotiation, perhaps ironically, sometimes increase the prospects for successful use of cooperative or problem-solving tactics later in the negotiation. Dean Pruitt, a social psychologist who has studied conditions that foster problem-solving bargaining, concludes that "successful problem solving is made possible, in part, by some of the activities in the competitive stage."[13] According to Pruitt, as the negotiation progresses, deadlock is likely because neither

---

11. Gulliver recognizes three separate phases in what is described here as the single stage of *convergence*. *See* GULLIVER, *supra* note 8, at 141–68. These stages are Gulliver's "Phase 4: Narrowing the Differences," "Phase 5: Preliminaries to Final Bargaining," and "Phase 6: Final Bargaining."

12. *See* PRUITT, *supra* note 8, at 131–32; RICHARD E. WALTON & ROBERT B. MCKERSIE, A BEHAVIORAL THEORY OF LABOR NEGOTIATIONS: AN ANALYSIS OF A SOCIAL INTERACTION SYSTEM 141–68 (1981).

13. PRUITT, *supra* note 8, at 135.

party can make unilateral concessions. If agreement is to be reached, therefore, cooperative or problem-solving moves are necessary. At the same time the negotiator herself is becoming more realistic, she understands that her counterpart's goals are being moderated as well. As a result, trust increases and cooperative and problem-solving bargaining becomes possible. To put it another way, a negotiator sometimes will not seriously attempt cooperative or problem-solving tactics until she realizes that her efforts to use competitive tactics, and to exploit the other side's weaknesses, have failed.

In summary, the negotiator should consider *timing* as an essential factor in deciding whether to use competitive tactics or the more collaborative tactics of the cooperative and problem-solving methods. In the earliest stages of the negotiation, cooperative and problem-solving tactics are less likely to be reciprocated than later in the negotiation. Early in the process, cooperative moves may be regarded by some negotiators as signs of weakness or inexperience. This is not to assert that meaningful collaborative negotiation is necessarily impossible before extended haggling occurs, but rather to suggest that the negotiator must be realistically confident that the other party is also willing to use cooperative or problem-solving tactics.

E. RELATIVE BARGAINING POWER

In choosing negotiation tactics, the negotiator also should consider the relative bargaining power of her client and the other party. *Power* can be defined as the capacity to influence the other party's negotiation behavior.[14]

The extent of a negotiator's power over the other party depends largely on how the two parties perceive their alternatives to a negotiated agreement.[15] If the other party perceives that a negotiation breakdown will produce severe detrimental consequences for him, then the negotiator has great leverage to dictate the terms of an agreement. Conversely, if the other party perceives that he has other viable options if negotiation fails, the negotiator has relatively little power. A negotiator's power also is affected by how favorably she views her own alternatives to a negotiated settlement. In the litigation context, for example, a negotiator's power is dependent on how each party evaluates the likely outcome at trial and her costs in proceeding to trial.

The value of a negotiated settlement to a client and the value to the other party also include factors other than the obvious, quantifiable

14. *See id.* at 87. *See also* SAMUEL B. BACHARACH & EDWARD J. LAWLER, BARGAINING POWER, TACTICS, AND OUTCOMES 37–40 (1981); Dean Tjosvold & Morris A. Okun, *Effects of Unequal Power on Cooperation in Conflict,* 44 PSYCHOL. REP. 239, 239–42 (1979).

15. *See* BACHARACH & LAWLER, *supra* note 14, at 60–62; FISHER ET AL., *supra* note 6, at

102–03. Fisher, Ury and Patton use the phrase "Best Alternative To a Negotiated Agreement" or "BATNA" to identify the standard against which any proposed agreement should be measured. *Id.* at 100. *See also* Roger Fisher, *Negotiating Power: Getting and Using Influence,* 27 AM. BEHAV. SCIENTIST 149, 156–57 (1983).

results of the negotiation. The value of the agreement is also subjective—strictly in the eye of the beholder. For example, avoiding delay in reaching agreement may be extremely important to one party or the other, and this concern may substantially reduce a party's bargaining power. Thus, concessions and other cooperative tactics become more attractive, because they may lead to a quick agreement. Likewise, clients often desire an early conclusion to negotiations: they may need settlement proceeds immediately, they may desire to minimize legal fees and other expenses resulting from prolonged negotiation, and they may want to minimize the psychological strain associated with continued conflict.

Unfortunately, outside pressures on counsel, such as the heavy caseload of an urban prosecutor or a public defender, often lessen bargaining power and force expeditious settlements. If the pressures on counsel result in her encouraging her client to accept a settlement offer not in the best interests of the client, the lawyer violates her ethical obligations to her client. The *Model Rules of Professional Conduct* require the "thoroughness and preparation reasonably necessary for the representation" of the client.[16]

When the client's power is greater than that of the other party, the negotiator may choose tactics from any one of the three strategies without considering the impact of relative bargaining power. A negotiator with a viable alternative to a negotiated agreement is exposed to minimal risk if she chooses competitive tactics, despite the increased risk of settlement impasse. In addition, the use of threats, a competitive tactic, by a powerful negotiator will be perceived as more credible by the other lawyer—and therefore will more likely be effective—than would similar threats by a less powerful negotiator. The less powerful negotiator has two options available: (1) she can attempt to change the perceived balance of negotiating power between the two parties, or (2) she can use either cooperative or problem-solving negotiation tactics.

The parties' perceptions of their own and their counterparts' bargaining power are not static; instead, they change throughout the negotiation. The negotiator can attempt to alter the relative distribution of power between the parties by convincing her counterpart that his initial perceptions of both parties' alternatives to a negotiated agreement were inaccurate. For example, in a personal injury settlement negotiation, the plaintiff's attorney can shift power by convincing her counterpart that her expert medical witnesses will convince the jury of higher damages than the other negotiator previously anticipated. If the negotiator succeeds in altering the power balance by changing the other negotiator's assessments of the alternatives to agreement, she increases her ability at a later point to employ effective competitive tactics, thus increasing her negotiation flexibility. This factor helps to explain the frequent use of competitive negotiation tactics in the early phases of negotiation.

16. MODEL RULES OF PROF'L CONDUCT R. 1.1 (2006).

Paid mediator likely to change reality?

For negotiators with less bargaining power, the collaborative tactics of the cooperative and problem-solving strategies are more effective than competitive tactics. When a low-power negotiator tries to use competitive tactics, for example, threats and a reluctance to concede, she generally fails because her competitive tactics are not viewed as credible. The negotiator with greater power does not respond to such tactics because he senses that he can extract further concessions. Therefore, the greater the other party's power over the negotiator, the greater the negotiator's incentive to engage in cooperative or problem-solving tactics. Competitive tactics simply do not work well.

Fortunately for less powerful negotiators, research suggests that powerful and high-status negotiators are likely to respond favorably to cooperative and problem-solving tactics.[17] This is true in part because normative concerns constrain the use of power—powerful negotiators are inclined to be generous toward less powerful negotiators.

Cooperative and problem-solving tactics, therefore, appear more likely than competitive ones to yield favorable results for a negotiator who faces a more powerful counterpart. However, some social scientists have reached a somewhat different conclusion that "[p]erhaps the only way to offset the disadvantage of low power is to be tough initially and then become more yielding over time."[18]

F. ONGOING RELATIONSHIPS

The terms of the negotiated agreement are only one part of the results of negotiation. Another outcome of the negotiation is the nature of the relationship between the parties, and between their attorneys, once the negotiation is concluded. Most negotiations do not occur in a vacuum, but rather as a part of bargaining networks or communities. Leaving aside, for a moment, the relationship between the negotiating attorneys, the attitudes that the parties develop toward one another during the bargaining process likely affect both their own ongoing relationship and their reputations among other individuals and organizations with whom they will be negotiating in the future. An agreement that achieves a two-percent cost savings for a client but which also results in a rupturing of future business dealings with the other party and a damaged reputation within the bargaining community is not an agreement which satisfies the client's interests.

When a relationship between the parties is likely to continue beyond the negotiation, use of either cooperative or problem-solving tactics is

17. *See* Karen S. Cook & Richard M. Emerson, *Power, Equity and Commitment in Exchange/Networks*, 43 Am. Soc. Rev. 721, 737 (1978); William A. Donohue, *Analyzing Negotiation Tactics: Development of a Negotiation Interact System*, 7 Hum. Com. Research 273, 285 (1981); Dean Tjosvold, *Commitment to Justice in Conflict Between* *Unequal Status Persons*, 7 J. Applied Soc. Psychol. 149, 160 (1977).

18. W. Clay Hamner & L. S. Baird, *The Effect of Strategy, Pressure to Reach Agreement and Relative Power on Bargaining Behavior*, in Bargaining Behavior 247, 265 (Heinz Sauermann ed., 1978).

recommended.[19] Competitive tactics often generate distrust and ill will, negative feelings that may impair future dealings with the other party. Competitive tactics also often result in social disapproval within the bargaining community and invite retaliation in the future for violating bargaining norms.

The negative consequences of using competitive tactics are most pronounced when such tactics are used late in a negotiation. Social research suggests that negotiators concerned about enhancing prospects for a good future working relationship with the other party should avoid beginning the bargaining with cooperative tactics if they plan to switch to competitive tactics at a later stage.[20] Goodwill between the negotiating lawyers is more likely to result when the negotiator changes from early competitive tactics to a more collaborative approach, employing either cooperative or problem-solving tactics.

Other research demonstrates that parties, in fact, are likely to reciprocate cooperative or problem-solving tactics when continued contact in the future is anticipated and when the negotiator displays cooperative tactics early in the negotiation.[21] This important finding shows that a negotiator's early cooperative moves are less likely to be exploited when the other party anticipates an ongoing relationship.

In many but not all instances, the issue of whether the parties will have an ongoing relationship depends upon whether it is a *transactional* or a *dispute resolution* negotiation. In *dispute resolution* negotiation, each party has the opportunity to litigate or have the case submitted to a third-party decision-maker if the bargaining fails to reach an agreement. Typical examples include settlement talks in any kind of lawsuit—personal injury negotiations, plea bargaining or settlement discussions after an antitrust suit has been filed—or the negotiation of an employee's grievance against the employer when the employee has a contractual right to arbitration. Dispute resolution negotiation generally is characterized by the parties trying to agree upon the historical facts that have led to the dispute and then invoking *norms* to resolve the dispute. These norms include the applicable substantive law contained in prior judicial decisions—for example, precedents which establish when a plaintiff may recover for intentional infliction of emotional distress—or prior settlement negotiations, which suggest a pecuniary value for the plaintiff's permanent psychiatric disturbance.

In contrast, *transactional* negotiations are those in which agreement depends entirely on the consent of the parties and neither party has the power to compel the other to submit the dispute to a third-party for

voluntary binding not granted — mediation

19. See PRUITT, supra note 8, at 39–40, 109–12 & 184; Kenneth J. Roering, E. Allen Slusher & Robert D. Schooler, *Commitment to Future Interaction in Marketing Transactions*, 60 J. APPLIED PSYCHOL. 386, 386–87 (1975).

20. E. Allen Slusher, *Counterpart Strategy, Prior Relations, and Constituent Pres-*

sure in a Bargaining Simulation, 23 BEHAV. SCI. 470, 476 (1978).

21. ... with ... tive E ... 403, 4

Pyrrhic victory — won the battle but at too great a cost.

resolution. In most instances, such negotiations are not premised on the "rights" or "entitlements" of the parties; they involve neither restoring the situation to the way that it was (tort liability) nor enforcing an expectancy that never occurred (e.g. contract liability). Instead, transactional negotiations are opportunities for the parties to agree voluntarily on the rules that will govern their affairs in the future. Examples include any purchase and sale agreement—whether the object of the transaction is a used car or a large corporation—as well as collective bargaining or international treaty making. To be sure, the distinction between dispute resolution and transactional negotiation may not be as clear as it first appears. When the attorneys for the government negotiate a consent decree in a prisoners' rights case or a consent decree in a complex antitrust suit, such negotiations have elements of both dispute resolution and transactional negotiation. Either party may compel adjudication and may claim certain rights and entitlements, but the agreement between the parties is designed to govern their future conduct.

For the lawyer as a negotiator, whether the negotiation involves dispute resolution or a transaction often—but not inevitably—has two consequences. First, the parties in dispute resolution negotiations frequently are engaged in "one-shot" negotiations; they do not have a continuing relationship. In transactional negotiations, this is somewhat less likely to be true. On one hand, many transactional negotiations—such as the sale of a parcel of real estate—are isolated transactions without any continuing relationship between the parties. On the other hand, in many transactional negotiations, the essence of the issues to be negotiated is generally how the parties will conduct themselves in their future relationship. Accordingly, not only the substance of the agreement to be reached in transactional negotiations is important, but so is the negotiating process itself.

Threats and blustering that might be appropriate or effective negotiating techniques in some dispute resolution negotiations will be counterproductive in most transactional negotiations for two reasons. First, the other negotiator probably responds by terminating the negotiation and seeking other business partners or other persons to whom to sell his real estate. A lawyer negotiating in a dispute resolution context does not have the same freedom to change with whom she is negotiating. Second, in the large number of transactional negotiations that are not "one-shot" deals, extremely competitive tactics jeopardize the continuing partnership or relationship between the parties.

Often transactional negotiations also present more opportunities for value creation and the use of problem-solving tactics. Frequently, there are multiple issues, thus presenting integrative potential for logrolling—the mutually advantageous exchange of concessions on issues upon which the parties place differing priorities. Further, because transactional negotiations involve ongoing relationships between the parties, the positive working relationships established by problem-solving tactics are attractive.

Whether the likelihood of a continuing relationship between the parties occurs in a transactional negotiation, or in a dispute resolution negotiation, the use of cooperative or problem-solving tactics, particularly in later stages of the negotiation, makes sense. If, on the other hand, the negotiating party knows that the negotiation is a one-shot situation, then his interests will not necessarily be adversely affected by the use of competitive tactics.

A potential ethical concern arises when the attorneys focus on their own ongoing relationship in choosing negotiation tactics. Many negotiations which are "one-shot" transactions from the standpoint of the parties—such as plea bargaining or personal injury negotiations—involve attorneys who deal with each other on a continuing basis. The risk is that the public defender, in an effort to maintain a credible and cooperative working relationship with the prosecutor, will not negotiate as competitively as she would if she did not need the prosecutor's continued goodwill. Similar conflicts may exist in civil cases. An attorney who vigorously represents her client's interests and refuses to accede to the pressures for accommodative working relationships between attorneys may be dismissed as a lightweight who "can't control" her client.

A comment to *Model Rule of Professional Conduct 1.7* states that "a conflict of interest exists if there is a significant risk that a lawyer's ability to consider, recommend or carry out an appropriate course of action for the client will be materially limited as a result of the lawyer's other responsibilities or interests."[22] If the lawyer believes her client's particular interests would be best served by competitive negotiation tactics, is she committing an ethical violation if she does not pursue such tactics because she fears repercussions in subsequent negotiations? What is involved in this issue is not only a trade-off between the client's interest and the attorney's desire for comfortable working relationships with other attorneys with whom she will have contact in the future, but also potentially her effectiveness in representing future clients. To some extent, the attorney can minimize the conflict by packaging competitive negotiation tactics, when called for, in a cooperative style. This may facilitate continued contact with the other negotiator, even when the client's best interests dictate competitive tactics.

The reality is that lawyers often do respond to pressures from their negotiating counterparts and pursue settlements that are fair and just to both parties. The pressure on the lawyer to use cooperative and problem-solving tactics results not only from the expectation of future contact with the other lawyers, but also from the traditions of courtesy and fair play among lawyers.

The effective lawyer must consider the norms of the bargaining community of which she is a part. Negotiation behavior varies greatly

22. MODEL RULES OF PROF'L CONDUCT R. 1.7 cmt. 8 (2006). Rule 1.7(a) itself arguably addresses this concern by limiting conflict of interest obligations to those instances where the representation of one client is "*directly* adverse to the interests of another client" (emphasis added).

from one specialized area of practice to another, and among geographical districts. The lawyer who uses competitive tactics, such as the threat of filing a lawsuit, in a commercial or real estate dispute where bargaining tends to be accommodative, invites ill will from her colleagues in the bargaining community, and possible retaliation. A novice public defender in a rural area that plea bargains aggressively likely will be told by both the judge and the prosecutor "That's not the way things are done here." Obviously, the negotiator's tactics should not be dictated solely by standard operating practice within the bargaining community in which she bargains. At the same time, she must be aware of negotiating behavior norms, and consider them along with other factors in choosing effective negotiation tactics.

G. ATTITUDE OF THE LAWYER'S CLIENT

Legal negotiation is negotiation on behalf of a client. As previously discussed, the American Bar Association's *Model Rule of Professional Conduct 1.2* provides that decisions as to whether to accept a settlement proposal are to be made by the client.[23] Although lawyers generally decide what "means" or methods and tactics they use in the representation of clients, *Model Rule of Professional Conduct 1.2* further requires the attorney to consult her client regarding the "means" of representation.[24] Arguably, this provision requires the attorney to consult with the client regarding negotiation tactics she intends to use.

If not required as a matter of professional obligation, then certainly as a matter of client relations and good business practices, the lawyer should consider the client's input regarding negotiation tactics. Sometimes the client's legitimate concerns relate to one of the factors described previously, for example, the impact of the choice of negotiation tactics on continuing relationships between the parties. In other instances, the attorney's desire to maintain rapport with an adversarial or angry client may necessitate that she adopt competitive tactics in bargaining on behalf of the client.[25] A client not inclined to trust his attorney may be convinced by visibly competitive tactics that she is representing his interests, and is not "selling out" to the other party. In simulated negotiations, social scientists have found that representatives who are accountable to constituents are more likely to be tough and to use competitive tactics.[26]

H. THE NEGOTIATOR'S PERSONALITY

A fundamental thesis of this book is that the negotiator's personality does not necessarily dictate her choice of negotiation tactics. Personal

23. *Id.* R. 1.2.

24. *Id.* R. 1.2(a).

25. *See* PRUITT, *supra* note 8, at 41–45 MCKERSIE, *supra* note 12, at 417–19; Helmut Lamm, *Group–Related Influences on Nego-* *tiation Behavior: Two–Person Negotiation as a Function of Representation and Election, in* BARGAINING BEHAVIOR 284, 297–302 (Heinz Sauermann ed., 1978).

26. *See* PRUITT, *supra* note 8, at 42, 120–21 & 196; Lamm, *supra* note 25, at 297.

traits, however, inevitably affect the ability of the negotiator to carry out certain tactics. The negotiator who instantly dominates the room when she walks in is going to have an easier time using competitive negotiation tactics effectively than will a more reserved peer. On the other hand, the more assertive and aggressive negotiator may find it difficult to employ collaborative strategies that may seem to her needlessly "touchy-feely" or even convoluted.

As you initially study negotiation tactics, it is recommended that you try a variety of negotiation techniques and, in effect, engage in role-playing behavior in order to use those tactics that may not come naturally to you. Ultimately, you probably will find yourself comfortable with certain tactics that you would not use if you were negotiating "naturally." These tactics can become a part of your negotiation repertoire, to be used at appropriate times. On the other hand, your preferred negotiation tactics, even after studying negotiation and trying out various approaches, probably will reflect, to some extent, your basic personality and the negotiating style you have used, more or less habitually, in the hundreds of negotiations that ordinary, non-legal life demands from us all.

I. BUT HOW DO YOU CHOOSE
THE BEST TACTIC?

This chapter discusses various factors to consider in choosing effective negotiation tactics at each and every point during the negotiation. Table 2–1 presents a summary of how the issues considered in this chapter influence the choice of effective negotiation tactics.

The factors influencing the choice of negotiation tactics often point in contradictory directions regarding which tactics will be effective. Unfortunately, there is no method for either ranking the importance of the factors or for weighing the effects of various factors. As with all strategic decisions made by lawyers—whether during appellate argument, trial or interviewing and counseling—tactical negotiation choices are matters of individual judgment. Nevertheless, the lawyer who systematically considers the full array of factors involved in making such choices is more likely to make an informed and effective decision.

TABLE 2-1

CHOOSING EFFECTIVE NEGOTIATION TACTICS: A SUMMARY

ISSUE INFLUENCING CHOICE OF TACTICS	TYPE OF TACTIC SUGGESTED BY "YES" ANSWER	TYPE OF TACTIC SUGGESTED BY "NO" ANSWER
Will *other negotiator* continue *competitive tactics*?	Competitive	Any
Does bargaining context offer *integrative potential*?	Problem-solving	Competitive or Cooperative
Is negotiation in *early phases*?	Often Competitive	Increasing Possibility of Problem-solving or Cooperative
Does Negotiator possess *superior bargaining power*?	Any	Cooperative, or Competitive Followed by Cooperative or Problem-solving
Is there an *ongoing relationship* between the parties?	Cooperative or Problem-solving	Any, including Competitive
Do competitive tactics violate *bargaining norms*?	Cooperative or Problem-solving	Any
Does *client's input* favor competitive display?	Competitive	Any
Does *negotiator's own personality* make her more comfortable with collaborative tactics?	Cooperative or Problem-solving	Any

Chapter Three

NEGOTIATION PLANNING

A. AN OVERVIEW OF STRATEGIC PLANNING

Planning for legal negotiation consists of two discrete tasks: subject matter preparation and negotiation strategy preparation. The more important of these, subject matter preparation, will be mentioned only briefly here. The lawyer must understand thoroughly the subject matter of the case or transaction being negotiated. Otherwise the prosecutor who has not yet examined the case is not in the strongest possible negotiating position when confronted in the courthouse halls by a well-prepared defense attorney. Effective negotiation is also difficult for the inexperienced plaintiff's personal injury attorney unaware of the local norms in personal injury settlements when she bargains with a wizened veteran. Insofar as the other party's competitive tactics are designed to induce the negotiator to lose confidence in her case, nothing assures his success as the negotiator's own sense that she does not understand the case and is inadequately prepared. The lawyer's legal and factual preparation provides the substance of her arguments and her questions during negotiation, and helps her evaluate the case. This chapter, however, discusses the other kind of negotiation planning: strategy preparation.

The lawyer cannot script the negotiation process in the same way that a trial lawyer can prepare an opening statement or questions for direct examination. The lawyer's second and third communications in a negotiation depend upon the other negotiator's initial responses. Although negotiation is somewhat unstructured and spontaneous, the lawyer who has not considered her strategy in interacting with the other party is at a severe disadvantage. What then can be done to prepare for the strategic aspects of negotiation?

For several reasons negotiation planning should be a joint process between lawyer and client. First, ultimately the client will need to approve any agreement reached by the negotiating lawyers, and therefore it is sometimes desirable to have the client approve any proposals or concessions made by his lawyer in advance.[1] Second, as suggested in the

---

1. On other occasions, there are tactical reasons to avoid giving the attorney author- ity to settle the case. *See infra*, at pages 72– 74.

47

previous chapter, the choice of tactics often affects the client in ways other than success in achieving a desirable agreement, and therefore he should have a role in formulating them. Third, the client is usually more knowledgeable about both the dispute or transaction being negotiated and his own interests in it; this familiarity allows him to assist his lawyer in developing negotiation proposals, arguments and other tactics.

In some instances, it may be more feasible or advantageous for the lawyer to do the negotiation planning without significant assistance from the client. If the attorney and client have had a long-standing relationship and the lawyer understands the transaction thoroughly, a client may decide to delegate all responsibility for negotiation planning to the attorney. For example, a business client and his lawyer may decide in the interest of time and money that it is not desirable or realistic for them to consult extensively about the negotiation for a collection of a modest overdue debt.

The lawyer and client should discuss the following topics prior to beginning bargaining:

(1) What are the client's interests that will be affected by the results of the negotiation and by the negotiation process itself?

(2) What alternatives to a negotiated agreement are available to the client, and what is the least advantageous outcome of the negotiation (the "reservation price" or "reservation point") that the client would prefer to these alternatives?

(3) What alternatives to a negotiated agreement are available to the other party, and what is the least advantageous negotiated outcome that he probably would prefer to these alternatives?

(4) What implications, other than the result of the negotiation, does the lawyer's negotiating behavior have for her client?

The remaining topics of the planning conference between lawyer and client depend upon whether the lawyer anticipates using predominantly competitive, cooperative, or problem-solving negotiation tactics, or a mixture of tactics. If the lawyer plans on using competitive tactics, she should also discuss the sources of leverage and power that the client has over the other party. If cooperative tactics are to be used, the lawyer should investigate with her client the potential sources of objective criteria that she could use to resolve a dispute. The problem-solving approach to negotiation suggests that the lawyer and client formulate solutions that will satisfy the parties' underlying interests. Also, in anticipation that the lawyers may "horse-trade" on the various issues, this approach requires the client to determine her relative order of preferences among these issues.

B. DETERMINING THE CLIENT'S INTERESTS

The quality of a negotiated agreement is determined by the extent to which it serves the client's interests.[2] Accordingly, the lawyer must

---

2. According to an American Bar Association committee report:

The purpose of settlement negotiations is to arrive at agreements satisfactory to

accurately understand the client's interests before beginning to bargain. This often is not as simple as it initially seems. When questioned about what he expects from a negotiation, the client often responds with a "bottom line" or negotiating *position.* For example, consider a negotiation between Katie Eisinger, the attorney representing Professor Anton Volkov, and Jonathan Prevas, counsel for Banting Medical Technologies, Inc. Professor Volkov has recently pioneered a new method for genetically modifying viruses in order to treat diseases, a technology he calls "Viral Sharpshooter." Under his newly patented method, Dr. Volkov removes the viral DNA from a well-known virus, such as a specific type of influenza virus, replaces the viral DNA with healthy DNA, and injects the modified virus into the diseased patients' bodies. Once injected, the modified virus attacks diseased cells and replaces them with healthy DNA cells. Though the procedure is neither FDA approved nor proven replicable on a large scale, Dr. Volkov believes that his patented technology may one day cure diseases caused by viruses—including some forms of cancer.

Jonathan, as attorney for Banting, has offered Dr. Volkov a lump sum payment of $300,000 for exclusive worldwide manufacturing and distribution rights for Viral Sharpshooter. While this price is modest, Rachel Goldberg, Banting's Vice–President for Research and Development, believes that Viral Sharpshooter is an unproven technology and that the expenses involved in further testing and FDA approval will be very substantial, possibly without yielding a commercially viable technology. Dr. Volkov, whose research has been highly acclaimed by peers in the medical research community, is infuriated by what he regards as an insulting "low ball" offer from a greedy corporation, and insists that Katie counter-offer with a figure of $400,000,000. He tells Katie that such a price is highly reasonable for the sale of a technology that will lead to the eventual eradication of some forms of cancer, HIV, influenza, the common cold, and all other viral illnesses! Negotiation stalemate and breakdown appear to be imminent.

If Katie, as Volkov's lawyer, probes beneath her client's stated *position* to determine his *underlying interests,* however, agreement may be possible.[3] Focusing on the underlying interests of the parties instead

those whom a lawyer represents and consistent with law and relevant rules of professional responsibility. During settlement negotiations and in concluding a settlement, a lawyer is the client's representative and fiduciary, and should act in the client's best interest and in furtherance of the client's lawful goals.

Ethical Guidelines for Settlement Negotiations, 2002 A.B.A. SEC. OF LITIG. § 2.1 (2002).

   3. In some instances, the client's "bottom line" might be determined more by

market prices or "what the market will bear" than by the client's underlying interests. In all but the simplest and most routine legal negotiations, however, market price is not a sole determinant of the client's "bottom line" because potential partners to a transaction and what they have to offer are not fungible. This lack of fungibility suggests the limitations of price alone as a proxy for client satisfaction.

of on positions is an important part of problem-solving negotiation. Consider how Jonathan and Rachel might explore Banting's underlying interests in the negotiation:

1—Jonathan: How did you decide that our initial offer to Dr. Volkov should be $300,000?

2—Rachel: It's the most we ever pay for a new drug or technology that has neither been tested on humans nor approved by the FDA. There are just too many long-shot possibilities out there, and we cannot gamble more than that on any one of them. The costs of the FDA approval process and testing on humans can easily run into the millions!

3—Jonathan: I think you did tell me before that the upside potential of the Viral Sharpshooter is greater than anything you've ever seen. But it's still too big a risk?

4—Rachel: Definitely. And we cannot set a precedent for other unproven technologies.

Here Jonathan has delved beneath Banting's stated position and has learned that its underlying interests include:

(1) A desire to avoid being stuck with both a large licensing fee owed to Volkov and the considerable expenses of human testing and FDA approval, while at the same time shouldering the substantial risk that Viral Sharpshooter ultimately may not become a marketable technology; and

(2) The need to avoid creating a precedent that would cause other researchers to demand substantial lump-sum licensing fees.

A variety of negotiation proposals now can be devised that adequately will protect these interests at the same time that they meet Banting's needs. For example, Volkov might agree to a smaller guaranteed "up front" licensing fee if he receives royalty payments on revenues earned from the Viral Sharpshooter technology. Further, he might also agree to keep the amount of the royalty payments confidential so that it does not establish a trend for agreements with other scientists in the future.

One classic example of an agreement that became possible when the negotiators focused on the underlying interests of the parties and not on their stated positions was the peace treaty negotiated by Egypt and Israel in 1978 at Camp David.[4] Egypt's stated demand was the return of the entire Sinai Peninsula, captured by Israel in the 1967 War. Israel's

---

4. *See* ROGER FISHER, WILLIAM URY & BRUCE PATTON, GETTING TO YES: NEGOTIATING AGREEMENT WITHOUT GIVING IN 41–42 (2d ed. 1991); HOWARD RAIFFA, NEGOTIATION ANALYSIS: THE SCIENCE AND ART OF COLLABORATIVE DECISION MAKING 321–25 (2002).

seemingly irreconcilable position was its continued possession for security purposes of at least a portion of the Sinai. The underlying interests of the parties, however, were not inherently incompatible. Israel's interest was security: to prevent Egyptian forces from being poised in the Sinai to launch an invasion of Israel. As a matter of principle and national pride, Egypt's interest was the Sinai's return to its sovereignty. At Camp David, the two sides agreed to return the Sinai to Egyptian sovereignty, but to demilitarize major portions of the peninsula so as not to pose a military threat to Israel. In this case, stated *positions* previously had obscured the fact that the *interests* of the parties were not inherently in conflict.

These two examples, one from a technology transfer negotiation and the other from the world of international diplomacy, show the importance of determining the client's underlying interests. How does the lawyer accomplish this? As demonstrated by Jonathan, the basic approach is to delve behind the client's stated position and ask *why* the client articulates his position as he does. Negotiating positions are inherently conclusory statements that hide the specifics of the client's needs.

It is important not to construe the client's interests too narrowly. Too often, when lawyers consult with clients about negotiation, they focus exclusively on monetary and other easily quantifiable factors. The client's interests in the negotiation are not only economic, but also psychological and professional or social. For instance, reaching agreement reduces anxiety for clients and their executives, regardless of whether the client's alternative to a particular negotiated agreement is to forego a potentially lucrative medical technology or is to proceed to trial. The client's interests are also professional or social: how will researchers who licensed their technologies to Banting in the past react if the "new kid on the block" gets a break on the amount of the licensing fees? Thus, to produce a negotiated agreement that is satisfying to the client, the lawyer should be aware of all of the client's interests in the matter, including economic, psychological, professional and social ones.

C. CONSULTATION CONCERNING NEGOTIATION STRATEGY

The client's interests affect not only the substance of negotiation proposals and positions, they also should influence the choice of negotiation tactics. One consequence of the choice of negotiation strategy warrants reiteration at this time because of its considerable impact on the client's interests. The lawyer and client should explore, during a pre-negotiation conference, the implications of negotiation tactics on the future relationship between the client and the other party. If the parties anticipate a continuing relationship, either cooperative or problem-solving bargaining tactics usually will be preferred,[5] because competitive

---

5. *See* ROBERT M. AXELROD, THE EVOLUTION OF COOPERATION 129 (1984); DEAN PRUITT, NEGOTIATION BEHAVIOR 39–40, 109–12 (1981); Kenneth J. Roering, Allen E. Slusher &

tactics often generate distrust and ill will. Further, competitive tactics may not serve the client's best interests because they often result in social disapproval within the business community and invite later retaliation for violating fairness norms. On the other hand, a particular client might prefer the use of competitive tactics in a negotiation with a party with whom it has a continuing relationship because the client believes such tactics establish a strong bargaining image and discourage future attempts at exploitation by the other party. The client's input into the lawyer's choice of negotiation tactics is critical precisely because of the different concerns clients may have about how their lawyers' negotiating behaviors affect their own relationships with other parties.

D. THE CLIENT'S "BEST ALTERNATIVE TO A NEGOTIATED AGREEMENT" AND RESERVATION POINT

The most important aspect of determining the client's interests in the negotiation is to ascertain what alternatives the client has to a negotiated agreement and, perhaps, what negotiated agreement is least advantageous, yet acceptable, from his viewpoint. The least advantageous settlement acceptable to the client, or the "bottom line," is referred to as the client's *reservation point* or *reservation price*.[6] The advantage of determining a reservation point in advance of the negotiation is that a quantified "bottom line" prevents both the client and the negotiator from being "swept away" during the negotiation process. Without an explicit reservation point, a lawyer occasionally accepts a bad deal for her client because she becomes anxious or is persuaded by the other party's assertions during bargaining.

Determining the client's reservation point in advance of the negotiation, however, may be both unrealistic and undesirable. Any consideration of a "bottom line" prior to the negotiation requires an understanding of both the alternatives to settlement and the likely settlement outcome. At this early stage, though, the information available to lawyer and client usually is incomplete; lawyers typically begin negotiating prior to completing their own investigation of facts, legal research and discovery. In addition, the lawyer is unaware at this stage of how the other side views the case and of additional facts and information that will be gleaned from the other party during the bargaining process. The lawyer, therefore, should make disclaimers about the adequacy of her information during her counseling sessions with the client concerning alterna-

Robert D. Schooler, *Commitment to Future Interaction in Marketing Transactions*, 60 J. APPLIED PSYCHOLOGY 386, 386–87 (1975); Jeffery Z. Rubin, *Negotiation: An Introduction to Some Issues and Themes*, 27 AM. BEHAVIORAL SCIENTIST 135, 137 (1983).

6. The first edition of this text used the term "minimum disposition" to express this idea. *See also* GARY BELLOW & BEA MOUL-

TON, THE LAWYERING PROCESS: MATERIALS FOR CLINICAL INSTRUCTION IN ADVOCACY 487 (1978). More recently, however, the term "reservation value," "reservation price" or "reservation point" has become the generally accepted term. *See* RAIFFA, *supra* note 4, at 110; *see also* Russell Korobkin, *A Positive Theory of Legal Negotiation*, 88 GEO. L.J. 1789, 1792–93 (2000).

tives. These same factors suggest that any reservation point determined by the client at this time be regarded as flexible and subject to change as the negotiation continues.

Fisher, Ury and Patton, leading proponents of problem-solving bargaining, go further and suggest that a client should not set a "bottom line" prior to bargaining.[7] They offer two justifications for their position. First, the bottom line is likely to be set too high. Before hearing from the other party, and at a time when uncertainty prevails, it is very easy for the client and the attorney to assess the client's situation through "rose-colored glasses." There is a natural tendency among most people, including lawyers, to defer bad news as long as possible; one reason is that lawyers may believe that good news facilitates client relations. After all, the other party's unwillingness to fulfill the client's expectations always can be blamed on "unreasonableness." If a rigid reservation point is set too high, according to Fisher, Ury and Patton, the client may subsequently decide to reject a negotiated settlement that meets his interests.

In addition, as with the adoption of a fixed negotiation position, a specific reservation point inhibits problem-solving bargaining. If Banting establishes a reservation price of $300,000, it would reject any licensing scheme calling for a lump sum licensing agreement of $1.5 million, even if the university that employed Volkov or the National Institutes of Health agreed to pay some or all of the costs of further testing or the FDA approval process.

Regardless of whether a lawyer believes that on balance it is good negotiation practice to establish a reservation point, she should review with the client his alternatives to the negotiated agreement and determine his "Best Alternative to a Negotiated Agreement" or "BATNA."[8] Fisher, Ury and Patton use this term to represent the option available to the client that best satisfies his interests if the negotiation is unsuccessful; they suggest that the client's BATNA be the standard against which any negotiated agreement be measured. In many cases, the client's explicit awareness of his BATNA prevents him from being too optimistic about his prospects if negotiation deadlock occurs. In other cases, it prevents the client from being overly pessimistic and entering into an agreement that is not as satisfactory to him as an available alternative.

One of the most valuable types of expertise that the experienced lawyer brings to her professional relationship with her client is knowledge and inventiveness about possible alternatives to the negotiated agreement. For example, if Katie, Dr. Volkov's attorney, is an experienced intellectual property and tech-transfer attorney, she knows that pharmaceutical manufacturers and medical technology companies frequently pay royalties on the subsequent sales of products and services incorporating patented research. She also likely knows about additional sources of funding for the required regulatory approvals of Viral Sharpshooter and associated human testing. In many instances, the client will

7. FISHER, URY & PATTON, *supra* note 4, at 98–99.

8. *Id.* at 104.

know more about the alternatives than anyone else, and sometimes he will have his own professional experts such as business consultants, investment counselors or accountants to rely on. In other situations, however, depending upon the nature of the relationship agreed upon by the lawyer and the client, the lawyer also might be expected to provide advice of this kind. If the lawyer is not aware of the necessary information from her own professional experience and background, she needs to research her client's alternatives by consulting with other appropriate professionals.

In personal injury negotiations, plea-bargaining or other litigation settlement talks, the expected trial outcome usually is the client's alternative to a negotiated agreement. The lawyer takes the lead in describing for the client both the expected trial outcome and the probable range of any negotiated settlement.[9] Lawyers use a variety of methods to predict jury verdicts in litigation. Sometimes in a routine case the experienced lawyer can predict confidently for the client the likely legal consequences of the trial alternative. For example, assume a defendant who has been charged with driving under the influence of alcohol and who:

(a) recorded a blood alcohol breath test result of .11% alcohol in the blood by weight;

(b) was observed by a police officer for a distance of one-half mile weaving left of center;

(c) has three prior convictions for DUI; and

(d) could not touch his finger to his nose.

An experienced lawyer who routinely handles DUI cases (driving under the influence of alcohol) in a particular jurisdiction and locale typically can predict both the expected trial outcome and the prosecutor's plea bargaining position with some accuracy.

Suppose, however, that the lawyer has never handled a similar case before, even though the case is not extraordinary. As an example, consider the case of a chemical engineer who leaves his employer and sets up a competing business, even though his contract with his original employer included agreements precluding him from using either trade secrets or customer lists after his employment ended. Even if the legal issues are clear, the lawyer probably does not have sufficient information from her practice experience to predict how the jury would react to the liability and damage issues. Under these circumstances, the inexperienced lawyer should seek the advice of more experienced attorneys who have handled similar cases. Indeed, ready sharing of this kind of information among lawyers is one of the benefits of practicing with a large

9. *See* DAVID A. BINDER, PAUL BERGMAN & SUSAN C. PRICE, LAWYERS AS COUNSELORS: A CLIENT CENTERED APPROACH 337–40 (1991). The process of decision analysis in choosing between settlement and litigation alterna-tives is analyzed in RAIFFA, *supra* note 4, at 32–33, and in Peter T. Hoffman, *Valuation of Cases for Settlement: Theory and Practice*, 1991 J. DISP. RESOL. 1 (1991).

firm or maintaining good relations with other attorneys in the community.

Finally, consider the "big case" or another unusual case for which there are no precedents in a particular locale. How is it ever possible to predict trial outcomes so that the client knows whether she is better off to settle or to go to trial? First, it is important to acknowledge that valuing cases and predicting trial outcomes is far from an exact science. Douglas E. Rosenthal, in his seminal work on client counseling, *Lawyer and Client: Who's In Charge?*,[10] reports on a survey in which he asked three experienced personal injury lawyers and two insurance company representatives to place a settlement value on sixty-one personal injury claims after looking at the actual case files. In one of the cases, the highest valuation by an expert was $30,000; the lowest was $2,000. Differentials of 600% in the other cases were not unusual.

Assume however that the plaintiff is Tamiqua Lewis, the mother of Malik, the lead poisoned child. Tamiqua and Michelle Chang, her attorney, have retained an expert medical witness that will testify that Malik's cognitive functioning has been significantly and permanently harmed by the lead poisoning and that Malik also suffers from attention deficit hyperactivity disorder (ADHD) as a result of the exposure. What are these claims of Malik, now nine years old, worth? Neither Michelle nor any attorney in her office ever has represented a plaintiff with identical injuries or with identical facts on liability. Yet she must advise her client of the alternatives she has to acceptance of the latest settlement offer from Piccolo Property Management. In this context, the lawyer must predict:

(1) how the trial court judge will resolve all legal issues;

(2) the credibility of her own liability witnesses, including those testifying regarding Piccolo's property maintenance procedures (or the lack thereof), and the credibility of Piccolo Management Company's employees and/or experts;

(3) whether the jury will believe that Piccolo's actions were negligent and whether such negligence caused Malik's impairments;

(4) whether the jury will find her own client to be credible and likable or will, for legitimate or illegitimate reasons, implicitly blame the mother for the child's difficulties;

(5) the credibility of the plaintiff's damages witnesses including the treating physician, the childhood lead poisoning medical and rehabilitation expert, and the economist;

(6) the amount of damages, if any, that the jury will award; and

(7) whether the judgment of the trial court will be upheld on appeal.

Presumably both law school and practice teach lawyers something about predicting the legal decisions of trial and appellate courts. Common sense, educated by trial practice and evidence courses—and especially by

10. Douglas E. Rosenthal, Lawyer and Client: Who's in Charge? 200–08 (1974).

experience—makes lawyers more capable of predicting the factual findings of the jury. How, then, can the lawyer predict damages?

Once again, in fairly routine cases, the lawyer can rely upon her experience or that of her colleagues. In the more unusual case, there are several tools that may be of assistance. Historically, trial lawyers sometimes used various formulae to predict personal injury verdicts. But the "three times specials" or other multiples of the plaintiff's "out of pocket" expenses that have often been used as a rough approximation of a claim are generally inadequate and out of date. Of more use are services, such as *Mealey's Litigation Reports: Lead*, that report on the liability and damages facts of recent settlements and are currently available through the Lexis/Nexis database. Similar *Mealey's Reports* are available for many other specialized types of personal-injury claims, as well for general damage verdicts and settlements in certain jurisdictions. Other guides are available as well. The *Personal Injury Valuation* Handbook[11] or the *AAJ Law Reporter*,[12] for example, report the amount of settlements and jury verdicts for various types of injuries and also frequently provide some description of the characteristics of the jurisdiction in which the award was granted—that is, whether juries are likely to be liberal or conservative in estimating damages. Finally, experts can be retained who value personal-injury claims by looking at cases with comparable liability and damage issues in similar jurisdictions. A large number of these valuation experts advertise on the world-wide web.

The methods used for valuing personal injury claims are only examples of the wide array of approaches that lawyers use to predict the legal consequences of the trial alternative in a litigation context. It is important to reiterate that the psychological, economic and social consequences for the plaintiff of proceeding to trial are also important factors in describing and evaluating the alternatives to a negotiated settlement. These factors often are highly personal to the client, and weighing these factors is a uniquely individual decision. Tamiqua Lewis's lawyer might conclude that she has an eighty percent chance of a favorable verdict and the likely amount of that verdict would be $1.2 million dollars. Nevertheless, the client may legitimately decide to accept any settlement offer in excess of $400,000. From a strictly economic standpoint, has the client behaved irrationally? Perhaps, but it is the client and her son who will live with the consequences of her decision, while the lawyer goes on to her next case.

Regardless of whether the lawyer and client decide upon a rigid reservation point prior to negotiation, or only evaluate the client's Best Alternative to a Negotiated Agreement, either of these approaches serves as a check on the negotiator. Many lawyers also establish a negotiation *target*. The *target* is set at some level above the reservation point

---

11. JURY VERDICT RESEARCH, INC., PERSONAL INJURY VALUATION HANDBOOKS.

12. *Law Reporter Injury Collections*, AMERICAN ASS'N FOR JUSTICE (formerly Ass'n of Trial Lawyers of America), *available at* http://www.atla.org/LegalResearchServices/ Tier3/lawreporterdocs.aspx (last visited, April 25, 2007).

acceptable to the client, and provides a higher level of satisfaction to the client than an agreement that achieves only the client's reservation point. Interestingly, the empirical work of Chester Karass suggests that negotiators who have "higher targets" or greater aspirations achieve more for their clients in negotiations than others.[13] In addition, a negotiation target can serve as a "tripwire" in a negotiation; when the negotiator makes a proposal on an issue that is less advantageous than the negotiation target, she knows the bargaining is approaching her client's minimum requirements.

The lawyer should also evaluate the other party's alternatives to the negotiated agreement. It is useful to the lawyer to understand the other party's probable BATNA for prediction of eventual agreement and detection of bluffing. Understanding the other party's interests also assists the lawyer in her efforts to use problem-solving methods.

In summary, prior to the negotiation, the lawyer and client dyad should discuss the client's interests, the chosen negotiation strategy's implications for the client, and alternatives to a negotiated agreement for both the client and the other party. The balance of the pre-negotiation planning conference depends upon whether the issues to be negotiated have integrative potential or are predominantly distributive ones, and upon whether the lawyer intends to use competitive, cooperative, or problem-solving tactics, or a mixture of strategies.

E. IDENTIFYING INTEGRATIVE POTENTIAL

In preparing for negotiation, the lawyer should explore if there are any integrative opportunities (opportunities for value creation) in the bargaining situation, that is, whether the parties could resolve their differences in ways that provide a high degree of satisfaction for both parties. This result can be achieved in one of two possible ways, as described in Chapter Two. First, is there a potential solution to the parties' respective problems that will satisfy both their underlying interests? Second, are there multiple issues involved in the negotiation which the parties prioritize differently? If so, the parties may be able to "logroll"—each will concede on issues of less importance to him or her. The resulting exchange of concessions will yield greater joint benefit than if each side makes concessions on all issues.

The appropriate time for the lawyer to begin to identify any integrative potential is prior to the negotiation. The mere presence of integrative potential, which would allow the lawyer to use problem-solving tactics, however, does not necessarily dictate that the lawyers should use such tactics. In some circumstances, the lawyer may decide that it is in her client's best interests to use competitive tactics, even if a problem-solving approach also could be used.

13. *See* CHESTER KARASS, THE NEGOTIATING GAME 12–26 (1970); Charles B. Craver, *The Negotiation Process*, 27 AM. J. TRIAL ADVOC. 271, 281 (2003).

How can the lawyer decide what integrative potential exists in a bargaining situation? The analysis begins when the lawyer and client discuss the underlying interests of the client and those of the other party. The process continues with possible identification of potential solutions to problems facing both parties that would satisfy their underlying interests.

1. "BRAINSTORMING"

One of the techniques to be used in developing proposals that satisfy both parties' interests is "brainstorming."[14] The purpose of brainstorming is to produce as many potential solutions to the parties' problems as possible. The participants in brainstorming, in this case the client and his attorney, are encouraged to articulate whatever possible solutions come to mind, regardless of how ridiculous or non-viable they initially appear. The lawyer and client suspend critical evaluation and judgment until all possible proposals have been listed, and only at that point do they consciously and systematically consider the viability of each option and its advantages and disadvantages. This technique mitigates the possibility that a viable option will not be carefully considered because the participants have excluded it as a result of intuitive or subconscious prejudices that, upon further reflection, are not valid. Brainstorming also serves to counteract the tendency of many lawyers to be too critical and, as a result of either their personalities or their legal training, to seek only the "best answer."

To illustrate the use of brainstorming as part of a client counseling session prior to the negotiation, consider the pre-negotiation counseling session between Jonathan Prevas and Rachel Goldberg, Banting's Vice President for Research and Development. Rachel is unwilling to pay Dr. Volkov more than a flat $500,000 lump sum licensing fee, both because of the substantial possibility that the technology will not pan out and because she does not want to create a costly precedent for the acquisition of other technologies in the future. In the following example, observe as Jonathan actually educates his client about the use of brainstorming techniques. This is not unique, however, as lawyers frequently teach their clients about other aspects of the legal process such as cross-examination or depositions:

1—Jonathan: Rachel, I'm scheduled to meet with Katie Eisinger, the attorney representing Dr. Volkov, tomorrow to see whether we can work out an agreement for the licensing of the Viral Sharpshooter technology. I think the most contentious issue will be how much we pay Volkov as a licensing fee. He seemed insulted by our earlier offer, claiming that a cure for viral illnesses is worth virtually unlimited royalty payments. As I recall, you told me before that I

---

14. *See* Fisher, Ury & Patton, *supra* note 4, at 60–69.

was not authorized to pay anything more than $500,000. Is that still the case?

2—Rachel: Chances are this technology is worth nothing. It simply costs too much to test and get approved. Meanwhile, we would be communicating to every other researcher that Banting is handing out billions.

3—Jonathan: Well, what I'd like to do today, Rachel, is to see if we can come up with some ideas that would be fair to Volkov if this turns out to be the real thing, but does not bankrupt you if it is just another false hope and, at the same time, does not invite other researchers to expect a huge handout. If we can, I'll propose it to Volkov's attorney tomorrow. I've done some work in this area before and I have some ideas, but I really wanted you involved in this process because your superior background and experience in technology acquisition should provide us with additional ideas.

What I have found usually works best is for you and me simply to throw out ideas that might work, regardless of how crazy they might sound. We'll just list the ideas and come back later to evaluate each of the options. That way we won't subconsciously discard what might be a good idea. Do you have the idea?

4—Rachel: I think so. You mean just to talk about whatever crazy ideas come to mind? They teach you that in law school?

5—Jonathan: (laughs) I think you've got the idea. And yes, they're starting to teach such things in law school.

Here the lawyer has educated the client about the technique of brainstorming.

Brainstorming often initially seems uncomfortable and unconventional to some clients. Sometimes the lawyer can ease this threatened loss of rapport by reporting how well it has worked with other clients. Brainstorming seldom will be appropriate in the first encounter between lawyer and client, but hopefully by this time in Rachel's relationship with Jonathan, she has enough trust in him that she will go along with what initially appears to be a strange and crazy idea. After this introductory phase, the actual brainstorming begins:

6—Jonathan: Let's begin, then. Any ideas on how we could work something out with Volkov?

7—Rachel: Obviously he believes that this really will cure viral illnesses including some forms of cancer and if it does, that he is entitled to much more than $500,000. Sometimes in the past, researchers who license their technologies to us receive royalty payments, a percentage of the revenues earned from the technology.

8—Jonathan: Yes, I've worked with that kind of an agreement in the past. Good, we'll write that down and come back to it in a minute. Do you have other possible approaches?

9—Rachel: We could agree to additional payments as the development of the Viral Sharpshooter technology reaches certain benchmarks. I think, for example, that we would be willing to pay a great deal more when the FDA licensed Viral Sharpshooter.

10—Jonathan: Good!

11—Rachel: Or perhaps we could even make substantial payments at earlier benchmarks, like achieving certain results in the clinical trials. But maybe that's not such a good idea. What happens if the clinical trial results are ambiguous or conflicting as they often are?

12—Jonathan: Let's wait till we've listed all the options that we can think of before we start evaluating and criticizing the various possibilities. I don't want you to get cautious in suggesting options because you are thinking about the problems with them.

In this sequence, both lawyer and client contribute options through a joint brainstorming process. Jonathan writes each one down, but does not pause for evaluation or either favorable or critical comments. His responses of "good" to Rachel's various suggestions are *recognition* comments on how well she is doing in the brainstorming process itself, not evaluations of her substantive suggestions. In segment number 11 of the exchange, Rachel begins to evaluate one of the options she has mentioned and suggests that it is not viable. Jonathan points out that this contribution is evaluative and discourages it.

Together, Jonathan and Rachel so far have identified those options that come readily to mind because they relate directly to the structure of the payments for licensing the Viral Sharpshooter technology. Observe as Jonathan tries to keep the brainstorming process flowing by broadening the scope of the inquiry:

15—Jonathan: What else?

16—Rachel: That's about it.

17—Jonathan: So far we've mostly talked about altering the format for compensating Volkov for the licensing of his technology. In what other ways can we change the situation?

18—Rachel: Perhaps we could work jointly with Volkov to get NIH [National Institutes of Health] funding or even a direct Congressional appropriation. If we did that, it would lower our testing costs and we could afford to pay Volkov more.

19—Jonathan: Good. Is there any chance that if Volkov's university were to get a cut of the royalties they would provide some of the testing services for free or at least reduce their usual overhead charges?

20—Rachel: That might work. We'd have to check. Perhaps we could even do some of our own fundraising among family-members of those suffering from currently incurable forms of cancer.

21—Jonathan: I'll write that down. Anything else?

22—Rachel: I'm out of ideas.

23—Jonathan: What about Banting agreeing to provide Volkov with a long term consulting agreement to work on this medical technology or other new ones? Let's consider that.

Other than that, I can't think of anything else either. Now let's go back and decide which of these ideas are serious possibilities.

Jonathan's extra prodding produced a number of different options. Some of these options probably will be quickly discarded, but others, such as hiring Volkov on a long-term consulting contract, may be viable ones that might not have surfaced except for the free-flowing brainstorming processes. A conscious and systematic evaluation of their viability may reveal that at a minimum they should be proposed to the other party during the negotiation session itself.

The biggest advantage of brainstorming techniques is that they tend to prevent the lawyer and client from prematurely excluding possibilities on the basis that they either "sound crazy" or are not the usual way of doing things. During the second stage of brainstorming, the lawyer and client consciously and systematically evaluate the feasibility and the advantages and disadvantages of each option. Later, during the negotiation itself, the two lawyers also evaluate the proposals.

Pre-negotiation brainstorming often includes not only the client and the attorney, but also appropriate experts. Accountants or investment bankers, for example, often are capable of devising creative ways of structuring financial transactions that are not readily apparent to even the sophisticated client and his experienced counsel. Similarly, annuity experts may be able to suggest a structured settlement approach for the injured personal injury claimant.

Fisher, Ury and Patton emphasize brainstorming as an important ingredient in their approach of "principled negotiation."[15] They suggest a number of ways in which bargaining situations with possibly little or no integrative potential still can benefit from a problem-solving approach. For one thing, they argue that greater problem-solving opportunities exist if the participants in brainstorming *expand the agenda*, that is, consider enlarging the issues to be included within the proposed agreement. The brainstorming session previously described between Jonathan and Rachel illustrated a number of instances of *agenda expansion*, such as reaching an agreement with the university to pick up some of the testing costs in exchange for a share of the royalties or placing Volkov on a long term consulting contract. Neither of these issues was previously present in the negotiation, but each provides an alternative that benefits both Banting and Volkov. By expanding the agenda as a result of the brainstorming process, the lawyer and client have discovered integrative potential that was not readily apparent.

2. PREPARATION FOR OTHER PROBLEM–SOLVING TACTICS

The lawyer and client, during the pre-negotiation counseling session, should discuss the possible use of other problem-solving techniques. First, the lawyer should determine the relative importance of the issues to the client. Most negotiations involve multiple issues. For example, the technology transfer agreement between Banting and Volkov involves not only the compensation to Volkov for the licensing of his patented technology, but also the duration of the licensing agreement, the potential confidentiality of any agreement, and perhaps many other issues such as an ongoing consulting relationship between Banting and Volkov. One problem-solving technique, "logrolling,"[16] consists of conceding on some issues while the other party concedes on other issues. To the extent that the parties place differing emphasis on the various issues, logrolling increases the parties' joint benefit beyond what it would be if each party conceded an equivalent amount on each individual issue. In other words, when logrolling each party concedes more on the issue about which it cares less. To be effective, logrolling requires the lawyers to clearly understand their clients' relative priorities among the multiple issues.

15. *Id.* at 70–71.   16. *See* PRUITT, *supra* note 4, at 153–55.

Do not underestimate the importance of either the logrolling technique or the accompanying need to counsel continually with the client regarding his relative preferences among the various issues. In actual negotiation, the fact that parties place differing priorities on various issues is a significant reason why agreements are reached in most cases. Therefore, discussing the logrolling process and ascertaining the client's priorities prior to the negotiation are important aspects of negotiation planning.

The lawyer also should anticipate, during the planning conference with the client, the possibility of using two other problem-solving negotiation techniques, *cost-cutting* and *compensation*.[17] If one party to a negotiation is to achieve its goals, this often imposes significant *costs* on the other party. Cost-cutting and compensation are two methods of making such an agreement less painful to the other party while allowing the first party to achieve its goals. In *cost-cutting*, the parties find ways of making the concessions less onerous. For example, Banting is concerned that any royalty payments in excess of $500,000 will create a precedent that would encourage other researchers to demand exorbitant payments in future negotiations. This cost can be "cut", however, by a confidentiality clause that provides that Volkov will not disclose to anyone else the amount paid by Banting.

Compensation is a problem-solving tactic in which the negotiator provides substitute satisfaction in exchange for the other party conceding on an issue. Obviously, logrolling is one form of compensation: the negotiating party is compensated for making a concession on one issue by receiving a concession on the other issue. Both cost-cutting and compensation will be discussed more fully in Chapter Eight, "Narrowing of Differences and Closure: Problem–Solving Tactics."

F.   DISTRIBUTIVE ISSUES

Not all issues in negotiation have significant integrative potential; some issues remain predominantly distributive ones. When the insurance company's lawyer and the paraplegic plaintiff's lawyer negotiate a settlement in a personal injury action, they are somewhat concerned with structured settlements or with having both parties avoid the costs of litigation. Neither party, however, would suggest that its primary interest is anything other than the dollar amount to be paid on the claim, a distributive situation. In the negotiation between the criminal defense attorney and the prosecutor over the length of a sentence recommendation, the lawyers perceive that their interests directly conflict. Even in the negotiation situation between Banting and Volkov, used to illustrate brainstorming techniques, the single most important issue to both parties probably is the amount of compensation Volkov will receive for the technology transfer.

How does the lawyer plan for negotiation on distributive issues? This chapter previously described the idea of a reservation point, that is,

17. *Id.* at 142–53.

the least advantageous settlement acceptable to the client. The client, of course, prefers an agreement more advantageous to her than her reservation price. For example, even if Banting were able and willing to pay a lump sum payment of $1 million and an additional payment of ten percent of all revenues generated by the Viral Sharpshooter technology, Banting's executives and shareholders would be even more pleased to pay only $500,000 and five percent of all revenues. There may be limits, of course; if the agreement is excessively favorable to Banting, it may justifiably fear that its future relationship with Volkov and other researchers will not be an entirely positive and comfortable one.

Theoretically, at least, a *range* of solutions to the matter being negotiated will always be present. Even if these solutions do not fit into readily quantifiable variables, such as dollars, it still is possible to rank-order the various negotiated settlements according to the client's relative order of preference. For example, Banting might list the options previously developed during the brainstorming session into the following sequence with the least desirable option listed first and the most desirable option listed last:

1. Pay Volkov a very large lump sum payment by raising funds through appeals to family members of cancer patients;

3. Agree to give the university a share of royalties in exchange for providing in-kind services for the required testing;

4. Pay Volkov a very large lump sum payment in exchange for his obtaining funds for further testing, customarily financed by the pharmaceutical company, from the National Institutes of Health;

5. Provide additional compensation to Volkov by hiring him as a consultant on a long-term basis;

6. Make additional incremental payments to Volkov when certain benchmarks are achieved, e.g., completion of clinical trials or licensing by FDA;

7. Make royalty payments to Volkov strictly on the basis of a percentage of revenues derived from the Viral Sharpshooter technology.

It would be possible to place each of these options sequentially on a horizontal line graph with the distance from the beginning point of the line graph at the left end representing Banting's level of satisfaction with the agreement:

FIGURE 3-1

BANTING'S LEVEL OF SATISFACTION

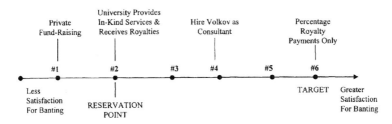

If it is assumed that option number 2, agreeing to give the university a small percentage of revenues in exchange for testing the technology, is the least attractive option which would be acceptable to Banting, then this option is Banting's reservation point. On the other hand, Banting realistically hopes that Volkov will agree to option number 6, that he be compensated strictly on the basis of royalties from the sales of the technology. Accordingly, option number 6 would be Banting's *target point*. The negotiator's goal or *target point* often reflects her prediction of what terms constitute the other side's reservation point.

The analysis of reservation point and target point is much easier in a truly distributive bargaining situation where the parties are confronted with a single issue consisting of a fixed quantity which must be divided between the parties. Consider a personal injury case. Michael Van Meter, a truck-driver, is rendered a paraplegic as a result of a collision between the truck he is driving and a railroad locomotive. His lawyer, Maria Santiago, brings an action against the railroad alleging negligence on its part. The evidence obtained during discovery shows that the railroad arguably was negligent in a variety of ways, including operating its train at an excessive rate of speed, allowing brush and shrubbery to grow near the tracks that made it impossible to see down the tracks from the highway, and failing to use statutorily required "cross buck" warning signs. The attorney for the railroad, Ashton Crutchfield, asserts that liability should be precluded, or at least damages reduced substantially (in a comparative fault jurisdiction in which the defendant's liability is reduced, but not eliminated by the plaintiff's own negligence), because of Michael's contributory negligence in not looking more carefully for an oncoming locomotive and in driving across the railroad tracks when his visibility was obscured.

In analyzing Michael's case after extensive discovery, Maria reaches the conclusion that Michael has approximately an eighty percent chance of proving the railroad's negligence. She also determines that on the comparative negligence issue there is about a sixty percent chance the jury will find Michael negligent and that if it does, the jury probably will assess his comparative degree of fault in the twenty to thirty-five percent range. In other words, the probabilities are that Michael will recover, his recovery probably will be reduced somewhat by his own contributory negligence, and that the likelihood is that this reduction in the damages will be in the range of twenty to thirty-five percent. From Michael's perspective, a settlement value must begin with the jury's likely estimate of the value of Michael's damages and then reduce it by the estimated twenty-percent possibility that the jury would find that Baltimore & Western Railroad had not been negligent. Finally, this figure should be reduced by the sixty percent probability that the jury will reduce its award between twenty and thirty-five percent because of Michael's own comparative fault.

Maria believes the most likely result is that the jury will assess Michael's total damages at roughly $2.7 million dollars. Based upon his counsel's predictions and his moderate adverseness to risk, Michael reasonably establishes his reservation point as being $1.8 million. He hopes for a better result, however, and establishes a target point of $2.1 million based upon his counsel's most optimistic predictions about the trial results and the additional costs to the railroad of trying the case. These reservation and target points are illustrated as follows:

FIGURE 3-2

MICHAEL'S LEVEL OF SATISFACTION

Michael would reject any offer from the railroad or its insurer of less than $1.8 million, his reservation price. Michael would accept any settlement in excess of $1.8 million and his level of satisfaction, theoretically at least, would increase proportionately with the increase in the dollar amount. Michael would have achieved his target or goal if the settlement exceeded $2.1 million.

What possible significance does the client's subjective goal or target have for the negotiation? Chester Karass, in his research on negotiation, established that those negotiators with high aspiration levels, or target points, did better in negotiations than negotiators with lower aspirations.[18] In other words, negotiators who expected more, in fact received more.

Most often, but not inevitably, the other party also will have some idea as to what constitutes its reservation point. Of course either party's

18.   KARASS, *supra* note 13, at 42.

reservation price may change, and often does change, during the course of the negotiation itself. The most typical bargaining situation, therefore, is one in which at the beginning of the negotiation, each party knows its own currently-evaluated reservation point, but has only probabilistic information, based upon its own knowledge of the bargaining problem and prior communications with the other party, about the other's reservation point.[19]

Looking at the bargaining situation from an omniscient perspective, instead of the actual perspective of one party with only limited information, the interval between the two parties' reservation points defines the *bargaining range*. If the two negotiating parties behave rationally, an agreement will be reached at some point within the bargaining range, because by definition both parties prefer a negotiated agreement within this range to the other available alternatives. For example, if the railroad determines that it is in its best interests to offer Michael $2.0 million rather than to face the risks of a larger judgment after trial, then its reservation point is the payment of $2.0 million to Michael. Its level of satisfaction increases to the extent it can settle the claim for *less* than its reservation price. If Michael is willing to accept any amount in excess of $1.8 million and the railroad is willing to pay up to $2.0 million dollars, then it is in the interests of both parties to settle for an amount somewhere between $1.8 million and $2.0 million.

Graphically, it looks like this:

FIGURE 3-3

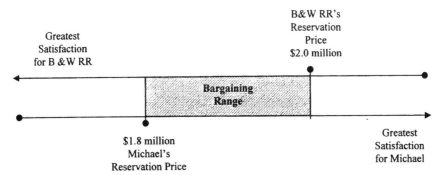

As the negotiated agreement approaches a party's reservation price, the party's level of satisfaction decreases. In other words, the more that the railroad pays and the closer it comes to paying $2.0 million, the less satisfied it is. Conversely, as the amount of the settlement increases, and the amount by which it exceeds Michael's reservation price increases, Michael's level of satisfaction increases.

It is possible that there is no bargaining range in which the parties both prefer agreement instead of pursuing the alternatives. In a litiga-

19. *See* RAIFFA, *supra* note 4, at 111–12.

tion situation such as this one, if Ashton valued Michael's chances for recovery and the probable amount of his recovery far more conservatively than did Maria, then both parties would believe that it was in their interests to proceed to trial rather than to accept the most favorable proposal of the other party. Similarly, in the technology-transfer negotiation between Volkov and Banting, a transactional negotiation, Volkov might decide that he was better off talking with other medical technology companies rather than accepting Banting's best offer of a lump sum payment of $500,000. In these two situations, the only bargaining range is a "*negative*" one,[20] and if the parties behave rationally, they will forego settlement and pursue other options.

Frequently, parties fail to reach a negotiated agreement even when their reservation points overlap, and there is a bargaining range where both parties prefer an agreement to the available alternatives. This is one of the risks of bluffing during negotiation. If Maria continues to assert vigorously throughout the negotiation that Michael would not accept any amount less than $2.5 million, then Ashton may decide either that Maria is not negotiating in good faith or that the parties have an honest disagreement as to the settlement value which makes continued negotiation futile. He may break off negotiation, even though in reality his client would be willing to pay more than Michael's reservation price of $1.8 million.

1. THEORETICAL OVERVIEW OF COMPETITIVE GOALS

In a distributive or value-claiming bargaining situation, the negotiator using competitive tactics views her goal as the acquisition of the largest possible share of the bargaining range for her client. The competitive negotiator considers the other negotiator as an "opponent" or "opposing party"; her function is to convince the other negotiator to settle on terms favorable to her own client. The way to accomplish this, according to the competitive negotiator, is to demonstrate to the opposing negotiator that he could not obtain a better deal for his client either through further negotiation or by pursuing his alternatives to a negotiated settlement. Ashton, the lawyer for the railroad, may try to show Michael's lawyer, Maria, that if Michael does not accept the railroad's offer of $900,000, no further offers will be forthcoming, and that at trial the jury will return a defendant's verdict. If Banting's lawyer uses competitive tactics, he may assert that only his company has the research and production facilities to rapidly bring pharmaceuticals based on the Viral Sharpshooter technology to the market place, and that Banting believes that competing technologies being developed by other researchers are even more promising than Volkov's.

Returning to the concept of bargaining range, the competitive negotiator attempts to do several things. First, she hides her reservation point from the other negotiator and tries to convince him that her

---

20. *See* RICHARD E. WALTON & ROBERT B. MCKERSIE, A BEHAVIORAL THEORY OF LABOR NEGOTIATIONS 17, 43 (1965).

reservation point is higher than it is. The lower limit of the bargaining range thus becomes the other side's *perception* of the client's reservation point and *not* the client's *actual* reservation point. For example, Maria wants to convince Ashton that her client, Michael, will not settle for less than $1.95 million.

Graphically, the bargaining situation looks like this:

FIGURE 3-4

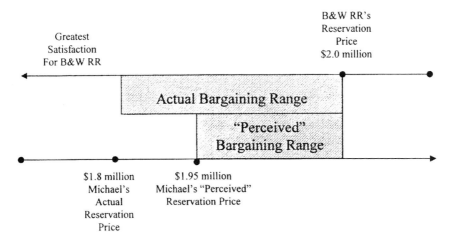

Subsequent chapters describe the various specific competitive tactics that can be used to conceal a negotiator's reservation point and to establish a bargaining range containing a range of more desirable solutions than the reservation point.

The second objective of the competitive negotiator is to determine the agreement most advantageous to her client that also is acceptable to the opposing party. In a true distributive context where the utility of the agreement for one party is inversely proportional to the utility of the agreement to the other party, determining the agreement most advantageous to the client that also is acceptable to the other party is the same as determining the other party's reservation point. More often, however, negotiations offer opportunities for value creation (integrative opportunities). Therefore the other party's reservation point early in a negotiation will not reflect all that your client can gain by the end of the negotiation, because working together, the two negotiators will create new value to be divided between the parties that was not evident when the negotiation began. Nevertheless, determining what agreements are acceptable to the other side is a critical function in negotiation. This goal permeates many different types of techniques used by the negotiator, but is most directly connected with the information gathering tactics discussed in Chapter Five.

Finally, competitive tactics can be used to change both the other party's reservation point and his target. In many cases, the specific techniques used to convince the other party that the negotiator's reservation point is less flexible than it is in reality are the same techniques used to induce the other party to change his reservation point or target. Once again, the basic approach is "If you don't settle on these terms and conditions favorable to my client, your client will be disadvantaged." Discussed in Chapter Seven, "Narrowing of Differences and Closure: Competitive and Cooperative Tactics," arguments and threats are among the primary competitive tactics to be used in this manner.

2. ANALYZING SOURCES OF LEVERAGE AND POWER

The negotiator with a competitive orientation views the process as one in which she is trying to influence the other party to do what is in the best interests of her own client. As part of the preparation for negotiation, therefore, lawyer and client together should consider what sources of influence, leverage and power they hold over the other party. The kinds of leverage and power available to the negotiator form the substance of competitive arguments and threats. Later in this section, the potential sources of influence that form the basis for the different kind of argument employed as a cooperative tactic will be examined.

What constitutes power in negotiation is not always self-evident and in fact may be counterintuitive. As Nobel Prize winner Thomas C. Schelling suggests, no one may have more bargaining power than the poorly dressed man with bloodshot eyes that knocks at your door and says that he will stab himself unless you give him twenty dollars![21]

The most important determinant of the negotiator's power over the other party is the nature of the alternatives to a negotiated agreement available to both the client and the other party. In Schelling's example, being forced to deal with someone who has stabbed himself on your front porch is a pretty unpalatable alternative to a negotiated agreement. To the extent that the competitive negotiator is able to argue successfully that her own alternatives are more desirable than previously perceived by the other party, her ability to influence the terms of the agreement increases. For example, if the woman answering the door is the police chief and her husband is an emergency room physician, the bargaining power of the man threatening to stab himself may decrease somewhat (Perhaps not! Think of the publicity and the investigation!). Similarly, her bargaining leverage increases when she convincingly argues that the other party's alternatives to an agreement are less palatable than they first appeared ("If you stab yourself, you'll simply end up in a mental facility.").

While the comparative disadvantages of the parties' alternatives to a negotiated agreement are the most important determinants of bargaining power, other factors influence power as well. These other factors often are more easily controlled by the skillful negotiator than the alternatives to a negotiated agreement. For example, the party's level of *commitment* to the matter being negotiated affects its bargaining power.

---

21. *See* Thomas C. Schelling, The Strategy of Conflict 22 (1960).

Consider the criminal defendant charged in a case that both the prosecutor and the defense attorney agree is almost certain to result in conviction, but one that will require substantial resources to try. Even though the defendant's alternative to a plea bargaining agreement initially seems bleak, by refusing to "cop a plea" he imposes considerable costs on the government. Accordingly, his level of commitment to not pleading guilty gives him bargaining power he would otherwise not have. Similarly, the legal services attorney who is prepared to contest her client's eviction all the way to the United States Supreme Court has considerable bargaining power with the landlord's attorney, even if the letter of the law clearly suggests the eviction was lawful.

The lawyer also may increase her client's bargaining position through her expertise and preparation. As mentioned previously, the lawyer who knows everything about the case or the transaction being negotiated often is able, during the course of the negotiation, to undermine the confidence of the other party in his original negotiation target and even in his reservation point. If a negotiator has superior knowledge of the situation, there is a natural human reaction to credit her evaluations and proposals. Accordingly, the well-prepared negotiator with expertise is in a more powerful negotiating position than the less capable one in the same situation.

In the planning process, the lawyer and client also should consider whether bargaining power can be augmented by *external rewards* that a negotiator is capable of bestowing on the other party or *external punishments* that she can inflict upon him. These rewards and punishments result from something other than the consequences of the breakdown of the negotiation. For example, it is possible that Dr. Volkov is a close friend of a colleague whose recent discoveries pave the way for the elimination of heart disease. Volkov, therefore, has additional power in its negotiation with Banting because Volkov might be able to influence his colleague to license his discovery to Banting. Further, most negotiations involve continuing relationships, not "one-shot" deals. A party possesses additional bargaining power if it has the capacity to bestow benefits or inflict punishments on the other party in future negotiations, or in other interactions.

The lawyer also must consider how past relationships between the two negotiators affect the lawyer's ability to influence the other negotiator. If past dealings suggest to the other negotiator that a plaintiff's personal injury attorney fairly and accurately values her cases, and that she has the capability to represent her client effectively in the courtroom if the negotiation breaks down, then her prior reputation substantially increases her bargaining power.

The parties' alternatives to a negotiated settlement and their relative needs for an agreement remain the most important factors in determining their respective levels of bargaining power. One aspect of the other party's need for an agreement warrants separate mention because the negotiator frequently can manipulate it. This factor is *time*.

If Michael Van Meter is not able to work as a truck driver any longer because of the injuries he sustained in the train accident, and he lacks private disability insurance, the railroad company may possess additional leverage because of Michael's need to replace all or some of his income in order to support his family. If a criminal defendant is incarcerated pending trial because he cannot post bail, the passage of time creates an additional hardship on him. His attorney's bargaining power is comparatively weaker because the defendant is interested in *any deal* that would end his incarceration. Negotiators often seek to exploit time pressures on the other party, and even to create time pressures.

3. PREPARATION FOR COOPERATIVE TACTICS: OBJECTIVE STANDARDS

As previously discussed, the orientation of the negotiator using cooperative tactics is to reach a solution that is fair and just to both parties. Proponents of the cooperative strategy believe that negotiators are motivated not only to gain as much as possible for their clients, but also to reach a fair solution.[22] Arguments in the cooperative strategy are addressed to what is "fair and just," not to disparaging the other negotiator's alternatives to a negotiated agreement; accordingly, the cooperative negotiator frequently refers to objective criteria.

To prepare for making such arguments, the negotiator and her client should discuss which normal practices or other objective standards would be useful in resolving the dispute with the other party. For example, in the technology-transfer agreement between Volkov and Banting, what is the usual or typical arrangement? Is it simply an upfront lump sum payment? A percentage royalty agreement? Or a combination of the two? In the settlement discussions between Michael Van Meter and the railroad, either side may try to locate similar cases that have settled or have been tried and argue that those cases establish an objective value for Michael's claims. Such criteria then form the basis for arguments on Michael's behalf that a "fair and just" value of his claims is $2.2 million or whatever other figure is suggested by the outcomes of comparable cases.

Past practice or precedent plays an important role in determining what is "fair." In a study conducted by Daniel Kahneman, a recent Nobel Prize winner in economic science, and his colleagues, the authors conclude, "A central concept in analyzing the fairness of actions in which a firm sets the terms of future exchanges is the *reference transaction,* a relevant precedent that is characterized by a reference price or wage."[23] Eighty-three percent of people surveyed by Kahneman and his

---

22. Otomar J. Bartos, *Simple Model of Negotiation: A Sociological Point of View,* 21 J. CONFLICT RESOL. 561, 567–570 (1977) *reprinted in* THE NEGOTIATION PROCESS: THEORIES AND APPLICATIONS 13, 19–24 (I. William Zartman ed., 1978). *See also* OTOMAR J. BARTOS, PROCESS AND OUTCOME OF NEGOTIATIONS 44–47 (1974); PRUITT, *supra* note 4, at 91–135.

23. Daniel Kahneman, Jack L. Knetsch & Richard H. Thaler, *Fairness as a Constraint on Profit Seeking: Entitlements in the Market,* 76 AM. ECON. REV. 728, 729–30 (1986).

colleagues regarded it was unfair to lower the wages of existing workers, even if market conditions made it possible to do so:

> Question 2A. A small photocopying shop has one employee who has worked in the shop for six months and earns $9 per hour. Business continues to be satisfactory, but a factory in the area has closed and unemployment has increased. Other small shops have now hired reliable workers at $7 an hour to perform jobs similar to those done by the photocopy shop employee. The owner of the photocopying shop reduces the employee's wage to $7.
>
> (N = 125) Acceptable 17% Unfair 83%[24]

This pervasive belief that treatment in accordance with past practice is "fair" underlies the use of past practice as a persuasive basis for cooperative argument.

Past practice, of course, is but one of many possible norms used as justifications in cooperative arguments. Fisher, Ury and Patton, as part of their approach of principled negotiation, suggest the use of objective criteria based upon market value, precedents, professional standards, established moral standards, tradition, equal treatment, principles of reciprocity, scientific judgment, and efficiency.[25] Note that cooperative arguments are different than competitive ones. Ashton's cooperative arguments on behalf of Baltimore & Western Railroad do not try to persuade Michael and his counsel that he would be better off in his own right to settle for $1.6 million; rather, Ashton asserts that this is the fair and just, or objective, value of Michael's claims.

The ability to argue effectively using objective criteria depends upon prior preparation by the lawyer and the client. Most often the client knows more about market values, professional standards, scientific judgments and costs than does the lawyer. In some instances, the lawyer and client may decide to use experts or other professionals in establishing criteria such as fair rental values or professional standards. Further, a professional economist could project the lifetime earnings of Michael Van Meter and determine the present discounted value of his income stream. The argument constructed from this data is not "Look what we can prove to the court," but rather "This is a fair value for Michael's lost income."

4. THE LAWYER'S AUTHORITY TO NEGOTIATE

During the pre-negotiation counseling session, the lawyer and client also should consider the lawyer's authority to enter into an agreement binding on the client.[26] The type of authority a client delegates to his

---

24. *Id.* at 730.

25. *See* FISHER, URY & PATTON, *supra* note 4, at 85–88.

26. According to the *Restatement of Law Governing Lawyers*:

As between client and lawyer ... the following and comparable decisions are reserved to the client except when the client has validly authorized the lawyer to make the particular decision: whether and on what terms to settle a claim....

See RESTATEMENT (THIRD) OF THE LAW GOVERNING LAWYERS § 22(1) (2000). Similarly, the *ABA Litigation Section Ethical Guidelines*

lawyer ranges from unlimited authority, which gives the lawyer *carte blanche* to enter into an agreement on behalf of a client,[27] to authority which authorizes the lawyer to negotiate, but does not give her any authority to enter into a binding agreement.[28]

The type of the authority granted by the client affects both the negotiation process itself and the prospects for a client-centered counseling process. In some simulated negotiations, social scientists have found that attorneys held strictly accountable to their clients, and given only *limited* authority, are likely to be vigorous and "tough" in their use of competitive tactics.[29] Attorneys given *unlimited* authority are less competitive. Surprisingly, on the other hand, some studies have shown that attorneys with unlimited authority behave more competitively than those whose authority is *nominally limited* by the client.[30] In these cases, the clients authorize settlement within an extremely broad range that is readily obtainable, and the attorneys accordingly behave even less competitively than if the clients have given them unlimited authority. Apparently the broad authority explicitly granted by the clients relieves the attorneys, to some extent, of their sense of obligation to obtain the best deals possible for their clients. When the lawyer intends to engage in problem-solving bargaining, a grant of unlimited authority however, gives her greater flexibility to consider proposals from the other party and to invent solutions for the parties' problems.

Even though granting the lawyer broad authority facilitates problem-solving and cooperative negotiation tactics, a more restricted grant of authority also has distinct advantages both as a competitive negotiation tactic and as a means of facilitating client-centered advocacy. If the client grants his attorney only limited authority to enter into an agreement, the lawyer can tell the other lawyer that she does not have authority from her client to accept his proposal, without facing the question of whether a false denial of authority is ethical.[31] Denying that

for Settlement Negotiations provides, "the degree of independence with which the lawyer pursues the negotiation process should reflect the client's wishes, as expressed after the lawyer's discussion with the client." *Ethical Guidelines for Settlement Negotiations*, 2002 A.B.A. SEC. OF LITIG. § 3.1.3 (2002).

27. The client may always revoke such authority. *See* RESTATEMENT (THIRD) OF THE LAW GOVERNING LAWYERS § 22(3) (2000).

28. According to a comment to the *Restatement*, "in the absence of a contrary agreement or instruction, a lawyer normally has authority to initiate or engage in settlement discussions, although not to conclude them." *Id.* § 22(3) cmt. c.

29. *See* PRUITT, *supra* note 4, at 42, 120–21 & 196; Helmut Lamm, *Group–Related Influences on Negotiation Behavior: Two–Person Negotiation as a Function of Repre-*

sentation and Election, 7 BARGAINING BEHAVIOR: CONTRIBUTIONS IN EXPERIMENTAL ECONOMICS 284, 297–302 (Heinz Sauermann ed., 1978).

30. *See* RAIFFA, *supra* note 4, at 50.

31. *Model Rule of Professional Conduct 4.1* prohibits a lawyer from knowingly making a false statement of material law or fact to a third party, including opposing counsel. MODEL RULES OF PROF'L CONDUCT R. 4.1 (2006). How should Michelle Chang, representing Tamiqua Lewis in her own right and on behalf of her son, respond when asked by Patrick Quinn, counsel for the Piccolo Management Company, whether $975,000 will settle the case when in fact he knows that his client's reservation point is only $900,000? If Michelle answers "no," she violates the literal language of *Rule 4.1*. On the other hand, if she answers "yes," the negotiation concludes immediately and her client loses the chance to obtain an

she has authority is an excellent means of justifying why a concession cannot be made or why a concession must be limited in amount.[32] Claim adjusters or attorneys representing insurance companies in personal injury negotiations sometimes use this technique.

Restricting the lawyer's authority to enter into an agreement binding on the client also aids client-centered advocacy because the client retains greater control over his attorney's conduct during the negotiation. A series of incrementally increasing grants of authority during the course of the negotiation guarantees regular attorney consultation with her client. Presumably, lawyers precede such requests for additional authority with reports on the current status of the negotiation, and thus keep the client better informed about the negotiations and more directly involved in them. Similar reasoning appears to undergird the Committee Notes to the negotiation guidelines promulgated by the American Bar Association's Section of Litigation, at least in the litigation context:

> Irrespective of the breadth of the settlement authorization the client has apparently provided ... best practices dictate that the lawyer communicate to the client the full terms of a proposed final settlement agreement and obtain the client's specific consent to the settlement before agreeing to it on the client's behalf. This precaution is warranted by the potentially binding nature of the lawyer's actions combined with the possibility that the client or lawyer may be confused about, may not have precisely defined, or may not fully understand the precise breadth of the authority the client has conveyed and the lawyer has obtained.[33]

G. CONCLUSIONS

Nothing in this chapter should suggest to the beginning lawyer that a negotiation can be scripted in advance. The negotiator will not be able to plan intricately the exact content, timing and sequence of her concessions or other negotiating proposals, or the precise words to be used in her arguments. Negotiations are interactive events between at least two individuals, both of whom are trying to control the process and outcome. Any attempt to execute a detailed plan prepared in advance imposes a

even larger settlement. Finally, if Michelle avoids answering or even hesitates in answering, perceptive opposing counsel realizes that she has authority to accept the $975,000 offer. *See* James J. White, *Machiavelli and the Bar: Ethical Limitations on Lying in Negotiation*, 1980 AM. B. FOUND. RES. J. 926, 932–35 (1980); Thomas Guernsey, *Truthfulness in Negotiation*, 17 U. RICH. L. REV. 99 (1982). Addressing this dilemma, comment 2 to Rule 4.1 provides that "[u]nder generally accepted conventions in negotiation, certain types of statements ordinarily are not taken as statements of material fact." MODEL RULES OF PROF'L CONDUCT R. 4.1 cmt. 2 (2006). The

comment lists "a party's intentions as to an acceptable settlement of a claim" as an example of the type of statement that ordinarily is not taken as a statement of material fact. *Id.*

32. Recognizing this, many judges now require that attorneys come to pre-trials either with full authority to settle, or accompanied by the client or a client representative with settlement authority.

33. *Ethical Guidelines for Settlement Negotiations*, 2002 A.B.A. SEC. OF LITIG. § 3.2.1, Committee Notes (2002).

counterproductive straitjacket on the negotiator. This is not direct or cross-examination in the courtroom where the trial attorney controls the stage and frequently prepares his questions in advance. Nor is it client interviewing and counseling where the effective lawyer generally guides the interview through an established structure,[34] even if she does not control the content.

General approaches to negotiation, potential proposals, opening demands or offers, concessions and other negotiating tactics, however, should be thought about in advance. Whether the negotiator actually uses a specific tactic, and the timing of its use, are dependent upon the other negotiator's behavior and the flow of the negotiation process. This is not a new idea for a law student. Preparing for negotiation is like preparing for law school examinations. Students do not prepare the exact answers to exam questions in advance. Instead, they learn about rules, doctrines and policies and a process for analyzing legal problems. When they confront the first exam question they are better "prepared" than they would have been without preparation. No one familiar with law school examinations would suggest that preparation is unimportant merely because answers to exam questions cannot be written and memorized in advance. So it is with negotiation planning.

34. *See* BINDER ET AL., *supra* note 9, at 25–30.

Chapter Four

THE RELATIONSHIP BETWEEN THE NEGOTIATORS: INITIAL ORIENTATION

A. BEGINNING NEGOTIATION: AN OVERVIEW

The primary goal of negotiation is to have the other negotiator agree to a resolution that satisfies your client's interests. The nature of your personal relationship with the other negotiator during the bargaining, in and of itself, is important in achieving this objective.

Chapter One used the attorney's goals in establishing relationships with the other negotiator as a criterion for classifying negotiation tactics. To review briefly, competitive tactics are negotiating behaviors designed to undermine the other negotiator's confidence in his bargaining position and to induce him to enter into an agreement less advantageous to his client than he would have prior to the negotiation. The negotiator using cooperative tactics seeks an agreement which is fair and just to both parties and hopes to develop a relationship with the other party that is characterized by goodwill and trust. Finally, when the negotiator uses problem-solving tactics, she hopes to develop a relationship with the other negotiator that will permit them to search together for solutions to their clients' mutual "problems."

Because the underlying psychological relationship between the negotiators is a critical variable in negotiation, the effective negotiator must be aware of psychological factors and seek to influence them to achieve her client's objectives. Every contact between two negotiating attorneys is part of the negotiation process, because each passing comment, letter or telephone call—no matter how seemingly innocuous—affects the relationship between them and the ultimate resolution of the dispute. Indeed, the current negotiation must be considered in light of the prior professional and social contacts between the two negotiators that obviously affect their present relationship.

Negotiations do not always begin the same way. Early phases of a negotiation typically include one or both of the following: (1) information gathering and disclosure and (2) exchange of initial proposals. The sequence of such processes varies from one negotiation to the next. For example, in personal injury negotiations such as Michael Van Meter's claims against the Baltimore & Western Railroad, the bargaining often begins with an initial proposal in the form of a demand letter from the plaintiff's lawyer to the insurance company adjuster or the defendant. This letter includes a specific demand figure calculated to establish both the bargaining range and the initial tone of the relationship between the parties. In addition, the demand letter is accompanied by documentation and arguments—sometimes even a "settlement brochure" presenting the plaintiff's liability and damage claims in a perspective most appealing to a jury. In other negotiations, such as Banting Medical Technologies, Inc.'s technology transfer licensing negotiation with Dr. Volkov, the bargaining typically begins only with an extremely broad initial proposal: "We would like to obtain licensing rights to the Viral Sharpshooter technology." In all probability, neither party in this tech-transfer negotiation will present an initial proposal including such terms as licensing fees until after the parties have shared information and bargained for some period of time. Prior to these initial proposals, both parties disclose certain information about their clients' needs and expectations and attempt to gather information about the other party's situation. In other words, in this second negotiation, information disclosure and gathering precede the exchange of opening proposals. Occurring in either order, *initial proposals* and *information exchange* are important interactions in all negotiations. Both processes occur in a wide variety of forms and contexts, and each activity is the subject of a chapter of this book. It is important to remember, however, that in any particular negotiation, the sequence of these activities may differ from the sequence in which these behaviors are analyzed in this text.

Regardless of whether the negotiation begins with an exchange of initial proposals or with information bargaining, the negotiators also are establishing both a personal relationship and at least the initial "tone" of the negotiation. Skilled negotiators focus not only on the beginning substantive tactics of a negotiation, but also on tactics explicitly designed to affect the relationship between the parties instead of the substance of the negotiation. First impressions are as important in negotiation as they are elsewhere in life.

This chapter considers the tactics employed for this purpose. These tactics are loosely grouped in this chapter according to whether they are a subset of negotiation tactics from the competitive strategy, the cooperative strategy or the problem-solving strategy. Many of the same orientation issues arise, however, regardless of what strategy is used. Therefore, even though the issues of "Physical Arrangements at the Negotiation Site" and "Agenda" are discussed under the heading of "Competitive Orientation Tactics," the manner in which these issues are handled by negotiators using cooperative or problem-solving tactics are considered in these initial discussions. Similarly, the discussion of "Cooperation

Facilitators" describes tactics that play important roles in the problem-solving strategy as well as in the cooperative strategy.

B. COMPETITIVE ORIENTATION TACTICS

Simply stated, the goal of the negotiator employing predominantly competitive tactics is the pervasive projection of power through means that are as subtle as possible.[1] How can the other party be made to feel uncomfortable about the prospects of disagreeing with the negotiator? How can the negotiator seize a psychologically dominant position? Subsequent chapters discuss competitive negotiation tactics such as extreme opening demands, threats and arguments. A dominating personality, enabling the negotiator to be the focus of attention whenever she enters a room, is certainly a big advantage, but unfortunately, one that cannot be learned through reading this text. This section describes a variety of competitive tactics that some negotiators believe achieves a "psychological edge" in negotiation that can be learned.

1. BARGAINING SITE

Negotiation folklore uniformly holds that the negotiator who operates on "her own turf" is at an advantage in the negotiation. Indeed, empirical research confirms that the negotiator who bargains on her own territory is likely to increase both her assertiveness and the chances of a favorable negotiation outcome.[2] Diplomats appear to respect this claim and frequently negotiate at a site in a neutral third country, such as Geneva, Vienna or Helsinki. In sports competition, few doubt the existence of a "home-field advantage."

The presence of an advantage for the negotiator who bargains on her own turf makes sense, especially if viewed from the perspective of competitive negotiation tactics. Because the competitive negotiator seeks to undermine the other party's confidence in his judgments about the bargaining situation, anything which produces doubt or psychological discomfort in the other negotiator is an advantage. Most people are more comfortable and less likely to lose confidence in themselves in familiar surroundings; they are more naturally assertive as hosts than as visitors. The attorney from a small firm in a rural area may be more comfortable and assertive negotiating the sale of a small company to a large multinational corporation if the talks are held in her office than she would be if the bargaining takes place in New York City's financial district, or even more acutely, Tokyo's financial district. Similarly, legal services attorneys sometimes attempt to arrange negotiations with attorneys from

---

1. In her attempts to dominate her opponent and wrest from him a more favorable outcome for her client, the competitive negotiator has goals similar to those of a nation at war. *See generally* CARL VON CLAUSEWITZ, ON WAR (Michael A. Howard & Oaeter Paret trans., Princeton University Press 1989).

2. JEFFERY Z. RUBIN & BERT R. BROWN, THE SOCIAL PSYCHOLOGY OF BARGAINING AND NEGOTIATION 82–88 (1971); David A. Martindale, *Territorial Dominance Behavior in Dyadic Verbal Interactions*, 6 PROC. OF THE 79TH ANN. CONVENTION OF THE AM. PSYCHOL. ASS'N 305–06 (1971).

large firms and banks at offices in low-income neighborhoods, expecting that these unfamiliar surroundings will make the other lawyer uneasy.

Scheduling negotiations at one's own office also has a variety of tangible advantages. Administrative and other support personnel are available to assist if needed. More control may be asserted over factors such as interruptions and seating arrangements.

On the other hand, there are definite tangible benefits to negotiating at the other attorney's office. Most importantly, at his own office the host negotiator has greater access to his complete files, including documents that might disadvantage his client if shared with the opposing lawyer. Thus, it is difficult for him to refuse access to such documents, if the visiting lawyer requests them. Conversely, the visiting attorney does not have immediate access to documents or statements. Further, on rare occasion, a negotiating attorney may want to terminate a negotiation abruptly by walking out; it is difficult for her to walk out of her own office.

Ultimately, the "home-turf" advantage means only as much in a negotiation as the visiting attorney allows it to mean. The important thing is for the visiting attorney not to let unfamiliar surroundings create discomfort which then affects her negotiating behavior. Awareness of this possibility, and the concomitant ability to guard against it, usually is all that is required to neutralize any advantage. The disadvantage of negotiating at someone else's office is probably greater for the novice attorney who feels somewhat insecure about the negotiation process, the prospect of facing more experienced counsel, her new professional persona as an attorney, or the novelty of the type of case. Experienced attorneys who are more professionally secure generally are less affected when negotiating at the other attorney's office.

Awareness of the advantages of negotiating on one's own territory should not lead the lawyer to overemphasize the issue of negotiation location. It is difficult to imagine, for example, a situation in which a routine legal negotiation should break down over the site of the negotiation. If both negotiators feel this strongly about the venue issue, the bargaining can be conducted in a neutral location such as a restaurant or courthouse conference room that gives neither side a psychological advantage.

If the lawyer negotiates at the other attorney's office and senses psychological disadvantage, what can she do about it? A simple rule of thumb would be that the negotiator should not concede anything to the other party when extraneous factors are making her uncomfortable. Analogously, trial practice manuals have suggested that key witnesses become familiar with the courtroom prior to their testimony so that they are not as uncomfortable.

Many negotiations, of course, do not occur in a single session scheduled in advance. Negotiation proposals are often traded during telephone calls or in courthouse halls following a deposition on an entirely different case. It is as important for the negotiator to feel comfortable operating under these often hurried and chaotic conditions, as it is for her to feel comfortable negotiating in someone else's office.

2. PHYSICAL ARRANGEMENTS AT THE NEGOTIATION SITE

Physical arrangements at the negotiation site may have subtle psychological effects on the negotiators, but the extent of these effects should not be overestimated. During the negotiations that ended the war in Vietnam, the shape of the table around which the negotiators were to sit was debated at length. In the barbershop scenes of Charlie Chaplin's classic film, *The Great Dictator*, Hitler and Mussolini each consecutively raises his barber's chair to a level higher than the other's in order to gain a perceived power advantage. Physical arrangements can prove discomforting when, for example, during a job interview with a prestigious law firm, a law student is asked to sit in a soft, low chair facing a senior partner who is seated behind an immense mahogany desk in an eight-foot, high-backed, leather chair.

Research does suggest some helpful conclusions about physical arrangements and their effects on negotiations.[3] Accommodative interpersonal relationships, such as those needed if cooperative and problem-solving tactics are to succeed, are facilitated if the negotiators sit at adjoining sides of a rectangular or square table or adjacent to each other at a circular table. This configuration allows them sufficient physical proximity to maintain verbal communication, while engaging in as little or as much eye contact as is comfortable. Conversely, the preferred configuration for competitive relationships, according to social scientists, is face-to-face, such as on opposite sides of a desk or table.

3. BARGAINING WITH CREDENTIALS

Within a bargaining relationship, the perception of power depends not only upon the merits of the matter being negotiated, but also upon the aura of power generated by the negotiator. The novice attorney often feels somewhat uncomfortable when negotiating with a seasoned veteran. A lawyer from a two-person practice often approaches the city's most prestigious law firm with some trepidation. Occasionally such discomfort is heightened by the other party's surroundings, office furnishings and dress that all exude professional and material success. The *coup-de-grace* is complete when the young negotiator observes the carefully framed letter from the Chief Justice of the United States thanking the host lawyer for helping him out of a dire personal crisis.

Once again, these perceptions of power and influence matter only if the negotiator allows them to matter. President Franklin D. Roosevelt's words, "The only thing we have to fear is fear itself," apply perfectly to these circumstances. As the lawyer matures, she becomes more secure

---

3. *See* JEFFERY Z. RUBIN & BERT R. BROWN, THE SOCIAL PSYCHOLOGY OF BARGAINING AND NEGOTIATION 88–91 (1964). For an in depth analysis of physical arrangement's effect on negotiations, *see generally* Jeffery S. Wolf, *The Hidden Parameter: Spatial Dynamics and Alternative Dispute Resolution*, 12 OHIO ST. J. ON DISP. RESOL. 685 (1997).

with her own professional identity and realizes that her own clients are not at a disadvantage. For the novice attorney, preparation is the most important ingredient in negotiation. Preparation goes a long way toward compensating for a lack of experience and can be more important than the other negotiator's reputation or ability to intimidate.

Delaying serious negotiation until the attorney overcomes any discomfort generated by the negotiation site or the credentials of the other negotiator minimizes the potential psychological disadvantage. Sometimes preliminary small talk offers opportunities for the beginning attorney to discuss her own past relevant professional and educational experiences in ways that may help neutralize any psychological disadvantage. Any aggressive attempt to strut one's own qualifications, however, will probably be seen by the other negotiator as a sign of insecurity and have exactly the opposite effect of what was intended.

4. NUMBER OF NEGOTIATORS

Because the psychology of bargaining power is sometimes primitive in nature, multiple negotiators for one party may sense a psychological advantage if they "outnumber" the other side. When a lone attorney finds herself negotiating with six representatives of a corporation, her psychological sense of being overwhelmed numerically may be very real.

Aside from pure intimidation value, multiple negotiators often dominate a discussion by participating more as a unit than as lone negotiators. Dividing negotiation responsibility among associates may prevent them from tiring, thus reducing the risk of ill-advised concessions influenced by fatigue. Further, additional negotiators can carefully observe the verbal and nonverbal cues of the other side's lawyer while their partner is actively interacting. On the other hand, often there are advantages to being outnumbered by the other side. A skilled negotiator may be able to read the non-verbal reactions of one of the several less experienced negotiators representing the other party. A member of the other side's "negotiating committee" sometimes reveals information or makes a concession that the principal negotiator would not have made if she were negotiating alone.

5. TIMING OF NEGOTIATIONS

Patience is power in negotiation. The competitive negotiator is aware that most serious bargaining is accomplished as deadlines approach. Personal injury cases frequently settle, figuratively and even literally, on the courthouse steps. Labor contracts sometimes are reached either immediately before or even after a strike begins. In bargaining in which competitive tactics predominate, the most serious concessions occur at or near a deadline, because each side expects that if it waits as long as possible, the other party will say "chicken."

These realities have implications both for those who intend to use competitive tactics and for those who negotiate against someone using these tactics. Let's first consider the defensive implications. In many contexts, serious negotiation will not occur until the last possible moment; all offers and proposals prior to that time probably do not represent the best possible deal for the lawyer's client. In one personal injury case in which the author was involved, for the first two years after the filing of the case, the defendant's attorney offered only to settle "for court costs" despite a settlement conference in which the trial judge strongly encouraged both parties to settle. Then, within one week of the scheduled trial date, the defendant's attorney started to ask questions such as "What would it take to settle this case?" and initially offered $200,000, in an era in which that sum still constituted real money. The case ultimately settled. Patience pays.

In addition to time deadlines set by others, negotiators should be aware of their own abilities to set time deadlines within a case in order to induce settlement. For example, Dr. Volkov might schedule a meeting with a European or Asian pharmaceutical or medical technology company, and let Banting Medical Technologies, the American competitor, know the date of the scheduled meeting. As that date approaches, Banting will probably feel pressure to make a realistic proposal so that Volkov will not sign a licensing agreement with another pharmaceutical company.

Even deadlines that are internal to the negotiation or that affect only the attorney and not his client may produce pressure to concede. If an attorney from Sacramento is visiting New York and is leaving on an evening flight, she probably feels pressure to concede and reach an agreement—or at least to achieve progress—before she leaves the city. Certain days of the year, such as the day before the negotiator's two-week family vacation begins, or December 31, may help to induce settlement. The negotiator's awareness of this psychological tendency may prevent, or at least lessen, the rush to agreement, because she can guard against hurried and ill-advised concessions.

6. PRESENCE OF THE CLIENT

Most negotiations occur between two or more lawyers without the presence of their respective clients. The theory behind the competitive negotiation strategy offers several justifications for the client's absence in most cases. Unless the client is a skilled and experienced negotiator in his own right, and the client and attorney have discussed their negotiation strategy extensively, a lawyer's plan to negotiate competitively in the presence of her client is likely to be a risky venture. The client's verbal and non-verbal reactions to the other party's proposals and questions will probably be unguarded and may allow the other side to accurately gauge the client's reservation point. Your client is unlikely to recognize when the other lawyer is "bluffing" and may lose confidence in your own case evaluations too quickly. Furthermore, many clients are obstreperous and may be unable to participate personally in the process of identifying potential solutions and compromises. The "give and take" that lawyers typically engage in as a part of negotiation sometimes appears to the client to be acts of disloyalty. In short, one of the advantages of negotiation by representatives is that attorneys are less likely to be emotionally involved with the issues and less susceptible to being influenced by the fears, anxieties and angers that clients typically experience as part of the negotiation process.

There are exceptions to the general rule that clients should not participate directly in the negotiation process. The presence of the client during all or part of the bargaining can serve either competitive or problem-solving goals. For example, in a sex discrimination action or in a housing code violation class action, a committed plaintiff sometimes can be more effective in convincing defense counsel that litigation will be pursued unless justice is done. Further, direct client involvement in negotiation can be a virtue in problem-solving negotiation because clients may be more readily able to identify their respective underlying interests. Sometimes their detailed understanding of the subject matter of the negotiation also makes them principal players in identifying integrative bargaining solutions.

7. AGENDA CONTROL

Because every interaction between lawyers involved in negotiation is a part of an ongoing process that affects later bargaining, the *agenda* for the negotiation session, or the order in which the issues are considered, often has important implications. In most instances, parties do not explicitly bargain over the negotiation agenda. Nevertheless, when Ashton Crutchfield, the railroad's attorney, asks Maria Santiago, Michael Van Meter's attorney, "How much is it going to take to settle this case?," he begins to define the negotiation agenda by indicating his desire to negotiate the amount of the claim before considering such peripheral issues as whether or not the payment is to be made in a lump sum or through a structured settlement. In more complex negotiations, such as those involving international diplomacy, labor relations or corporate mergers and acquisitions, the negotiation agenda sometimes is explicitly negotiated.

The order of issues to be negotiated, whether decided through explicit bargaining or more subtle suggestions, or by default, often affects the negotiation outcome. The negotiator employing predominantly competitive tactics sees the ability to control the agenda as an initial indication of the bargaining power of each negotiator. Both the selection of issues chosen by the negotiator for initial consideration and the other negotiator's reactions to her proposed agenda indicate much about their respective priorities and values. For example, suppose Katie Eisinger, representing Dr. Volkov, begins her bargaining with Jonathan Prevas by discussing the amount of money that Volkov will receive up front. By stressing the up-front payment, she sends a strong message to Jonathan that this issue is an important issue, perhaps the *most* important issue, to Volkov.

A negotiator can achieve far greater control of an agenda by presenting the other party with an initial draft agreement or written offer. The natural tendency is for negotiators to work from the draft and to consider the issues in the order that they are presented. If the other negotiator wishes to depart from this agenda, he assumes a subtle psychological burden to justify a different sequence.

Agendas frequently change or are modified during the course of a negotiation. Three basic agenda strategies, however, are possible in multiple issue negotiations: (1) considering the most important issues first; (2) considering the least contentious issues first; or (3) simultaneously considering multiple issues.

a. Considering the Most Important Issues First

Perhaps the most common practice is to address the one or two most important issues first. The expectation here is that once the negotiators reach agreement on the major issues in dispute, they will resolve the minor issues quickly. Presumably once resolution is reached on the major issues, the parties will have established an accommodative working arrangement and will not want to jeopardize the agreement on these issues by bickering over details. The risk, of course, is a greater possibility of a deadlock if major contentious issues are considered first. Also, animosity resulting from contentious bargaining over the major issues may overflow into negotiation on less important matters.

Addressing the most important issues first probably is good practice in transactional negotiations in which the parties are trying to create a relationship where none existed before. In these cases, the parties perceive that it may not be worthwhile negotiating over the details if agreement cannot be achieved on the major points.

b. Considering the Least Contentious Issues First

Why would a negotiator sometimes want to negotiate first on the least contentious issues? Dealing with the easiest issues first helps to build rapport between the negotiating parties because they jointly experience bargaining success and this creates a sense of momentum.[4] This accommodative working relationship can then facilitate resolution of more difficult issues. Addressing the least contentious issues first also prevents a premature breakdown of the negotiation during the earliest phases when the parties might engage in substantial competitive posturing.

How can a negotiator identify in advance which issues are likely to be least contentious? Such issues are ones where the differences between the parties as revealed through prior communications are relatively small, where the issues are relatively unimportant, or where the issues do not include substantial emotional or symbolic implications. Often, however, it is not possible to identify which issues can be easily resolved before some initial bargaining on the entire range of issues.

4. *See* Peter H. Gulliver, Disputes and Negotiations: A Cross-Cultural Perspective 145–47 (1979); Rubin & Brown, *supra* note 3, at 148.

c. Simultaneous Consideration of Multiple Issues

The third option is to consider multiple issues simultaneously. In the abstract, such a suggestion may seem unwieldy, yet many agreements are reached because the parties engage in *"logrolling"* or trade concessions on different issues on which they have differing priorities. Volkov may be most interested in the amount of money he receives "up front," but Banting Medical Technologies may be most interested in the confidentiality of the licensing agreement. If Banting agrees to a large up-front payment, it seems likely that Volkov would agree to keep the amount of such a payment confidential. Logrolling on these issues thus requires simultaneous consideration of the amount of the payment and confidentiality.

Considering multiple issues together exponentially expands the number of combinations of proposals that may be available to address the issues. As such, this sequence facilitates the problem-solving approach to negotiation. If issues are considered together, a party may propose a "package deal" designed to resolve a number of issues. The other party may respond either by modifying some elements of the package or by proposing his own package deal.

Even when negotiators consider a single issue at a time, they often agree that final agreement on that issue is contingent upon agreement on all issues. Unless this is made explicit, issue reconsideration may be seen as a breach of an often-observed negotiation norm of not reopening an issue once it is decided.

Tying resolution of the issue under consideration to agreement on other issues can be used as both a competitive tactic and a problem-solving tactic. As a competitive tactic, it serves notice that everything remains up for grabs until final agreement, thus creating additional pressure on the other side to concede on other issues. As a problem-solving technique, it preserves maximum flexibility, allowing negotiators to go back and engage in logrolling later in the negotiation.

C. COOPERATIVE ORIENTATION TACTICS

Inherent in most negotiations are conflicting needs for the negotiators to cooperate and to compete. On one hand, the negotiator's need for something that the other party can provide is what brought her to the negotiation table, and cooperation is necessary in order to achieve this goal. On the other hand, in most cases the parties compete, at least to some extent, to determine how satisfied each will be with the eventual agreement.

The competitive element in most negotiations often leads to a counterproductive emotional cycle. The recognition by the negotiator that she needs or desires something from the other party, coupled with the realization that the parties' needs conflict, sometimes feel threatening to the negotiator. When the other attorney does not view the bargaining situation in exactly the same way as she does, the negotiator may unintentionally display anger. The negotiator's anger often exacerbates the other lawyer's own level of fear and produces a cycle of recurring reciprocal anger and fear. This cycle may obscure opportunities for mutual gains and for compromises which both parties otherwise would view as fair and just.

Negotiators using either cooperative or problem-solving negotiation tactics seek to emphasize the benefits of cooperation. Sometimes past experiences with the other negotiator, or other factors, suggest that cooperation with him, and trust in him, are likely to be reciprocated. Many times this will not occur until a negotiation has progressed through initial competitive stages. What techniques can the negotiator use specifically to facilitate a trusting relationship between the other negotiator and herself?

Many law students analyze factors inhibiting rapport and techniques used to develop a trusting relationship when they learn to establish rapport with the client in the interviewing and counseling process.[5] Certainly the relationship between negotiating attorneys differs significantly from the relationship between attorney and client, but many of the same rapport-building techniques are useful in both situations.

1. COOPERATION INHIBITORS

The goal of the negotiator who wants to use cooperative tactics is reciprocation of cooperative negotiation behaviors by the other negotiator so that together they can reach a fair and just agreement without a contentious negotiation process. What factors, then, inhibit the other negotiator from cooperating?

a. The Opportunity Costs of Cooperative Tactics

The other negotiator may be reluctant to use cooperative tactics, thinking he can achieve a better deal for his client by using competitive tactics, particularly if there is a possibility of exploiting his counterpart's trust. As discussed previously, if a competitive negotiator is bargaining with a negotiator who persists in cooperative behavior, the competitive negotiator may be able to exploit the cooperative negotiator's trust and achieve an agreement that is disproportionately favorable to his client. When faced with an opponent using cooperative negotiation behaviors, the competitive negotiator interprets concessions as signs of weakness and grants fewer concessions. There is no reason for the competitive negotiator to use cooperative negotiation tactics if he does not value his relationship with his opponent and if the opponent allows himself to be exploited.

---

5. See DAVID A. BINDER, PAUL BERGMAN & SUSAN C. PRICE, LAWYERS AS COUNSELORS: A CLIENT CENTERED APPROACH 34–45 (1991).

b. Fear of Exploitation

If a negotiator decides it is to her client's advantage to use predominantly cooperative tactics, the biggest factor inhibiting her use of such tactics is the possibility her own cooperation will not be reciprocated, but will be exploited by the other party. If the negotiator concedes and the other lawyer does not reciprocate, the parties are no closer to an agreement, and the negotiator loses bargaining power. If the negotiator shares information with the other lawyer, this information might be used to determine her weaknesses rather than to find an agreement that is fair and just to both parties.

c. Image Loss and Professional Role Expectations

The negotiator may be reluctant to cooperate because she fears counsel on the other side will see her as a "weak" or ineffectual negotiator and that image will affect her negotiating posture with him not only in future phases of the instant negotiation, but in any future negotiations as well. Further, how will the negotiator view her own performance as a legal professional? Finally, how will those involved in the present bargaining characterize her negotiating behavior to other attorneys with whom she likely will work in the future? The lawyer's role as an advocate for a client inherently places her in a position of possible conflict with counsel negotiating on behalf of the other party. The legal profession generally is viewed, often but not always accurately, as highly adversarial. Thus, an attorney considering a cooperative or problem-solving approach to a negotiation may confront the expectation that "real attorneys are tough negotiators and do not cooperate." Professional role expectations may be particularly powerful inhibitors of cooperative behavior for new or insecure attorneys who fear that they are not representing their clients' interests vigorously enough.

d. Client Expectations

Lawyers as negotiators represent the interests of clients. In terms of effective professional service and good business relations, lawyers need to respect the expectations of their clients in the negotiations process. Often, clients approach negotiation in a more adversarial manner than attorneys, and these expectations may inhibit the lawyer-negotiator from negotiating cooperatively.[6] Visibly competitive tactics may convince a client who is not inclined to trust his attorney that his attorney is representing his interests and is not "selling out" to the opponent.

e. Personality Conflicts

Even though negotiation behaviors can be analyzed, negotiators are not robots. Instead, negotiations are intensely human interactions heavily influenced by the personalities of the negotiators. Personality conflicts, or other emotional reactions between the negotiating attorneys,

---

6. See RICHARD E. WALTON & ROBERT B. MCKERSIE, A BEHAVIORAL THEORY OF LABOR NEGOTIATIONS 417–19 (1965).

often inhibit negotiation. It is difficult to work cooperatively with someone you consider a "jerk," or worse.

Conscious and unconscious emotional reactions toward the other negotiator sometimes make cooperation more difficult. These reactions include the negotiator's responses to the other negotiator's bargaining behavior as well as the negotiator's distorted perceptions arising from subconscious association of the other negotiator with significant figures in her life. Psychiatrists refer to this collection of feelings as transference.[7] For example, if the lawyer negotiates with an older male with behavior or personality characteristics similar to her father, it is possible that the older male negotiator will invoke in her some of the same emotional reactions she previously experienced on a regular basis when she interacted with her father. When responding during the bargaining, for example, she might be influenced by either an unconscious excessive desire to please the father figure and to concede, or an unconscious urge to rebel. Either response could be counterproductive to the establishment of a trusting accommodative negotiation relationship.

f. Negotiation-Generated Emotions

Negotiations frequently are rife with conflict and strong emotions. As previously discussed, fear often is inherent in negotiation; fear leads to anger, and a cycle of fear and anger result. Perhaps a majority of all negotiations produces stages where one negotiator does not believe that her counterpart is bargaining in good faith or seeking a fair and just agreement. Such anger and mistrust obviously inhibit cooperation.

2. COOPERATION FACILITATORS

The factors described above make it a challenge for the negotiator to achieve the accommodative working relationship necessary to use successfully either the cooperative or the problem-solving approaches to negotiation. What techniques can the negotiator use to mitigate the effects of these cooperation inhibitors and to achieve the necessary rapport between negotiators?

a. Answering Competitive Tactics

If the other lawyer begins with the goal of exploiting the negotiator's naiveté by using competitive negotiation behaviors, then the negotiator who wants to use a cooperative or problem-solving approach must first demonstrate to the other lawyer that his competitive tactics will not succeed. Truly productive and fruitful cooperative and problem-solving negotiations often result only when the other negotiator believes that he cannot "win" by using competitive tactics.[8] Frequently, negotiations initially progress through competitive stages before the parties turn to more productive cooperative or problem-solving approaches.

---

7. *E.g.*, ANDREW S. WATSON, THE LAWYER IN THE INTERVIEWING AND COUNSELING PROCESS 21–23, 75–92 (1976).

8. *See* DEAN PRUITT, NEGOTIATION BEHAVIOR 37, 113–14 (1981).

b. Initiating Trusting Behaviors

If both lawyers mistrust one another when bargaining begins, the cycle of mistrust and competitive bargaining behavior needs to be broken if the lawyers are to engage in cooperative or problem-solving bargaining. The most significant way a negotiator can establish trust and encourage cooperative negotiation by the other lawyer is to begin with cooperative tactics, such as reasonable opening offers or demands, concessions or information-sharing. Such behavior can be a gamble. The other negotiator may be dedicated to the use of competitive tactics. If so, he sees the reasonable opening offer or the concession as a sign of weakness. He does not respond in kind, instead he becomes increasingly convinced that his toughness is working. If the cooperative negotiator shares information with the other lawyer hoping that he will use it to the mutual advantage of the parties, he may instead use it to determine the negotiator's points of vulnerability.

For these reasons, the cooperative negotiator must not "give away the store" in the opening moves of the negotiation. If Maria Santiago, the attorney representing Michael Van Meter, believes that a fair and just settlement value of claims against the railroad is $2.0 million, it probably is unwise to begin initially with a settlement demand of $2.2 million unless she has already developed a trusting bargaining relationship with the other attorney. Trusting negotiation behaviors can be initiated on smaller issues where the risk is not so great if the other lawyer exploits the opportunity created by the negotiator's reasonable valuation instead of reciprocating it. In some cases, the negotiator may be able to phrase cooperative tactics in ways that clearly indicate that such proposals are contingent upon their reciprocation.

The advice in this subsection is unavoidably inconsistent with that in previous paragraphs. On one hand, the negotiator is told to initiate trusting behaviors. On the other hand, it is suggested that competitive tactics be answered with competitive tactics. If the negotiator cooperates, she is vulnerable to exploitation; if the negotiator does not initiate cooperative negotiation behaviors, the cycle of mistrust and competitive behavior remains intact.

This section simply restates the central issue in all negotiations— when should the negotiator trust and cooperate and when should she act competitively? The answer to this question, like so many others, is really the product of a cost-benefit analysis performed at every moment in the bargaining. What does one risk for her client if the other negotiator does not respond cooperatively to a cooperative tactic? Will a reasonable offer or concession at this point in the negotiation move the parties out of the distrust-competitive cycle into a situation where both parties are working in good faith to reach an agreement satisfactory to both?

The answers to these questions turn upon a wide variety of contextual factors, largely surveyed in Chapter Two, "Choosing Effective Negotiation Tactics." What does the negotiator know about the other negotiator's negotiation behavior or personality? Are there signs in the negotiation that the parties are ready to cooperate? Are the risks of misplaced confidence in the other negotiator manageable ones that will not seriously impair the client's interests? The negotiator's judgment about these issues, even though imprecise and often risky, offers the best available guidance on the question of whether to cooperate or to compete.

c. *Explicit Discussion of the Benefits of Cooperation*

Because lawyers do in fact frequently negotiate regarding the type of tactics they will employ during the bargaining process, often it is appropriate to explicitly discuss the benefits of a cooperative or problem-solving negotiation strategy. However, such discussion often must be introduced obliquely. Otherwise, the negotiator sounds either naive or "preachy" when she talks about the benefits of negotiating in some way other than competitively. The discussion should be as specific and subtle as possible, and should focus on the lawyer's own negotiation preferences, not on how the other negotiator "should" negotiate.

The negotiator who wishes to discuss the process with her counterpart directly can make two kinds of appeals to him. First, she can suggest that she would welcome and reciprocate any cooperative or problem-solving moves from the other negotiator. Maria Santiago might suggest to Ashton Crutchfield that if the railroad makes a reasonable first offer, she will follow with a sizable concession designed to bring the parties quickly into a narrow bargaining range and avoid the expense of protracted negotiation or litigation. Second, the negotiator can explicitly discuss the advantages of cooperative or problem-solving bargaining. If Maria and Ashton have not previously negotiated personal injury claims, at an appropriate point she might raise the issue of their negotiating relationship:

1—Maria: You know, Ashton, I find that I negotiate with some defense counsel in a much different way than with others. Have you had that experience with plaintiff's counsel?

2—Ashton: You mean there are some who demand a million bucks on a thirty thousand dollar claim, holler and scream and shout, and others who work with you within reasonable ranges to determine the fair and just amount of a claim?

3—Maria: Exactly. I much prefer the more collaborative relationship. It makes my life more pleasant, and I think I do a better job for my clients.

The risk is that such an opening will be seen as a sign of weakness and an opportunity for exploitation by the competitive negotiator. As previously mentioned, the negotiator facing an unknown counterpart should not make concessions that, if not reciprocated, significantly impair her client's interests. However, there is little or no disadvantage in explicitly discussing a preference for a cooperative strategy when the other lawyer already has made a reasonable opening offer or meaningful early concessions.

d. Active Listening

Lawyers as negotiators are not computers programmed to respond to impulses from the other side. They are human beings with feelings generated by the bargaining process. Negotiations usually begin as conflict situations and, as such, generate feelings of mistrust, fear and anger that are counterproductive to establishing an accommodative relationship that facilitates the use of cooperative or problem-solving tactics.

The next several "cooperation facilitators" are designed to address the relationship between the two negotiators. If the negotiator uses techniques calculated to develop rapport with the other negotiator, the relationship necessary for cooperative or problem-solving negotiation strategies is facilitated without the negotiator "giving up" anything on the merits. In other words, interpersonal techniques that make the other negotiator believe the lawyer understands his concerns, and therefore facilitate cooperation, can be regarded as "the cheapest possible concessions."[9]

The most important of the interpersonal skills that can be employed as a cooperation facilitator in the negotiation context is *active listening.*[10] Active listening is the process of hearing what the other negotiator has said, understanding it, and responding with a reflective statement that mirrors what the negotiator has heard. Assume that Maria Santiago, the attorney representing Michael Van Meter, has made an initial demand in the case against the Baltimore & Western Railroad for $3.5 million. She believes this is a reasonable opening offer given recent jury trends in her jurisdiction, the expert opinions of her economists and physicians, and her careful review of all the circumstances. Ashton Crutchfield, representing the railroad, responds as follows:

> 1—Ashton: Don't be ridiculous. We can't even begin to talk about figures like that. I thought that we were developing a relationship during the discovery process where we could deal with each other in good faith. You're just like all the other plaintiffs' attorneys. You've been "sand-bagging" me all along. When are you folks going to get real?

The normal human response at this point is to get defensive and to counterattack:

> 2—Maria: What are you talking about? Let's just look at the facts of the case for a moment and the experts'

---

9. I am indebted to my former colleague Professor Don Peters of the University of Florida for this characterization.

10. *See* BINDER ET AL., *supra* note 5, at 46–68.

opinions. This number is a fair and just demand. You're the one who is playing games.

Assume, however, that Maria acts less defensively, breaks the fear/anger cycle, and employs an active listening response:

3—Maria: The high numbers are a surprise to you. You think I've been playing games with you and that this isn't a serious proposal.

Which response is most likely to result in Maria and Ashton engaging in serious dialogue about the value of the claim? In which case is serious consideration of the experts' reports more likely to occur during the remainder of the bargaining session?

What has Maria really conceded through an active listening response? She has neither conceded nor admitted that her initial demand was too high, and she has not shared information that a competitive negotiator could use against her. Perhaps the only trade-off is that if she had intended to use a pure competitive strategy/adversarial style negotiation combination in which the essential message was to be "You'd better pay up with mega-bucks or I'm going to clean your clock at trial," her initial use of the active listening approach is probably inconsistent with such an aggressive posture. However, few negotiators successfully use such a blatantly adversarial style of negotiation with long-term success.

This example demonstrates the use of active listening to facilitate cooperative or problem-solving negotiation tactics. Active listening is used to convey that the negotiator has accurately heard and understood the other negotiator's communications. When using an active listening response, the negotiator is also *non-judgmental* about the other negotiator's position. This does not mean that she accepts the other party's position, or finds it substantively reasonable, but only that she recognizes that the other side can take the opposite position without being a monster or a lower form of life. Most people are inclined to be more trusting and cooperative when they believe that others have listened to them and have understood their message.

Three types of messages in negotiations can provide opportunities for active listening:

(1) facts as presented by the other negotiator;

(2) negotiation proposals or positions presented by the other negotiator; and

(3) the feelings of the other negotiator.

One purpose of using active listening as a response to the facts and bargaining proposals of the other party is to be sure the negotiator has heard and understood them accurately. The emotionally laden and frenetic atmosphere in which bargaining often is conducted provides many opportunities for miscommunication. Negotiations where one party believes an agreement has been reached while the other party does not are common. Reflective statements capturing the essence of factual statements or negotiation proposals serve as a check on the potential for misunderstandings. Further, as discussed above, active listening responses to negotiation proposals or to the negotiator's emotional responses, as in the case of Maria and Ashton, facilitate the development of a bargaining relationship where the use of cooperative and problem-solving negotiation tactics are possible.

e. Other Responses to Anger

Anger is a frequently expressed emotion during a negotiation in which a negotiator's goals are frustrated by the other lawyer's negotiation behavior. Anger, unfortunately, obscures opportunities for cooperative and problem-solving bargaining. How should the negotiator who wants to establish an accommodative atmosphere conducive to the use of cooperative and problem-solving tactics respond to anger?

Anger—or any other emotion being experienced by the other side that is destructive to the bargaining relationship—often should be acknowledged and explicitly addressed.[11] When verbal or non-verbal communications lead the lawyer to believe that the other negotiator is angry, the relationship frequently improves with direct empathetic discussion of these feelings. The active listening response that Maria used in the previous section is a good example.

The goal in responding to the other negotiator's anger is not to respond substantively to the expression of anger, but instead to allow the other negotiator to express the anger directly so that it does not impair the development of an accommodative relationship between the negotiator in other hidden or subtle ways. If Ashton Crutchfield is extremely angry at Maria Santiago's initial demand, it is unlikely that the negotiation will be productive until Ashton has had a chance to ventilate. However difficult it may be, the negotiator should allow her angry counterpart an opportunity to "let off steam" without responding defensively or with interruptions. At the same time, the negotiator should not allow such emotional outbursts to affect her substantive positions or to cause her to lose confidence in herself or her case. In fact, it is sometimes ill advised for the negotiator to make any concessions or changes in her proposals immediately following an outburst by the other side unless the negotiator can make it clear that the concession was not a response to intimidation brought on by the display of anger.

D.   PROBLEM–SOLVING ORIENTATION

This section focuses on the ways in which a negotiator using problem-solving tactics attempts to establish a relationship between the negotiators that is different from the one preferred by the competitive

11. *See* ROGER FISHER, WILLIAM URY &   AGREEMENT WITHOUT GIVING IN 29–32 (2d ed. BRUCE PATTON, GETTING TO YES: NEGOTIATING   1991).

negotiator. This relationship is based on trust similar to that used in the cooperative strategy. At the same time, the atmosphere in the negotiation is one dedicated to finding mutual "solutions to problems," rather than to making concessions and expecting the other side to concede in return.

The techniques described in this section for achieving a negotiation ambience hospitable to problem solving are not necessarily designed for use in the earliest stages of the negotiation. As described previously, competitive phases of a negotiation often precede stages where cooperative or problem-solving techniques predominate. If the other negotiator's initial approach is competitive, the use of problem-solving tactics sometimes is not feasible until deadlock is achieved and both negotiators recognize that little or nothing will be accomplished unless their tactics change. Accordingly, the techniques described here for achieving a problem-solving orientation frequently are not profitably employed until the negotiation has proceeded for some period of time and circumstances suggest that a change to a more problem-solving approach would be reciprocated.

When the opportunity is ripe, the lawyer using problem-solving tactics attempts to create an orientation between the negotiators that resembles the atmosphere created in the problem-solving pre-negotiation planning session with the client. The lawyer views the subject matter of the negotiation as the *problem* to be solved by the negotiators and not as an opportunity for exchanging proposals.[12] The desired atmosphere is one where the negotiators attempt to maximize the joint gains of their clients, not divide a limited resource between the parties. The initial stage of a problem-solving negotiation, therefore, is characterized by attempts to uncover, identify, and understand the parties' problems. This process requires discussion of each side's underlying needs.

Success in the initial orientation of problem-solving negotiation depends upon achieving a psychological state characterized by the following:

(1) mutual trust between the negotiators;

(2) a shared desire to achieve joint gains;

(3) open, honest communication between the negotiators; and

(4) the negotiator's recognition that negotiation can be something other than merely "one-party wins, one party loses" positional bargaining.

Trust between the parties facilitates problem-solving. A trusting atmosphere encourages accurate communication about each party's needs, and facilitates creative solutions. Without trust, each negotiator carefully controls the dissemination of information about her client's needs out of fear that a competitive opponent will use such information to disadvantage her client. A lack of trust also leads the negotiator to

---

12. For an excellent theoretical overview of the initial orientation in problem-solving negotiation, *see* WALTON & McKERSIE, *supra* note 6, at 127–53.

question the veracity of the communication from the other negotiator, because she fears that he is acting competitively and is intentionally distorting information in order to gain a competitive advantage. Finally, a trusting relationship and negotiation ambience facilitates the creativity required to explore all possible solutions to a problem.

All the techniques previously described that are used to develop trust in the context of cooperative negotiation tactics can also be used to facilitate problem-solving tactics. Problem-solving bargaining additionally requires a motivation to achieve joint gains that flow from the realization that gains for the negotiator's client do not emanate exclusively from "losses" inflicted upon the other party. Assuming that a negotiator can achieve an initial trusting relationship, what else must the negotiator do to facilitate a problem-solving approach to the negotiation as opposed to a competitive or cooperative strategy? The key ingredient is to induce the other party to leave behind his familiar habits of positional bargaining, whether in the competitive vein or the cooperative vein, and to move to a negotiation process which focuses on the underlying interests of the parties.

A novice lawyer's pedantic lecturing to a more experienced attorney on the virtues of a new type of negotiation—whether termed "problem-solving" or "principled"—is likely to be ineffective. Implicit in such assertions are a thinly-veiled sense of moral superiority and a rejection of how the other negotiator has operated during his professional life. At best, such proselytizing behavior is ineffective and looks silly or naive; at worst, it is offensive.

Effective negotiators find more subtle ways to introduce problem-solving negotiation techniques. Assume that Jonathan Prevas, representing Banting Medical Technologies, Inc., insists that Banting cannot pay more than $500,000 as an up-front licensing fee for the Viral Sharpshooter technology pioneered by Dr. Volkov. How can Katie Eisinger, representing Volkov, move Jonathan away from his stated "position" and toward an exploration of Banting's underlying interests?[13] Initially, Katie should try to place herself in the position of Banting Medical Technologies' decision-makers and to understand what interests lie behind Banting's stated position. She can also ask Jonathan directly, "How did your client reach the decision that it cannot offer more than $500,000 up-front? Note that in either case, Katie does not admonish Jonathan that positional bargaining is inappropriate or that there is a better way to do things. Assuming that Jonathan answers that the amount of the up-front payment cannot exceed $500,000 both because it would create a dangerously expensive precedent for other licensing fees in the future and because it would be too expensive a gamble for Banting to make, this opens the door to ask Jonathan more questions about those issues and to begin candid discussions of alternatives designed to address these interests of Banting without sacrificing the interests of Volkov, her client."

13. *See* FISHER, URY & PATTON, *supra* note 11, at 44–50, 108–12.

In addition to discovering the other party's underlying interests, the negotiator using problem-solving tactics explicitly communicates her client's underlying interests to the other negotiator. Recall that one of the principal concerns of Banting Medical Technologies about paying Dr. Volkov a large up-front licensing fee was that such a payment might establish a precedent that would lessen its bargaining power in negotiations with other researchers regarding their pharmacological discoveries. If Jonathan, Banting's attorney, uses a problem-solving strategy, he will clearly communicate this concern to Volkov's attorney, Katie. Such explicit communication of needs may reduce Volkov's emotional reaction that Banting is simply making him a low-ball offer and does not appreciate the importance of his Viral Sharpshooter technology. It also clears the way for Jonathan and Katie to work together to identify mutually satisfactory solutions, such as keeping the amount of the up-front licensing fee confidential.

The statement of needs should be as specific and as concrete as possible. Often it is easier for parties to agree on specific solutions than on broad statements of general or abstract principles. Consider a labor negotiation between a health-care workers' union and a hospital over the issue of testing hospital workers for exposure to HIV. A broadly stated position of the hospital management might be: "A regular program for HIV testing of employees is absolutely essential in a health care facility where there is substantial contact between employees and patients." The union, fearing massive testing and immediate dismissal of employees with positive results, might respond with the position: "Mandatory HIV testing violates the employees' civil liberties and invades their privacy." Not much room for compromise! However, a *specific* proposal from management that limits testing to employees with direct patient contact where the exchange of bodily fluids is at least a remote possibility, ensures the privacy of those tested, and provides for alternative employment for those with positive test results, is far more likely to lead to an agreement.

The techniques for establishing a bargaining relationship conducive to problem-solving tactics are critical, because many attorneys representing other parties enter negotiation with backgrounds in oppositional bargaining and are unfamiliar with problem-solving approaches. The next two chapters, covering information bargaining and initial proposals, include sections that continue the discussion of how specific problem-solving tactics can be employed in the early phases of negotiation to encourage an orientation in which the lawyers search for integrative solutions.

Chapter Five

INFORMATION BARGAINING

A. A BROADER PERSPECTIVE ON INFORMATION GATHERING

No other aspect of negotiation is as important as the exchange of information between negotiators. Inherent in the negotiation process is the idea that each negotiator must learn enough about what the other party needs and wants to be able to propose an agreement that is acceptable to both her client and the other party.

Frequently, when negotiators begin to discuss their needs and aspirations, and to exchange information, this signals the beginning of genuine bargaining. In many negotiations, particularly transactional ones, substantial information bargaining occurs prior to the time when the parties make their initial proposals. In other instances, substantial information exchange is deferred until after the initial proposals. In either event, information exchange usually is an ongoing negotiation sub-process that, once begun, takes place throughout the negotiation.

At the same time that she is negotiating, the lawyer typically gathers information in other ways such as her own independent investigation of the facts and, in the case of dispute resolution negotiation, through discovery. For example, if the lawyer is negotiating to purchase a small corporation owning a chain of nursing homes, and her independent inquiries establish that other parties who were once prospective purchasers are now no longer interested in buying the corporation, the lawyer may infer that the present owners of the corporation might accept less in exchange for their shares of stock. Further, such circumstances might also prompt the lawyer to investigate why other prospective purchasers have backed away from the sale.

The progress of the negotiation itself also implicitly communicates information about the other party's needs and expectations. If the other party persistently refuses to change its position on a particular issue despite the negotiator's urging, the negotiator ordinarily may infer that the other party values that issue highly.[1] This chapter, however, focuses on more direct and conscious attempts to gain information during the negotiation process. Specific factual information about the matter being negotiated and the other party's attitude toward the transaction or the negotiation itself, as well as information about what he wants and expects from an agreement, all assist the negotiator in proposing an agreement that is both acceptable to the other party and advantageous to her client.

B. THE STRATEGIC IMPLICATIONS OF INFORMATION BARGAINING

This chapter discusses both the "offensive" and the "defensive" aspects of information bargaining. Tactics for gathering information from the other party and tactics for disclosing or concealing information are both considered. First, however, the differing perspectives of the competitive, cooperative and problem-solving approaches to information exchange are described briefly. The three approaches suggest different ways to handle (1) information gathering, (2) information concealment and (3) information disclosure.

1. THE COMPETITIVE APPROACH TO INFORMATION EXCHANGE

Because competitive tactics are designed to achieve an agreement as beneficial as possible to the client at the expense of the other party, the purpose of competitive information gathering tactics is to determine the other party's "bottom line." In other words, the negotiator seeks information that either directly or indirectly indicates the "opponent's" reservation point, that is, the terms of a possible agreement least satisfactory to the other side that it nevertheless would find acceptable. She also typically believes her opponent is approaching the negotiation competitively, and assumes that he will try to conceal information from her. Consequently, obtaining information becomes a game, albeit one with important implications for the parties.

Conversely, it is a competitive tactic to conceal from the other negotiator information that reveals, directly or indirectly, the negotiator's own reservation point, or otherwise weakens her bargaining power. Information that indicates to the opponent that the negotiator's actual reservation point is one less advantageous to her client than what she claims her minimal requirements to be (or what the other negotiator previously perceived her reservation point to be) weakens the negotiator's bargaining power. Similarly, it is a competitive tactic to conceal from the other lawyer information that would induce him to change his reservation point to one even less advantageous to the negotiator than the opponent's original reservation point.

---

1. Unless, of course, the other negotiator is making a false demand. *See infra* Chapter Six, "Initial Proposals," at page 129.

A competitive approach does not suggest that all information be concealed. The negotiator should share information that "strengthens her case" or suggests to the other negotiator that settlement is only possible on terms more favorable to the negotiator's client than the other side previously believed.

There are substantial limitations on the ability to conceal information from the other negotiator in the real world. First, there are practical limits on the ability to disclose "one-sided" information in negotiation. Even using the variety of subtle techniques described below to conceal information, at some point the competitive negotiator's efforts to disclose favorable information while concealing unfavorable information become obvious. In the event that the negotiator temporarily succeeds in one-sided disclosure, her credibility may be severely impaired if the other negotiator subsequently realizes the extent of the uneven and potentially misleading information disclosure. Second, in negotiation in the litigation context, the widespread availability of discovery makes it more difficult to conceal information. However, since full discovery is not always possible, negotiation can be used as an alternate form of discovery in those cases in which the full array of discovery mechanisms either is not feasible (e.g., in smaller cases) or is not available (e.g., criminal cases in some jurisdictions).

2. THE COOPERATIVE APPROACH TO INFORMATION EXCHANGE

Cooperative information bargaining tactics differ from competitive ones. The cooperative goal in information bargaining is to encourage and facilitate a full and accurate exchange of information so that the parties efficiently may achieve an agreement that is fair and just to both parties. In terms of information gathering, therefore, the cooperative approach functions similarly to the competitive approach—to gather as much relevant information as possible—but with a different purpose, a fair and just agreement.

The key difference between the two approaches to information exchange lies in the willingness of the cooperative negotiator to reveal information within her possession, even if it is potentially disadvantageous to her bargaining leverage. She risks this diminution of her bargaining position for two reasons. First, if the best possible negotiated result for the two parties is to be achieved, both parties require full and accurate information about the matter being negotiated and about which issues each party values most. Second, revealing information to the other negotiator is used as a tactic to obtain information from him. In other words, the expectation is to assume that the parties will trade information, just as they exchange concessions.

3. THE PROBLEM–SOLVING APPROACH TO INFORMATION EXCHANGE

Problem-solving information bargaining, like its cooperative counterpart, encourages the free flow of information between the parties. Full information about the parties' needs, goals and motivations is required if the negotiators are to devise mutually satisfactory solutions to address the parties' underlying problems. The negotiators also must exchange information about their clients' priorities among the issues if they are to engage in logrolling and trade concessions on different issues in a manner that maximizes joint gains.

C. INFORMATION GATHERING

Information gathering is an indispensable element in any negotiation strategy, regardless of whether it employs predominantly competitive, cooperative or problem-solving tactics. This section begins with a brief introduction describing how virtually any information—even seemingly irrelevant information—about the other party, other negotiator, or the case or transaction may be material to the bargaining. The section then goes on to describe a variety of specific information-gathering techniques.

1. A BROAD INTERPRETATION OF RELEVANCY IN INFORMATION GATHERING

The negotiator wants to know everything possible that might affect the other negotiator's bargaining behavior and the eventual negotiation results. Specifically, she wants to know anything that suggests directly or indirectly what the other party's requirements and expectations for an agreement are, and what his alternatives to a successful negotiation are. Therefore, her bargaining should include attempts to fill in information gaps about the matter being negotiated, as well as to ascertain the other party's perceptions of the negotiation situation. The skilled negotiator also uses to her advantage other kinds of information not directly tied to the transaction or the dispute itself. Is the other negotiator too busy or inexperienced to handle the negotiation properly? Is he scared to go to trial if the negotiation breaks down? An extremely competitive negotiator might want to know when the other lawyer intends to take a vacation with his family, so she can use the date of the approaching vacation to create an artificial time deadline.

Consider Jonathan Prevas's information gathering in the negotiation between his client Banting Medical Technologies, Inc. and Dr. Volkov. Jonathan tries to obtain information that indirectly tells him something about Volkov's reservation point and his negotiation target. Has Volkov had preliminary conversations with any other medical technology or pharmaceutical companies? If so, are these other negotiations ongoing or are they inactive? If they are inactive, why did the negotiations break down? Was it because the Viral Sharpshooter technology has problems of which Banting is not aware? Did the other prospective licensing companies become aware of competing technologies believed to be more valuable? Or were Volkov and his counsel unrealistically aggressive in their bargaining? Information about competing technologies or problems with the Viral Sharpshooter technology might yield valuable bargaining leverage for Banting.

Similarly, consider information gathering in the negotiation between Maria Santiago on behalf of her injured client Michael Van Meter and the Baltimore & Western Railroad. In addition to facts affecting the merits of the negligence case and the railroad's opinion of the liability and damage issues, Maria also is interested in the amount of any insurance coverage, because this may affect the willingness of the defendant and its insurer to settle the claim within a given range.

Information gathering can begin substantially in advance of any "formal" negotiation sessions. Off-hand comments by an attorney, complaining about her busy schedule when asking for leave to file an answer or a motion on a delayed basis, suggest that she may not have the time to properly prepare and litigate every issue if opposing counsel pushes the case forward quickly. References by an attorney to her experience or lack of experience in similar cases, or about her lack of enthusiasm for a difficult client, also are important facts that may affect settlement value and negotiation strategy.

2. QUESTIONING

The most effective way to gain information during negotiation is the most obvious—ask questions. Most individuals are socialized at a very early age to politely answer questions addressed to them, and such conditioning is reinforced by law school professors and judges who ask questions and expect answers. It is difficult to refuse to answer a question without giving a reason, and many negotiators feel uncomfortable about declining to answer questions even when they do give reasons. Even if a negotiating attorney is capable of finding means to fend off a question without answering it, either her client or an expert who is present at the bargaining session often will not have the poise or experience necessary to parry the question without answering it.

In some negotiations, direct questions about issues going to the heart of the matter often produce spontaneous and surprisingly revealing answers. Such questions include "What's your bottom line here?" or "What's it going to take to resolve this?" Direct questions are most likely to prompt accurate and meaningful answers if posed early in the negotiation, particularly if addressed to an inexperienced negotiator, or as part of a negotiation the other lawyer regards as being a "small matter."

When the other negotiator declines to answer a direct question or answers it evasively, slight variations in the same question frequently produce more information. For example, consider Maria Santiago's personal injury settlement talks with the Baltimore & Western Railroad. The most direct and blunt question to be asked by Maria would be "What's your client's bottom line?" or "Let's stop fooling around, how much will it take to settle this thing?" In all likelihood, that question will be answered evasively or dishonestly. The slightly more indirect variation of the same question would be "What do you expect the jury will do with this case?" The answer to this question may yield significant information for Maria about the railroad's reservation point, both because it is likely to produce quantifiably *more* information than the earlier question and perhaps because it will produce a more honest response. Finally, the negotiator can ask an even more indirect variation of the question, such as "What evidence do you expect to use at trial to prove your case?" Once again, the answer to this question tells the negotiator something indirectly about what the other attorney expects the results at trial to be, and therefore, about what constitutes his reservation point. By inquiring even more indirectly, however, the last question frequently produces both greater detail in the information and greater honesty than the questions described previously.

The negotiator should use varying *forms* of questions depending upon the following factors: how forthcoming the other negotiator is, the stage of the negotiation, and whether the parties are using predominantly competitive or predominantly cooperative and problem-solving negotiation tactics. The form of the question—that is, whether it is an open-ended, narrow or specific, or leading question—may affect the behavioral response of the other negotiator. The best-known example of this is the use of leading questions during cross-examination. Not only do the rules of evidence allow such questions, but leading questions also are most likely to control the content of the witness's testimony.

Open-ended questions are questions posed to the other negotiator which allow him to choose the topic, or which aspect of a broadly defined topic, to discuss. For example, Maria Santiago, Michael Van Meter's attorney, might ask the following open-ended questions in his negotiation with the attorney representing Baltimore & Western Railroad:

"How does your client view this case?"

"Why do you think this is a no liability situation?"

Open-ended questions posed to the other negotiator are productive when he is openly sharing information previously unknown to the negotiator and at least some of the information is relevant and useful. Open-ended questions are most likely to yield worthwhile information when the negotiators are using predominantly cooperative or problem-solving negotiation tactics, and therefore are committed to sharing information with each other. Incidentally, open-ended questions themselves facilitate the use of cooperative or problem-solving tactics by helping to develop rapport between the negotiators. Open-ended questions build rapport by allowing the other negotiator to choose the topics he is discussing and by giving him the sense that his client's interests in the negotiation are being fairly considered. Finally, open-ended questions usually are most productive early in the negotiation, when the negotiator has wide-ranging information gaps and needs to uncover general knowledge about the matter being negotiated and the other party's attitude toward it. Later in the negotiation, when the negotiator already has most of the information she needs, frequent use of open-ended questions is probably inefficient.

Specific or narrow questions are questions where the negotiator chooses the specific subject matter that she wishes the other negotiator to discuss. For example, Maria, as Michael's attorney, might ask Ashton Crutchfield, the railroad's attorney, the following specific questions:

"How fast was the train going at the time of the accident?"

"What procedures has Baltimore & Western established for keeping its crossings clear of overgrown brush and weeds?"

"When did the engineer first notice the truck approaching the tracks?"

The negotiator should ask specific questions when her informational needs are well-defined or when the other negotiator is not sharing relevant information openly. Specific questions are much more difficult for the other negotiator to evade than are open-ended ones. Thus, they are recommended when competitive tactics are predominant in the negotiation. Further, specific questions often are more fruitful later in the negotiation when the lawyer largely understands both the subject matter of the negotiation and the other party's views on the matter being negotiated, but still has information gaps about specific issues.

A leading question is an extreme form of a specific question that makes a statement and asks the other negotiator to confirm it. Strings of leading questions similar to those posed to hostile witnesses in a court-room during cross-examination are seldom, if ever, appropriate during negotiation. A courteous and cooperatively phrased leading question, however, may enable a negotiator to pin-down a point during bargaining. For example, consider the following questions interspersed by Maria Santiago in her conversation with the railroad's representative:

"So the engineer did not see the truck on the tracks until he was 80 yards away from the crossing?"

"You're telling me then that there wasn't any program of regular inspection of crossings to identify problems with visibility. Is that right?"

3.   ACTIVE LISTENING FOR CONTENT

The use of active listening as a cooperation facilitator in negotiation previously was considered in Chapter Four. You may recall that active listening was defined as the process of hearing what the other negotiator has said, understanding it, and responding with a reflective statement that mirrors what the negotiator has heard. In addition to the use of active listening primarily as a cooperation facilitator to reflect the other negotiator's feelings, active listening also can be applied to mirror factual statements by the other negotiator. When active listening is employed in this vein, it serves as a "content check" to assure the lawyer that she has accurately heard and understood the other negotiator. Thus, active listening for content is closely related to the noncombative cross-examination techniques described in the previous section.

Consider the following sequence in the negotiation between Maria and Ashton Crutchfield:

1—Maria: Tell me what measures your client took to be sure that visibility at crossings was not obscured by overgrown brush and weeds.

2—Ashton: My client's regular train crews were responsible for reporting whenever brush and weeds obscured vision at crossings.

3—Maria: So there weren't any routine inspections to check crossing visibility.

4—Ashton: That's right.

In segment number 3, Maria uses active listening to check her understanding that Baltimore & Western relied upon its train crews to report weeds and brush obscuring visibility and that it had no other regular inspection process. Ashton's response to this active listening parry *repeat back* consolidates the admission by Baltimore & Western's attorney that there was no process for regularly checking for visibility problems.

4. SILENCE

The most overlooked information-gathering tactic in negotiation is silence. Particularly because many negotiators frequently experience bargaining sessions as high anxiety events, lengthy pauses in the conversation usually feel unnatural and awkward. Accordingly, many negotiators are prone to fill gaps in the conversation by talking—and when they talk, they reveal information or—even better—make concessions. In educational programs for law school deans and development directors, they are taught that when asking a wealthy alumnus for a very large gift, "the first person that talks loses." In other words, if the fundraiser is sufficiently patient to wait until the prospect speaks, it is likely that the prospect will commit to making a charitable contribution.

The negotiator should not feel obliged to respond to every point made by her counterpart if his conversation is providing information helpful to her. The negotiator, however, needs to guard against the possibility that her counterpart will gain a real or perceived psychological dominance of the bargaining session by monopolizing the conversation.

5. DIRECT CHALLENGES

Another approach to obtaining information that the other negotiator is reluctant to yield is to "bait" him, or directly attack or challenge him in a way that yields a defensive outpouring of information. Assume that in Jonathan Prevas's negotiation with Dr. Volkov's attorney Katie

Eisinger, Katie has been evasive about revealing the results of some of the tests that Dr. Volkov supposedly has run on the Viral Sharpshooter technology. Both direct and indirect questions have failed to solicit these experimental results. Another approach would be for Jonathan to directly challenge Katie:

1—Jonathan: (obviously frustrated after a long bargaining session)

Katie, you keep telling me that your experimental results show that the Viral Sharpshooter technology will destroy at least some cancerous tumors. Yet we have yet to see the lab records with the experimental results. It almost makes me wonder whether Volkov completed those experiments at all or whether they show something that you would rather hide.

2—Katie: (while handing a binder to Jonathan)

Here, take a look at this. On page 37 you will see a table showing that Viral Sharpshooter significantly reduced or eliminated the tumor in 88% of the subjects, compared with positive results in only 17% of the control group.

In this case, Jonathan's direct challenge in the first statement puts considerable pressure on Katie to share the lab files and reports. Once Jonathan has access to these documents, he may find that they include a variety of other relevant information.

6. INTERPRETING PARALINGUISTICS AND NON–VERBAL COMMUNICATIONS

The ability to interpret non-verbal communication and paralinguistics can play a critical role for the negotiator. Paralinguistics are content-free vocalizations and pauses accompanying speech.[2] They include vocal qualities such as pitch and loudness, as well as speech disturbances such as stutter, omission, repetition, hesitation and unfilled pauses. Non-verbal communications, of course, refer to facial expressions, hand movements and body language.

The ability to read non-verbal communication and paralinguistics sometimes allows the negotiator to detect when the other party is using *competitive tactics* behind a *friendly-style* smokescreen.[3] In choosing between competitive tactics and more *collaborative* tactics, either *cooperative* or *problem-solving* ones, the most important factor is to predict

---

2. *See* DANIEL DRUCKMAN, RICHARD M. ROZELLE & JAMES C. BAXTER, NONVERBAL COMMUNICATION: SURVEY, THEORY AND RESEARCH 43–44 (1982).

3. *See* Aldert Vrij, *Nonverbal Communication and Deception, reprinted in* THE SAGE HANDBOOK OF NONVERBAL COMMUNICATION 342 (Valerie Manusov & Miles L. Patterson, eds., 2006).

accurately whether cooperative or problem-solving tactics will be reciprocated. The biggest danger for the negotiator is taking seemingly collaborative actions at face value when, in fact, they are competitive tactics disguised in a friendly style. The ability to recognize and interpret paralinguistic signals and non-verbal communication is often the most effective way to expose the competitive negotiator who seeks to mislead with a friendly style. The ability to read such communication also can expose specific substantive examples of deception and evasion by a competitive counterpart.

There is no simple Rosetta stone or index that tells the negotiator that a particular non-verbal communication invariably has a certain meaning. Individual non-verbal communications must be interpreted in the context of other non-verbal clues, the negotiation situation, and what is being verbally communicated.[4] On the other hand, interpreting non-verbal communications is not as complex or difficult as it first sounds because most people consciously or unconsciously interpret non-verbal messages on a regular basis.

No other part of the body is more expressive than the eyes—a fact frequently commented on by poets and proven by empiricists.[5] "Inquisitive looks," "icy stares," "shifty eyes," and "seductive stares" are all interpretations of mental states based upon visual cues. If the negotiator understands visual nonverbal communication, she often can use it to interpret the other negotiator's "eye messages." On the other hand, if the negotiator consciously focuses on her own visual behavior, she probably can manipulate, at least to some extent, her own visual messages.

Visual contact between the negotiators serves at least three functions. First, visual behavior is used subconsciously to signal to the other person when it is time to speak and when it is time to listen.[6] For example, when the other lawyer establishes direct eye contact with the negotiator during a conversation, it often signals his desire to speak. As a general rule, the negotiator has more eye contact with the other lawyer when she listens to him than when she speaks to him. The second function of looking at the other negotiator is to obtain information about him.[7] Research shows that frequency of gaze is an index of information seeking. Those who seek information about the other while controlling

4. *See* Judee K. Burgoon & Beth A. Le Poire, *Nonverbal Cues and Interpersonal Judgments: Participant and Observer Perceptions of Intimacy, Dominance, Composure, and Formality*, 66 COMMUNICATIONS MONOGRAPHS 105, 107–08 (1999).

5. *See id.* at 73–84 for a survey of research involving visual behavior.

6. *See generally* Michael Argyle & Roger Ingham, *Gaze, Mutual Gaze, and Proximity*, 6 SEMIOTICA 32–49 (1972) (exploring the relationship between distance, gaze and mutual gaze); Starkley Duncan, *Some Signals and Rules for Taking Speaking Turns in Conversations*, 23 J. OF PERSONALITY & SOC. PSYCHOL. 283–92 (1972) (studying the turn-taking mechanisms used by speakers); Adam Kendon, *Some Functions of Gaze-Direction in Social Interaction*, 26 ACTA PSYCHOLOGICA 22–63 (1967) (looking at the relationship between direction of gaze and the occurrence of utterances).

7. *See generally* Margaret Foddy, *Patterns of Gaze in Cooperative and Competitive Negotiation*, 31 HUM. REL. 925–938 (1978) (studying the frequency and duration of the gaze of negotiators).

information about themselves—a description fitting the negotiator using competitive information-bargaining tactics—frequently use short, frequent gazes. More sustained looks are characteristic of those who want to gather information about the other party while disclosing information themselves—such as negotiators willing to use cooperative or problem-solving tactics.

How can a negotiator become more effective by consciously controlling her own visual behavior? Studies suggest that a high degree of eye contact causes a presentation to be viewed as more authentic and a speaker to be seen as more poised.[8] Once again, however, the validity of this generalization depends upon the circumstances. Certainly, sustained staring often backfires and looks very awkward. Further, differences in the sex, race or cultural backgrounds of the negotiators sometimes mean that sustained eye contact may produce feelings of discomfort or even hostility.

Eye contact with another person also serves to communicate a willingness to collaborate—in the context of this text, either to engage in cooperative or problem-solving negotiation tactics. The average *duration* of gaze (eye contact) and mutual gaze have been found to be greater for cooperators than for competitors, while the *frequency* of gaze and mutual gaze were found to be the same for both groups.[9]

The negotiator also learns by watching for other non-verbal communications from her counterpart, including facial expressions and body language. Facial expressions probably convey the most specific information about the other negotiator's attitudes and emotions, but are more susceptible to conscious control by him.[10] Kinetics, or body language, including gestures, postural shifts and movements of the hands, head, feet and legs, has been extensively studied and classified.[11] Most often, body language conveys broad psychological states, such as anxiety, rather than specific intentions or emotions. Thus, patterns of body language may help reveal whether the other negotiator is behaving generally in a competitive or a collaborative manner, but they reveal little about the other negotiator's specific message.

Perhaps the most relevant research for negotiation students is a study by Daniel Druckman, Richard Rozelle and James Baxter, which

8. Robert E. Kleck & W. Nuessle, *Congruence Between the Indicative and Communicative Functions of Eye Contact in Interpersonal Relations*, 7 BRIT. J. OF SOC. AND CLINICAL PSYCHOL. 241, 246 (1968); William F. LeCompte & Howard M. Rosenfeld, *Effects of Minimal Eye Contact in the Instruction Period on Impressions of the Experimenter*, 7 J. OF EXPERIMENTAL SOC. PSYCHOL. 211, 219 (1971).

9. Foddy, *supra* note 7, at 936.

10. *See generally* DRUCKMAN ET AL., *supra* note 2, at 52–64 (discussing the role of facial expressions in nonverbal communica-

tion); GERARD I. NIERENBERG & HENRY H. CALERO, HOW TO READ A PERSON LIKE A BOOK 28–34 (1971) (discussing the vocabulary of body language); Alan J. Fridlund & James A. Russell, *The Functions of Facial Expressions: What's in a Face?, reprinted in* THE SAGE HANDBOOK OF NONVERBAL COMMUNICATION 299–319 (Valerie Manusov & Miles L. Patterson, eds., 2006) (arguing that facial cues are better seen as "social tools" modifying the trajectory of human social interaction).

11. *See generally* DRUCKMAN ET AL., *supra* note 3, at 64–73; NIERENBERG & CALERO, *supra* note 11, at 134–36.

measures the differences in non-verbal communications between subjects who were honest, those who were evasive, and those who were decep-tive.[12] The results of their research suggest that if the negotiator can observe her counterpart's degree of eye contact, frequency of leg move-ments and fidgeting with "objects" (e.g., pen, pencil, or jewelry), she may be able to predict whether he is being honest, deceptive or evasive.[13] Subjects who were deceiving others were found to have a higher number of speech errors, such as stuttering, repetition of phrases, broken phras-es and insertions of non-substantive phrases. "Deceivers" also spoke more rapidly and in a higher pitch. In addition, deceivers were more likely to "fidget" with objects and to avoid looking at the other party. Those who evaded answering questions were found to have more leg and foot movements than other subjects and to engage in more side-to-side head shaking, particularly early in the interaction. "Evaders" also avoided eye contact by gazing and fidgeting, particularly in the later phases of the interaction.

Negotiators often experience anxiety, discomfort, or defensiveness during bargaining. These emotional states may result either from decep-tion or evasion in negotiation behavior, or from other factors. In addition to some of the non-verbal communications previously described as char-acteristics of deceivers or evaders, other commentators have noted the increased frequency of throat-clearing and the presence of hands cover-ing or positioned near the mouth among those experiencing anxiety or discomfort.[14] In addition, arms crossed on the chest are a typical sign of defensiveness. Picture a manager leaving a dugout at a baseball game, rushing onto the field to dispute a call by the first-base umpire. How will the umpire respond? If sufficiently provoked, probably by ejecting the manager. Before things get to that point, however, the fans are likely to observe the umpire fold his arms across his chest.

Few negotiators will master the interpretation of all subtle non-verbal communication clues. One signal that most negotiators often can detect, however, is incongruity between the verbal message and the non-verbal communication. Assume that the response to the negotiator's demand is a slight pause or hesitation in the conversation and perhaps hints of a subtle smile by the other negotiator. When he then erupts with a statement that the demand is "OUTRAGEOUS" and that it is clear the negotiator is "wholly unrealistic about the case," the negotiator should not take these verbal statements at face value.

What other non-verbal behaviors may suggest a willingness of the other negotiator to engage in cooperative or problem-solving tactics? Perhaps the most obvious non-verbal behavior signaling openness or sincerity is "open hands" with the palms extended and facing up. I once

12. DRUCKMAN ET AL., *supra* note 2, at 109–75.

13. *See also* Letizia Caso et al., *The Impact of Deception and Suspicion on Different Hand Movements*, 30 J. NONVERBAL BEHAV. 1 (2006) (examining the effects of deception and raised suspicion on different types of hand movements).

14. *See* NIERENBERG & CALERO, *supra* note 10, at 44–104 for a fuller description of the specific non-verbal communications de-scribed in this section.

taught Torts to a class that included a hearing-impaired student who had become extremely adept at reading non-verbal communication. During one class, the student stopped her answer to a Socratic question in mid-sentence. When later asked about her unusual behavior, she responded that I almost always displayed "palms-up" and even pulled my hands toward me when I thought that a student's answer was a worthwhile contribution to class discussion. Conversely, she reported, I usually turned my hands over into a "palms-down" position when the student's answer did not please me. Therefore, when I changed my hand-position from "palms up" to "palms down" during her response to my question, she concluded that there was no reason to complete her answer!

Other gestures may indicate a readiness to engage in serious bargaining or to use cooperative or problem-solving tactics. Gerard Nierenberg and Henry Calero suggest, for example, that if the other negotiator is literally sitting on the edge of his chair, this signals a "readiness for action."[15] On one hand, this "action" may be a willingness to conclude the negotiation; on the other hand, it is also possible that the position indicates that the individual is about to walk out of the negotiation. However, if the other negotiator makes a "final and last offer" in this position, it is more likely that the offer is in fact "final and last" than it would be if he were leaning back from the table with his hands behind his head. Similarly, according to Nierenberg and Calero, if the other negotiator's hand or finger touches his chin or another part of the face, this often is an "evaluation gesture" suggesting that he is in fact seriously engaged in evaluating the lawyer's latest proposal.[16]

Any visual clues suggesting the other negotiator's degree of confidence obviously also are important. If the other negotiator is pursuing competitive tactics, non-verbal displays suggesting poise or confidence indicate that he believes his negotiation tactics are working. Conversely, if the negotiator herself is using competitive tactics in an attempt to undermine the confidence of the other negotiator, his body language may indicate whether her competitive tactics are effective in undermining his confidence. Probably the most clearly defined non-verbal communication suggesting confidence is "steepling," a hand position in which an individual joins the fingertips from one hand to the corresponding fingertips on the other hand to form a figure resembling a "church steeple." Nierenberg and Calero recommend that if you are playing poker and one of the players is steepling, "unless you have a very good hand, get out of the game."[17] Another gesture typically indicating confidence is leaning back with two hands laced behind the head. If the other negotiator displays these confident gestures, it suggests either that the negotiator's competitive tactics have not successfully undermined his confidence or that he believes his own competitive tactics are working.

---

15. *Id.* at 44–47.

16. *Id.* at 77–79, 81–83.

17. *Id.* at 93–104.

Like non-verbal communication, paralinguistic variables—content free vocalizations and pauses associated with speech—also can be used to detect anxiety. The frequency of speech disturbances, such as "ahs" and repetitions of words or phrases, increases with anxiety, whether that anxiety is caused by deception or other factors. In addition, the pitch or vocal frequency frequently becomes higher when a subject is lying.

The words chosen by the lawyer in negotiation also may communicate unintended messages. For example, when the other negotiator begins a statement about the limits of his authority with the preface "To be perfectly honest ..." or a similar phrase, the lawyer should be careful. Experience suggests that such statements frequently precede lies.

Similarly, careful listening can help the lawyer distinguish what actually was said from what the other negotiator hoped or expected that she would infer from the statement. Often negotiators will be careful not to tell a direct lie, but will purposely use words to mislead. For example, consider again the negotiation between Ashton Crutchfield and Maria Santiago in Michael Van Meter's personal injury case against the Baltimore & Western Railroad Company. Initially, the following statements by Ashton may appear to be saying the same thing:

(1) "My client cannot and will not pay more than $1.2 million."

(2) "I am not authorized to pay more than $1.2 million."

(3) "I am not authorized to offer more than $1.2 million at this time."

The first statement obviously is more absolute than the other two statements, posing less opportunity for subsequent changes in bargaining position. The second statement communicates implicitly that although the railroad attorney is not authorized to pay more, the amount of the settlement authority can be changed. The third statement is even more explicit, and virtually invites a suggestion from the negotiator that the other attorney return to his client to seek further authority.

The brief discussion of non-verbal communication and paralinguistics presented here is not exhaustive and will not make you an expert overnight. It is intended only to make you conscious of non-verbal communications and paralinguistics. Unconsciously, you always have read non-verbal communications. Greater focus and concentration on the other negotiator's non-verbal communication may assist you in answering the critical question of whether the other lawyer is acting competitively or collaboratively.

7. ADDITIONAL PROBLEM–SOLVING INFORMATION GATHERING TACTICS

The information-gathering tactics previously discussed can be used as problem-solving information-gathering tactics, as well as in competitive or cooperative bargaining. One additional major information-gathering approach for the problem-solving negotiator will be considered more fully in Chapter Six, "Initial Proposals." When the other lawyer begins with a traditional bargaining position, the negotiator can respond by asking her counterpart which of his client's interests are served by the proposal. In other words, she should ask "Why?" The answer to such an inquiry is likely to reveal the underlying interests of the other party. In addition, if the negotiator's own proposal is summarily rejected, she can ask "Why not?"

Another information-gathering, or more accurately, information-sharing technique, is for the negotiators to engage in informal problem-solving discussions outside the framework of formal negotiation sessions.[18] For example, labor negotiators frequently discuss the needs and interests of the union and of management more openly away from the formal, public bargaining sessions. They often do so with the understanding that such conversations are "off the record" and that they will not be held publicly accountable for any opinions or views expressed when the proposals are discussed.

D. INFORMATION CONCEALMENT

Information concealment is a competitive tactic. A negotiator using competitive tactics often avoids revealing information to conceal his reservation point or target or to prevent erosion of his bargaining leverage. By definition, problem-solving and cooperative information tactics involve disclosure, not concealment. However, even negotiators using predominantly problem-solving or cooperative tactics sometimes conceal information, such as when it is apparent that the other negotiator wants the information solely to weaken the negotiator's bargaining position.

This section begins with a discussion of the professional responsibility issues inherent in concealing information from the other negotiator or even misleading him. It then discusses a variety of techniques available to the lawyer to avoid answering the other negotiator's inquiries.

1. ETHICAL CONSIDERATIONS

Competitive tactics for concealing the client's minimum disposition, and even misleading the other negotiator about the client's interests in the negotiation, pose the primary set of ethical issues for the lawyer as negotiator. *Model Rule of Professional Conduct 4.1* explicitly provides:

In the course of representing a client a lawyer shall not knowingly:

---

18. *See* DEAN PRUITT, NEGOTIATION BEHAVIOR 98–99 (1981). In their book entitled *A Behavioral Theory of Labor Negotiations: An Analysis of a Social Interaction System*, Walton and McKersie discuss the effect of "off the record" conversations on the 1964 automobile industry negotiations. With both sides free to pursue alternatives in these conversations, tentative solutions were proposed and explored without fear of later accountability. RICHARD E. WALTON & ROBERT B. MCKERSIE, A BEHAVIORAL THEORY OF LABOR NEGOTIATIONS: AN ANALYSIS OF A SOCIAL INTERACTION SYSTEM 158–60 (1965).

(a) make a false statement of material fact or law to a third person; or

(b) fail to disclose a material fact when disclosure is necessary to avoid assisting a criminal or fraudulent act by a client, unless disclosure is prohibited by Rule 1.6.[19]

The Model Rules thus address the negotiator's deception, whether accomplished with an affirmative misstatement of fact (subsection (a)) or through an omission, at least in limited circumstances (subsection (b)).

The proper application of these seemingly straightforward prohibitions to the lawyer as negotiator remains obscure, but perhaps not as obscure as the existing prevalence of misrepresentation in negotiation would lead one to believe.[20] The inherent dilemma facing the negotiator using competitive tactics is how to comply with ethical constraints while simultaneously deceiving the other lawyer regarding her client's reservation point.

Certain types of statements used by the negotiator to deceive can be readily identified as falling on one side or the other of the ethical line. A statement by Maria Santiago that Michael Van Meter's past medical expenses were twice as great as they actually were is clearly a forbidden misrepresentation of material fact, as would be a false account of Dr. Volkov's experimental results. An extremely high initial demand by Maria, on the other hand, although calculated to deceive, is permissible. Similarly, "puffery," or misstatements of opinion about value, are not misstatements of material facts under conventional bargaining norms and therefore are permissible,[21] just as misrepresentations of the law-

19. MODEL RULES OF PROF'L CONDUCT R. 4.1 (2006). A few jurisdictions, including New York and Ohio, still have provisions modeled on *Model Rule of Professional Responsibility DR 1–102(A)(4) (1987)*, which states, "A lawyer shall not . . . engage in conduct involving dishonesty, fraud, deceit or misrepresentation." *See also* RESTATEMENT (THIRD) OF THE LAW GOVERNING LAWYERS § 98 (2000) ("A lawyer communicating on behalf of a client with a non-client may not (1) knowingly make a false statement of material fact or law to the non-client . . . or (3) fail to make a disclosure of information required by law."); *Ethical Guidelines for Settlement Negotiations*, ABA SEC. OF LITIG. §§ 4.1.1–4.1.3 (2002); Charles B. Craver, *Negotiation Ethics: How to Be Deceptive Without Being Dishonest / How to Be Assertive Without Being Offensive*, 38 S. TEX. L. REV. 713 (1997) (discussing circumstances when misrepresentations may be appropriate); Barry R. Temkin, *Misrepresentation by Omission in Settlement Negotiations: Should There Be a Silent Safe Harbor?*, 18 GEO. J. LEG. ETHICS 179 (2004) (exploring factual representations and omissions in settlement negotiations); Gerald Wetlaufer,

The Ethics of Lying in Negotiations, 75 IOWA L. REV. 1219 (1990) (arguing that lying in negotiations is effective, but not always justified by prevailing practice and lawyers' obligations to their clients).

20. A survey of lawyers conducted by the University of Michigan Law School in conjunction with the American Bar Foundation reportedly found that 18 percent of the national attorneys and 28 percent of Michigan attorneys surveyed believed that lawyers regularly or frequently make representations during negotiation that they believe are false. *See* ROGER HAYDOCK, NEGOTIATION PRACTICE 201–02 (1984).

21. MODEL RULES OF PROF'L CONDUCT R. 4.1 cmt. 2 (2006). The Restatement is less categorical on whether such statements should or should not be regarded as a misstatement of fact:

Certain statements, such as some statements relating to price or value, are considered non-actionable hyperbole or a reflection of the state of mind of the speaker and not misstatements of fact or law. . . . Whether a misstatement should be so characterized depends on whether

yer's authority to bind her client are not.[22] False demands also are a traditional and arguably inherent aspect of multiple-issue negotiations and thus probably do not constitute an ethical violation.[23] Finally, a negotiator presumably can argue a plausible interpretation of the law during negotiation—just as she can during argument to the court—while simultaneously entertaining private doubts about whether the law applies to the instant case.[24]

This list of exceptions to the prohibition against misrepresentation does not provide a clear standard against which to test the ethical propriety of the innumerable possible variations of deceptive statements during negotiation. Some commentators assert that bargaining conventions governing acceptable levels of deception vary from heterogeneous urban areas to more homogeneous rural communities, where a greater degree of "good faith" is expected of negotiators.[25] Further, they contend that traditional practice provides for a higher standard of ethical conduct in certain substantive practice contexts, such as securities practice, than in others, like personal injury practice. These practice differences arguably suggest that standards governing professionally acceptable levels of deception in negotiation vary according to the negotiation context.[26]

The questions regarding the ethical necessity to disclose certain kinds of information in negotiation are perhaps even more difficult than those relating to affirmative misrepresentations. Generally a negotiator is under no affirmative obligation to disclose or volunteer information that harms her bargaining position. What is Maria Santiago's obligation to the other lawyer, however, when Michael Van Meter informs her that some of the medical expenses he claimed earlier are fictitious? On one hand, *Model Rule of Professional Conduct 4.1*, as we already have seen, provides that "a lawyer must disclose a material fact" to the other negotiator "when disclosure is necessary to avoid assisting a . . . fraudulent act by a client . . ."[27] On the other hand, this obligation is trumped

it is reasonably apparent that the person to whom the statement is addressed would regard the statement as one of fact or based on the speaker's knowledge of facts reasonably implied by the statement or as merely an expression of the speaker's state of mind. Assessment depends on the circumstances in which the statement is made, including the past relationship of the negotiating persons, their apparent sophistication, the plausibility of the statement on its face, the phrasing of the statement, related communication between the persons involved, the known negotiating practices of the community in which both are negotiating, and similar circumstances. * * *

RESTATEMENT (THIRD) OF LAW GOVERNING LAW-YERS § 98 cmt. c (2000); *see also* James J. White, *Machiavelli and the Bar: Ethical Limitations on Lying in Negotiation*, 1980 AM. B. FOUND. RES. J. 926, 931 (1980) (sug-

gesting that the Model Rules refer to relative truth as determined by the situation); Craver, *supra* note 19, at 734 (discussing attorney motivation for ethical behavior).

22. *See supra* Chapter Three, "Negotiation Planning," at page 74, n. 31, for a full discussion of the ethical issues involved in a false denial of authority to settle a claim.

23. *See supra* Chapter Six, "Initial Proposals," at page 129, for a comprehensive discussion of the ethics of false demands.

24. *See* White, *supra* note 21, at 931.

25. *See* Thomas F. Guernsey, *Truthfulness in Negotiation*, 17 U. RICH. L. REV. 99, 100–01 (1982); White, *supra* note 21, at 929–30.

26. White, *supra* note 21, at 931.

27. MODEL RULES OF PROF'L CONDUCT R. 4.1(b) (2006). The provisions of the *ABA Ethical Guidelines for Settlement Negotia-*

by the lawyer's obligation to preserve the confidentiality of communications with the client.[28] In short, if the lawyer realizes that her prior statements to the other negotiator have included misstatements of material fact, she ought to inform the client of the client's obligation to set the record straight.[29] If the client does not now agree to the correction of these falsehoods, under most circumstances the lawyer is prevented by her duty of confidentiality from disclosing the misrepresentation. However, the lawyer also cannot continue to represent the client and therefore must withdraw from further representation of the client.[30] If this situation should arise, it is critical for the lawyer-negotiator to check a particular jurisdiction's ethical rules governing the lawyer's responsibilities. As the *ABA Ethical Guidelines for Settlement Negotiations* acknowledge:

> [S]tates have adopted different versions of these rules and there is considerable variation in the rules' applications by the states. Some states either allow or require disclosure in situations where the *Model Rules* do not. Accordingly . . . a lawyer should be careful to check the controlling ethical rules in the relevant jurisdiction. Moreover, even if a lawyer is not subject to discipline for failure to disclose, such failure may be inconsistent with professional practice and may possibly jeopardize the settlement or even expose the lawyer to liability.[31]

2. TACTICS TO AVOID REVEALING INFORMATION

As noted previously, there are practical, as well as ethical, limits regarding how one-sided even the negotiator using predominantly competitive tactics can expect the information exchange process to be. No experienced negotiator will reveal substantial information without reciprocity. Further, the tactics outlined in this section to conceal information succeed only if the other negotiator lacks the ability, persistence or

---

tions are even more explicitly relevant: "In the course of negotiating or concluding a settlement, a lawyer must disclose a material fact" to the other negotiator "when doing so is necessary to avoid assisting a . . . fraudulent act by a client." *ABA Ethical Guidelines for Settlement Negotiations*, ABA SEC. OF LITIG. § 4.1.2 (2002).

28. *Model Rule of Professional Conduct 4.1(b)'s* obligates the lawyer to affirmatively disclose a material fact "unless disclosure is prohibited by Rule 1.6." MODEL RULES OF PROF'L CONDUCT R. 4.1(b) (2006).

29. *Model Rule of Professional Conduct 1.6* (a) allows the lawyer to reveal the corrected facts gleaned from the client when "the client gives informed consent" or under very narrow circumstances in egregious situations:

> Ordinarily, a lawyer can avoid assisting a client's . . . fraud by withdrawing from

the representation. Sometimes it may be necessary for the lawyer . . to disaffirm an opinion, document, affirmation or the like. In extreme cases, substantive law may require a lawyer to disclose information relating to the representation to avoid being deemed to have assisted the client's . . . fraud.

Id. at R. 4.1, cmt. 3.

30. *Model Rule of Professional Conduct 1.2, comment 10* provides: "A lawyer may not continue assisting a client in conduct that the lawyer originally supposes was legally proper but then discovers is . . . fraudulent. The lawyer must, therefore, withdraw from the representation of the client in the matter. MODEL RULES OF PROF'L CONDUCT R. 1.2, cmt. 10 (2006).

31. *ABA Ethical Guidelines for Settlement Negotiations*, ABA SEC. OF LITIG. § 4.1.1, comm. notes (2002).

desire to follow up on his initial questions and to press for the information requested.

A complete array of tactics to avoid answering questions can be observed in any press conference held by a high government official or politician. Some of these tactics include:

a. Don't Answer the Question and Shift to Another Topic

Consider the following example from the Volkov/Banting Medical Technologies, Inc. negotiation:

1—Katie: Has Banting ever paid a researcher an up-front licensing fee of more than $500,000?

2—Jonathan: Banting's executives consider it poor policy to pay more than $500,000 in up-front licensing fees. Banting's research and development expenditures for a new technology are simply too great to allow it to pay more. Can Dr. Volkov assist us with these R & D costs by obtaining federal grants or help from the university?

Here Jonathan avoids answering the question asked about whether Banting *ever* has paid more than $500,000 up-front and reverts to a discussion of "poor policy" while restating Banting's justification for its figure. He effectively shifts the discussion to how Volkov might assist Banting by absorbing some of the research and development expenses.

b. Answer a Different Question Than the One Asked

An example from the negotiation between the attorneys for Michael Van Meter and the Baltimore & Western Railroad illustrates this tactic:

1—Maria: How many other car-train accidents have you had at this crossing?

2—Ashton: In all my years representing the railroad, we've never had a lawsuit from that crossing.

Ashton does not answer the question about the number of *accidents* at the crossing; instead, he answers the very different question of how many *lawsuits* have resulted from accidents at the same crossing.

c. Answer Incompletely

This evasive tactic is similar to the last one, as suggested by its application to the same situation:

1—Maria: How many other car-train accidents have you had at this crossing?

2—Ashton: To the best of my knowledge, there has never been one.

By limiting his answer to his own knowledge, Ashton answers incompletely. Maria does not learn the answer to the question, and unless she pursues the topic, Ashton is under no obligation to investigate the answer to the question.

d. Answer Only if Information Sharing Is Reciprocated

The negotiator agrees to answer the question, but only if the other party is prepared to answer a corresponding question. For example, let's consider again the negotiation between Dr. Volkov and Banting Medical Technologies:

1—Jonathan: Have you and Dr. Volkov had preliminary discussions with any other medical technology or pharmaceutical manufacturers?

2—Katie: I recognize that you would like to know what other alternatives we might have. My client would be prepared to share that information if you would tell us about any other negotiations you are having with medical researchers who have discovered technologies that may compete with the Viral Sharpshooter technology.

e. Delay

When asked a question she wishes to evade, the negotiator can promise to get the answer to the question and supply it at a later date. Often, however, she never does, and unless the information is important, the other negotiator frequently will not follow up on his request. The question has been effectively evaded.

f. Refuse to Answer and Explain Why

Frequently, a negotiator simply rules a question out-of-bounds. When asked how much authority she has from a client, she states, "That's between me and my client." When asked about negotiations with other researchers of anti-cancer technologies, Jonathan might respond that Banting always maintains the confidentiality of discussions with researchers who might license their technologies to Banting, and that Katie, as Volkov's attorney, certainly should appreciate that.

g. Beware of the Outright Lie

The *Model Rules of Professional Conduct* clearly state that misstatements of fact by attorneys during negotiations are prohibited and constitute violations of professional ethics.[32] Unfortunately, it is clear that some members of the bar do intentionally misrepresent facts during negotiation.

---

32. MODEL RULES OF PROF'L CONDUCT R. 4.1(a).

h. Say Little

If asked a specific question, it usually is not professionally or socially acceptable behavior to remain silent and say nothing. Over the course of a negotiation session, however, one of the best ways to reduce the amount of information being revealed to the other negotiator is to stay quiet and do little talking. As previously discussed, many lawyers representing other parties will fill silence by talking. Not only does the negotiator gain information while the other negotiator talks, during the time she listens, she also does not reveal any information to him.

i. Calculated Ignorance

One way to avoid sharing any information with the other negotiator is to avoid knowing anything. For example, Ashton Crutchfield, attorney for the Baltimore & Western Railroad, might make a calculated decision not to have any substantive conversations with representatives of his client prior to her first meeting with Maria Santiago, Michael Van Meter's attorney. A more extreme example is the law firm that sends an associate to a negotiation who knows very little about the case and who has no authority to settle it.[33]

E. INFORMATION DISCLOSURE AND ARGUMENT

It is difficult to conceive of any negotiation that concludes without both negotiators sharing at least some information with their negotiating counterparts. Unless the negotiator either discloses new information or demonstrates in new ways how the facts previously available to the other party support her own proposals and arguments, there is no reason for the other negotiator to change his initial proposal. Therefore, even the negotiator using predominantly competitive tactics discloses information that supports her proposals.

The negotiator using cooperative or problem-solving tactics goes further and discloses even information that conceivably could be used to harm her client's bargaining interests. The cooperative approach to information exchange is to encourage full and accurate disclosure of facts from both parties so that the negotiators together can determine what constitutes a fair and just agreement. One specific cooperative tactic is to initiate this sharing process by disclosing information and expecting reciprocation. The cooperative negotiator initially should choose carefully those items of information to be disclosed, so that if the other negotiator fails to reciprocate and instead seeks to use the disclosure to the detriment of the negotiator's client, any damage to the negotiator's bargaining position is limited.

Like cooperative tactics, successful problem-solving bargaining requires full and accurate information about each party's needs and preferences. Problem-solving information exchange occurs in two stages.

---

33. Some judges, perhaps responding to this tactic, now require attorneys attending pre-trial conferences either to have full settlement authority or to be accompanied by a client representative who does.

First, the negotiators exchange considerable information about each party's requirements before they initially suggest bridging solutions or logrolling exchanges of concessions. At a later point, the negotiators again freely exchange information about their preferences regarding each of the solutions that have been proposed.

Information disclosure during negotiation frequently occurs as the lawyer presents arguments in an effort to influence the other negotiator to alter his bargaining position. An *argument* is the invocation and reasoned elaboration of norms and their application to the subject matter of the negotiation. An argument is used either to support the lawyer's proposal or to critique the other negotiator's proposal.

Arguments, in part, are a form of information disclosure because they call for the other negotiator to reach conclusions based upon inferences from certain facts. Accordingly, the negotiator must present facts as a basis for her argument. For example, suppose that Katie, acting as Dr. Volkov's attorney, wishes to make an argument countering Banting's bargaining claim (an argument in itself) that a larger up-front lump-sum payment of licensing fees poses an unacceptable financial risk to Banting. Katie argues that the Viral Sharpshooter technology poses little risk to the acquiring corporation because existing experimental results show that the Viral Sharpshooter eliminates or substantially reduces tumors in 88% of all cases. In making this argument, Katie will disclose further details of the lab and clinical testing, and the results of such testing. Argument is probably the most important and frequently used form of factual disclosure during negotiation.

Arguments can be used as competitive, cooperative or problem-solving tactics. However, each variety of argument is different. Consider how Maria Santiago, Michael Van Meter's attorney in his case against the Baltimore & Western Railroad, would use the same liability expert for different purposes, depending upon whether she wanted to use competitive or cooperative tactics. If Maria uses the competitive argument tactic, she would take the approach, at least implicitly, that "I have an expert who will testify to these conclusions at trial, and as a result, your client is certain to lose." In contrast, if she uses cooperative tactics, her approach would be, "My liability expert's objective analysis suggests that the fairest way to resolve the liability issue is to agree that..." Finally, argument occurs as part of the evaluation process in problem-solving negotiation. When there are a variety of proposals on the table for consideration instead of two polar positions, the expert's analysis is then used to evaluate the advantages and disadvantages of the various proposals. This too is a form of argument.

Argument in negotiation is different from argument experienced in appellate or trial court proceedings.[34] After studying patterns of argu-

34. For a comprehensive description and analysis of argument in negotiation, *see* Robert J. Condlin, *"Cases on Both Sides": Patterns of Argument in Legal Dispute–Ne-* *gotiation*, 44 MD. L. REV. 65, 65–136 (1985). The reader is cautioned that Condlin classifies arguments into "cooperative" and "competitive" categories using different cri-

ment in legal negotiation, Robert J. Condlin describes it as "more akin to analysis than oratory."[35] He suggests that to avoid having a detailed argument come across as an awkward soliloquy that would be viewed suspiciously by the other negotiator, the lawyer should advance her arguments conversationally. A conversational tone suggests spontaneity, as opposed to the premeditated style of a well-prepared appellate argument.

Even for the competitive negotiator, the goal of argument is rarely, if ever, to browbeat her counterpart into confessing error and openly acceding to the negotiator's viewpoint. After all, the other lawyer's professional duty is to represent, as effectively as possible, his party's interests. Instead, effective competitive argument undermines the other negotiator's confidence both in his own analysis and in his negotiating posture. The most effective arguments, therefore, are ones that bring new facts or interpretations of facts to the other negotiator's attention, not predictable ones.

Conclusory and one-sided arguments, even if presented with great emotional vehemence, are unlikely to convince anyone who does not already agree with the negotiator—particularly someone who is paid to analyze the situation from the other party's viewpoint. To be effective, argument in negotiation should be detailed and balanced. The negotiator should begin her argument with facts, law, settlement procedures or principles that are difficult to dispute, and argue inferences from these details. In this manner, she is usually better able to persuade the other negotiator of the validity of her position than by simply using conclusory statements with no stated basis in fact. In most instances, competitive arguments presented in a friendly style—calmly, not angrily or sarcastically—are more likely to have an impact. There may be times, however, when it is to the negotiator's advantage to use anger when presenting an argument. Displaying anger as a competitive negotiating tactic is discussed in Chapter Seven.[36]

Information disclosure in negotiation sometimes takes the form of elaborate oral or written presentations that include both arguments and the information necessary to support such arguments. Some plaintiffs' personal injury attorneys prepare "settlement brochures" that provide a comprehensive and well documented presentation of the plaintiff's case on liability and damages. Similarly, a party to a transactional negotiation sometimes prepares a "prospectus," outlining the advantages to the other party of a sale of the business, merger or other continuing relationship.

teria than those used to make that distinction throughout this text.

35. *Id.* at 129.

36. *See infra* Chapter Seven, "Narrowing of Differences and Closure: Competitive and Cooperative Tactics," at pages 150–51.

Chapter Six

INITIAL PROPOSALS

This chapter focuses on the lawyer's first attempts during negotiation to frame and present her proposals for issue resolution. At this early stage of bargaining, as throughout the process, the negotiator chooses between competitive, cooperative and problem-solving tactics. Before describing these three types of initial proposals, however, this text considers when the negotiator should make her first proposal.

A. TIMING OF INITIAL PROPOSAL

As previously described, sometimes the negotiation process begins with a proposal from one of the two parties. Typically, for example, personal injury negotiations begin with a "demand letter" from the plaintiff's attorney. In other cases, the negotiators refrain from making initial offers until they have negotiated for some time. Instead, the parties begin by exchanging information about their respective interests and needs, and about the transaction at hand. A proposal is made only after information is exchanged and the parties have an opportunity to evaluate each other.

The timing of the negotiator's first proposal really depends on the negotiator's best judgment regarding two separate but intertwined sequencing issues. First, should she proceed with information gathering before making an initial proposal? And second, should she make the first offer or demand or encourage the other negotiator to do so?

As a rule of thumb, the lawyer should not begin the negotiation with a serious proposal when she is uncertain about what constitutes a likely or reasonable range for the eventual agreement. Some attorneys have had the experience of suppressing the desire to make an initial demand in the negotiation, only to have the other party offer more in its initial bid than the amount the attorney had intended to demand. For example, consider a university professor who has developed a new computer software system for predicting indemnity loss payment trends for liability insurance carriers. The professor, of course, knows that his software package is potentially valuable to insurance companies, but does not fully comprehend the considerable political value of his program in substantiating insurance company rate requests to various state regulatory authorities. On the other hand, the professor, unbeknownst to the insurance carrier, faces severe personal financial problems resulting from the cost of his children's college education and recent medical expenses. There is no "standard" price for such a software package. In a case like this, it is entirely possible that whichever party makes the first offer without extensive prior discussions will "lose" the negotiation.

Inventor Thomas Edison reportedly experienced a similar situation.[1] After inventing the "Universal" stock ticker that was widely used by brokerage houses for several decades, Edison was asked by one General Lefferts, the President of the Gold & Stock Telegraph Company, how much he thought he should receive for the invention. Edison describes what happened:

> I had made up my mind that, taking into consideration the time and killing pace I was working at, I should be entitled to $5000, but could get along with $3000. When the psychological moment arrived, I hadn't the nerve to name such a large sum, so I said: "Well, General, suppose you make me an offer." Then he said: "How would $40,000 strike you?" This caused me to come as near fainting as I ever got. I was afraid he would hear my heart beat. I managed to say that I thought it was fair.[2]

When the negotiator does not know the reasonable range of agreement between the parties, she has three options. She can:

(1) pursue information bargaining before making an initial proposal;

(2) encourage the other party to make the first proposal; or

(3) make an extreme proposal which allows enough leeway to protect her if she underestimates the value of what she has to offer.

In many cases, information bargaining should precede the negotiator's initial proposal. Almost inevitably, information gathering precedes the initial proposal if the negotiator begins the negotiation with a problem-solving strategy; this also is often true with either the competitive or cooperative strategies.

B. WHO SHOULD MAKE THE INITIAL PROPOSAL?

Assuming that the negotiator does have the information necessary to ascertain the reasonable bargaining range or the content of problem-solving proposals that might realistically move the negotiation forward, how should she determine whether it is best to make the first offer or demand or alternatively to allow her counterpart to do so?

1. *See* Frank L. Dyer & Thomas C. Martin, Edison: His Life And Inventions 132 (1929).

2. *Id.* (quoting Thomas Edison).

In many negotiation contexts, custom provides that one party or another should make the first proposal. For example, in personal injury negotiation, it is typical for the plaintiff to make his initial demand before the defendant makes a first offer. In many other areas of negotiation, however, there is no strong convention as to who should make the first offer. Under these circumstances, deciding whether it is advantageous for the client to make the first proposal can be made only by applying the criteria discussed in this section to the particular negotiation problem. In some cases these factors will point strongly toward either making or receiving the first proposal; in other cases the analysis will yield inconclusive results, suggesting merely that there are advantages and disadvantages to either approach.

The first proposal in negotiation, if credible and convincing, often becomes the focal point from which further bargaining proceeds. Hence, in some contexts, it can be an advantage to make the first proposal because it establishes the probable bargaining range. To accomplish this objective, the negotiator should make the initial proposal appear formal and carefully considered. For example, in the negotiation between Banting Medical Technologies and Dr. Volkov, Jonathan, as Banting's attorney, might present Katie, his negotiating counterpart, with a standard licensing agreement after carefully filling it in with provisions and numbers favorable to his client. The two attorneys probably will begin to bargain from these draft provisions. If they do, Jonathan has "anchored" the negotiation and strongly influenced the bargaining range on various issues by making a credible first offer. In other bargaining situations, however, it is extremely unlikely that the opening proposal will strongly affect the bargaining range. For example, many personal injury negotiations begin with extreme proposals from both sides. Because of this lawyering tradition, even a realistic initial proposal generally is not viewed as establishing a focal point for serious negotiation.

The other major advantage of making the first proposal is to elicit the other negotiator's reaction. If Katie's reaction to the draft licensing agreement is to tell Jonathan, "The draft needs some work, but it's a good place to begin," that tells Jonathan that his proposal is reasonably close to being acceptable to Katie. On the other hand, if Katie cancels a scheduled meeting after receiving a copy of Jonathan's draft, a very negative response is communicated. The negotiator, however, must anticipate the possibility that her counterpart may feign an angry response to an initial proposal.

At the same time, there are several disadvantages to making the first proposal. As suggested previously, the negotiator is generally ill advised to make the first offer if she does not know enough about the case to predict the probable range of the eventual agreement. In the most extreme situation, such as Edison's, the negotiator's first proposal may be less favorable to her client than the first offer she would receive from her negotiating counterpart if she were more patient. Even in a less egregious example, if the negotiator makes the initial proposal and lacks an accurate perception of strength of her client's bargaining position, she may begin the bargaining in a range less favorable to her client than otherwise would be possible. By making the first proposal, the negotiator also gives her counterpart the opportunity to adjust his first offer after measuring hers. Finally, in some litigation contexts, an immediate offer to settle may be interpreted by the other attorney as a sign of weakness; that is, the negotiator is too willing to compromise her client's interests because she is not ready to pursue vigorously her client's rights at trial.

The negotiator is ill advised to engage in first offer "ping-pong" where the parties argue over who will make the first offer. However, in some instances she can encourage the other lawyer to make the first proposal. If there is pressure for her to make the first negotiating proposal without enough information, the negotiator may respond by making an extreme and obviously unrealistic offer, thus protecting her from making an offer that is unknowingly disadvantageous to her client.

C. COMPETITIVE FIRST PROPOSAL TACTICS

Competitive negotiation tactics, as described in Chapter One, are designed to encourage the other party to enter into an agreement less advantageous to her client than she would have prior to the negotiation. Although additional principles governing competitive initial proposal tactics are discussed below, the most important competitive tactic is to make an extreme, but not totally unrealistic, first offer or demand.

1. AMOUNT (LEVEL OF EXTREMITY) OF THE INITIAL DEMAND OR OFFER

The lawyer using competitive tactics usually begins the negotiation with a high initial demand. Empirical research repeatedly demonstrates a significant positive correlation between the amount of the negotiator's original demand and her payoff.[3] A competitive initial proposal, therefore, is one substantially more favorable to the negotiator's client than she would settle for, but not one so extreme as to be blatantly unrealistic or ridiculous.

The principal purpose of the high demand or the low offer is to "anchor" or influence the other negotiator's perception of the eventual agreement between the parties. At the beginning of negotiation, generally there is uncertainty about the eventual range of agreement. In many instances, an extreme—but credible—initial offer determines the range in which the parties will eventually bargain. From the competitive negotiation perspective, the high demand or low offer also serves implicitly as a threat to the other negotiator: "If you are not willing to bargain in this range, there will be no agreement." It may be that the extreme

3. See, e.g., CHESTER KARASS, THE NEGOTIATING GAME 18 (1970); Adam D. Galinsky et al., Disconnecting Outcomes and Evaluations: The Role of Negotiator Focus, 83 J. PERSONALITY & SOC. PSYCHOL. 1131, 1134 (2002); Donald L. Harnett, Larry L. Cummings & W. Clay Hamner, Personality, Bargaining Style and Payoff in Bilateral Monopoly Bargaining Among European Managers, 36 SOCIOMETRY 325, 342 (1973); Russell Korobkin, Aspirations and Settlement, 88 CORNELL L. REV. 1, 27 (2002).

initial demand *should not* have this effect. If the other negotiator reasonably determines his reservation point, target, and initial offer, his counterpart's initial demand should have no effect. Nevertheless, negotiators frequently admit that their initial proposals were changed or modified after hearing their counterparts' first offers. In a similar vein, a high but realistic initial demand sometimes communicates to the other lawyer that a negotiator will not be exploited and is going to be a tough bargainer.

An extreme initial offer also provides the negotiator with a margin of error to protect her against undervaluing her case at a time when she has incomplete information. For example, in the previously described negotiation between the professor and the insurance company concerning the sale of the software package, an extreme early proposal from either side would have protected that party from entering into an agreement less favorable than the one its negotiating counterpart would have been willing to concede. Further, the extreme but seemingly credible early bargaining position allows the negotiator to probe for more information and for a sense of the other party's reservation point before making a serious settlement proposal. If the negotiator uses an extreme initial proposal and the opposing counsel responds with a mild, "That sounds a little high, but it's in a reasonable range," the negotiator has learned that she will probably realize more from the negotiation than she had expected. Thus, the extreme early proposal enables the negotiator both to hide her own reservation point in the beginning stages of the negotiation and to learn something about her counterpart's.

According to proponents of the competitive strategy, the high demand or low offer also allows the negotiator to make a series of meaningful concessions during later bargaining and to obtain concessions from the other party in exchange. If the negotiator's initial proposal is too close to her reservation point, there is no room to bargain.

The most prevalent risk of a competitive initial proposal is that the other negotiator will ignore the initial proposal and give it no credence. This is not really a detriment in and of itself; it is simply an acknowledgment that the technique will not work. It may lead, however, to a shift in bargaining power if the opponent is able to force the negotiator to make a second, more realistic offer before he begins bargaining. This second offer is, in effect, a major concession at a time in the negotiation process when the relationship between the parties is fluid and still in the process of being established.

The possible disadvantages of the extreme initial proposal fall into three categories. Such proposals (1) invite retaliation, (2) risk deadlock, and (3) may create a negative perception of the negotiator as being overly competitive.

A negotiator's early competitive tactics invite, and indeed virtually compel, the other negotiator to engage in similar behavior. If the other negotiator perceives the first offer as an extreme one, the appropriate response is probably to respond in kind. In addition, the extreme early offer may cause the other party to respond by concealing information and engaging in other competitive tactics, such as threats. Unless the negotiator successfully hides the extreme nature of the opening bid, she makes a competitive negotiation process likely.

Generally, it is believed that an extreme initial offer also risks a walkout or early termination of the negotiation.[4] The other negotiator may decide that the offer is so far out-of-line with what he could agree to that further negotiation would not be profitable. Further, an extreme opening proposal sometimes prompts the other party to decide that he does not want to do business with your "unreasonable" client who bargains in such a preposterous manner. In some cases, the walkout or early termination of the negotiation process is itself a competitive negotiation behavior; in other cases, it is a sincere and final termination to the negotiation, attributable to a demand grossly in excess of the client's genuine needs and expectations.

If the other lawyer perceives the initial bid as totally unrealistic, the extreme bid may cause considerable damage to the bargaining relationship and the negotiator's reputation. The negotiator risks becoming known in the negotiating community as unreasonable. Further, inflated demands frequently are viewed as signs of inexperience or perhaps as evidence that the lawyer is not fully prepared.

2. FIRMNESS OF INITIAL PROPOSAL

A competitive initial proposal most frequently communicates "firmness," that is, a commitment to that proposal and reluctance to modify it. This appearance of firmness is an important aspect of the negotiator's campaign to convince the other negotiator that she is not going to change her initial position easily and that he must change his if he wants to avoid a negotiation stalemate.

In presenting the initial proposal, the language chosen is crucial. If Maria Santiago, Michael Van Meter's attorney, begins the bargaining to settle Michael's personal injury claim for "something in the range of $2.5 million" or makes an initial demand of "$2.2 million to $2.5 million," she probably has communicated too much flexibility. Any demand containing two figures indicates to the other side that the negotiator is willing to settle for the lesser amount. Similarly, if Katie Eisinger, Dr. Volkov's attorney, makes a demand for an up-front licensing fee in the amount of "$2.5 million—negotiable," she similarly communicates a willingness to make substantial concessions. All blatant acknowledgments of willingness to compromise are usually superfluous and dangerous. Implicit in any initial proposal is an implied commitment to further bargaining. An explicit restatement of this willingness to

4. *But see* Russell Korobkin & Chris Guthrie, *Opening Offers and Out-of-Court Settlement: A Little Moderation May Not Go a Long Way*, 10 Ohio St. J. on Disp. Resol. 1, 11 (1994) (reporting experimental results showing that "moderate" first offers in fact lead to more negotiation breakdowns than extreme first offers). The Korobkin/Guthrie results are analyzed more fully at page 135 *infra*.

bargain, on the other hand, risks communicating an excessive desire to accommodate.

Richard Walton and Robert McKersie, in their definitive study of labor negotiations, provide an excellent analysis and an example of the importance of language in the initial proposal.[5] They argue that the degree of firmness of an initial proposal results from three factors: the degree of *specificity*, the degree of *finality*, and the *consequence* that will flow from the party's commitment. To illustrate this point, Walton and McKersie describe a hypothetical demand by a union negotiator to management during the final stages of a labor negotiation (obviously in an era prior to recent decades of price inflation!):

> "We must have the 12½ cent package and the seniority provisions which we proposed. We are prepared to strike, if necessary."

The provisions insisted upon, the "12½ cent package" and the "seniority provisions" are highly *specific*, according to Walton and McKersie. Less *firmness* would be communicated if the negotiator had demanded "the kind of package we have been talking about." Similarly the language "we must have" suggests a much higher degree of *finality* than a "suggestion" to management that it reconsider its position on these issues. Finally, the statement of the *consequences*—"we are prepared to strike"—is definitive. Alternative language, such as, "if you don't concede on these points, we are going to have a tough time selling this to membership," would have left more room to compromise at a later point in the negotiation.

3. JUSTIFICATIONS FOR THE PROPOSAL

The apparent level of the negotiator's commitment to her competitive initial proposal is also increased if she justifies the amount of the offer or counteroffer. For example, if Maria Santiago, Michael Van Meter's attorney, begins with an opening demand of $2.8 million that she has "picked out of the air" and cannot support with facts or reasonable arguments, the demand will probably have little effect on the railroad's evaluation of its case. On the other hand, if a settlement brochure justifying both the liability and damage claims accompanies the opening demand, the proposal likely will have more persuasive effect on the subsequent course of the negotiation. The demand in a personal injury case, such as Michael Van Meter's, ideally should include a detailed breakdown of past and future medical expenses, rehabilitation costs, and past and future lost earnings. Even the demand for "pain and suffering" damages should be justified in some manner, such as comparison to awards in similar cases or the use of a formula for calculation—for example, the product of the number of days of pain and suffering multiplied by an amount for each day. Such detailed justification lends an aura of legitimacy to the initial demand.

5. RICHARD E. WALTON & ROBERT B.   NEGOTIATIONS 93–95 (1965).
MCKERSIE, A BEHAVIORAL THEORY OF LABOR

At a later point in negotiation, this early articulation of the justifications for the demand provides an opportunity to explain changes in bargaining positions. As new information and arguments change the negotiator's evaluation of the factors originally used to justify a demand, she can make concessions and explain them as rational responses to new information and not the collapse of her bargaining will.

4. ESCALATION OF DEMANDS

Even among negotiators using competitive tactics, there is a general prohibition against either increasing the amount of an initial demand after it has been placed on the table or adding new demands. In most negotiation contexts, if the negotiator violates this strong norm, she probably either angers the other negotiator or appears to be inexperienced.

Sound reasons support this negotiation norm. Effective negotiations are impossible when the negotiator starts to concede an issue to meet the other negotiator's demands, only to have the other negotiator suddenly withdraw his proposal. An initial proposal from the other negotiator implies that if its terms are acceptable to the lawyer's client, an agreement can be reached on that basis, and the bargaining concluded. This allows the lawyer to evaluate the other negotiator's most recent bargaining position and make a decision on how, and whether, to negotiate further. Such evaluation is not possible if the other negotiator is continually and unpredictably increasing his demands. Further, the other negotiator's initial proposal contains the implicit message that these terms are acceptable to his client. How can the other negotiator subsequently argue with integrity and conviction that his own earlier proposal is now unacceptable to his client?

Every negotiation "rule" has its exceptions. Increasing the initial demand sometimes is appropriate if the negotiator warns the other party in advance and gives justifications for it. For example, the Baltimore & Western Railroad might announce that its $980,000 offer to pay Michael Van Meter for his injuries will expire next month at the time when house counsel for the railroad turns the case over to retained trial counsel. The removal of the offer, an "escalation" from the defendant's perspective, could be justified on the grounds that the railroad faces additional expense when outside counsel is brought in, and also that trial counsel will make all offers of settlement after that point.

What happens when, during negotiation, counsel discovers a "smoking gun" which substantially increases her bargaining power? Is she precluded from making new demands or increasing the old demands? Or what about the possibility of adding a last minute demand or a "rider," when it is clear that agreement is going to be reached on the major points?

There is nothing illegal about increasing demands under these circumstances, and it is done; however, many attorneys regard even these actions, except in extreme circumstances, as violations of norms.

Escalation tactics are unusually competitive ones. In most situations, when the negotiator increases her opening demand, she risks damaging ongoing and future bargaining relationships and her general reputation among lawyers.

5. FALSE DEMANDS

In addition to using extreme proposals as initial bids, the competitive negotiator sometimes also makes "false demands," that is, additional negotiation proposals insisting upon things that in reality have little interest or importance to her client. Why would any negotiator make such demands? To the extent that a false demand is made credibly and calls for concessions on important issues by the other party, the false issue becomes trade-bait. At a subsequent point in negotiation, the lawyer drops the false issue in exchange for a concession from the other negotiator on an issue she *does* care about. The value of the false issue in the negotiation depends upon how important the negotiator makes the issue appear to the other party. If the negotiator convinces the other party that dropping the issue is a great sacrifice, she can convincingly argue that she is entitled to a major concession in return.

However, the false issue strategy sometimes backfires. The other party occasionally decides to concede on the issue that the negotiator does not care about, and he expects a concession on another issue in return. The false issue strategy also damages the negotiator's future credibility and good will among other negotiators if it becomes apparent that she regularly employs this game-like strategy.

The use of false demands raises ethical issues similar to those previously considered in the context of false statements about the lawyer's authority, or lack of authority, to enter into an agreement binding on her client.[6] To review, *Model Rule of Professional Conduct 4.1* prohibits a lawyer from knowingly making a false statement of material fact. The lawyer using a false demand tactic makes a false statement when she explicitly states that her client is interested in an issue for which he has no bona fide concern. Nevertheless, false demands are routinely used in at least some negotiation contexts, such as collective bargaining. Presumably, false demands therefore fall within the exception for "certain types of statements ordinarily ... not taken as statements of material fact" under generally accepted conventions in negotiation.[7]

6. DEMANDS AS PRE-CONDITIONS FOR NEGOTIATION

Negotiators sometimes state a demand as a pre-condition for the "beginning" of negotiation. For example, Katie Eisinger, representing Dr. Volkov, might refuse to begin negotiations with Jonathan Prevas,

---

6. *See supra* Chapter Three, "Negotiation Planning," at 74–75, particularly 74, n. 31; *see also* James J. White, *Machiavelli and the Bar: Ethical Limitations on Lying in Negotiation*, 1980 Am. B. Found. Res. J. 926, 932 (1982).

7. Model Rules of Prof'l Conduct R. 4.1 cmt. 2 (2006).

counsel for Banting Medical Technologies, unless both parties agree that Banting will depart from its policy of capping up-front, lump-sum royalty payments at $500,000. Similarly, Maria Santiago, Michael Van Meter's attorney, could refuse to meet with Ashton Crutchfield unless Baltimore & Western recognizes that the case likely will lead to a liability judgment.

One of the most famous examples of the reciprocal use of pre-conditions to bargaining was the decades-long war of words between Israel and the Palestine Liberation Organization (PLO) during the 1960s through the 1980s.[8] Israel had continually stated as a pre-condition to any negotiation with the PLO that the PLO recognize the right of Israel to exist as a nation. Because this admission, although certainly understandable from the Israeli point of view, conflicted with the often-articulated positions of PLO representatives, any agreement by the PLO to negotiate on these terms would have involved a major concession. Conversely, the PLO implicitly insisted, as a pre-condition to negotiation, that Israel negotiate with the PLO as the representative of the Palestinian people. Obviously, any willingness on Israel's part to negotiate with the PLO in this capacity would have involved a major concession.[9]

Stating a demand as a pre-condition to negotiation serves several functions. First, if the other party accedes to the pre-condition in order to begin negotiations, the negotiator has gained substantively. This removes the issue from the bargaining session, and the negotiator is not required to make concessions in order to obtain the other party's agreement to this demand. Second, by agreeing to the pre-condition, the other party usually gives the negotiator a strong psychological advantage at the beginning of the negotiation. Finally, "impossible" pre-conditions often serve as a way of avoiding negotiation altogether when a party believes negotiation is futile or prefers other courses of action, but finds it necessary to explain to others his unwillingness to negotiate.

7. "BOULWARISM:" FIRST, FIRM, FAIR, FINAL OFFER

Although the typical competitive initial proposal consists of an extreme demand, an alternate competitive demand tactic exists. Under a tactic generally referred to as "Boulwarism," the party makes an initial offer that it believes is the basis for a reasonable agreement between the parties; in other words, this approach is directly opposite to the extreme initial proposal. The party making the offer then refuses to make any concessions or modifications of the initial offer: it is a "take-it-or-leave-it" proposition. There is no bargaining in the traditional sense.

8. *See* HENRY KISSINGER, YEARS OF UPHEAV-AL 197–99 (1982).

9. In 1993, Yassar Arafat signed the Oslo Accords, renouncing violence and implicitly recognizing Israel's right to exist by expressly shifting the PLO's central mission away from the destruction of Israel. As a result, Israel agreed to talks with the Palestinian National Authority for the first time in its history. With the upset election victory of Hamas in January of 2006, the Palestinian Authority once again refused to recognize Israel as a state, and the sides found themselves at an all-too-familiar impasse.

The term "Boulwarism" is taken from the name of Lemuel R. Boulware, a vice-president of General Electric during the 1950s who pioneered the use of this bargaining technique in labor relations.[10] Under his direction, General Electric developed what it believed was a series of fair proposals regarding matters scheduled for consideration in collective bargaining. General Electric then bypassed the union representatives and publicized the proposals directly to the workers. Most importantly, it refused to make changes in its positions unless the union presented facts that it had overlooked.

The combination of these bargaining practices was ultimately found to be an "unfair labor practice" by the National Labor Relations Board[11] because it constituted a refusal to bargain in good faith that undermined the union's position and the integrity of the collective bargaining process. Nevertheless, the term "Boulwarism" is now applied to the negotiation approach of developing a "first, fair, firm, final" offer and then refusing to make concessions. Boulwarism is more than a historical footnote. Among others, some insurance claims personnel sometimes use this approach. Frequently, prosecutors use this approach in plea bargaining, refusing to retreat from their original guilty plea offers to defendants.

Those who use Boulwarism as a negotiating tactic believe that it reduces the hassles, delays and expenses of the typical bargaining dance, and it yields superior bargaining power. Expense reduction alone suggests that the use of Boulwarism is often justifiable on economic grounds in smaller cases. Further, Boulwarism arguably increases bargaining power because it effectively serves the competitive goal of convincing the other party that he cannot obtain a better deal by using arguments, threats or other bargaining tactics.

Boulwarism, however, creates two substantial risks. First, it often leads to deadlock, particularly when the negotiators represent clients or other constituents. The expectation in negotiation is that both sides will compromise from their initial proposals and make concessions. When this does not occur, frustration results. Confronted with Boulwarism, the negotiator/attorney is not able to show her client that representation during the bargaining has accomplished anything. It is precisely this reasoning that led the National Labor Relations Board to declare Boulwarism an unfair labor practice, because it undermined the union as a representative of workers in the collective bargaining process. The possibility of damage to the attorney/client relationship when the other party refuses to make concessions often causes the attorney to respond to the other negotiator with anger when he uses the "first, fair, firm, final" offer approach.

The second obstacle to the effective use of Boulwarism is credibility. The method fails unless the other party believes the negotiator when she

---

10. NLRB v. Gen. Elec. Co., 418 F.2d 736, 740–46 (2d Cir. 1969).

11. Gen. Elec. Co., 150 N.L.R.B. 192 (1964), *enforced* NLRB v. Gen. Elec. Co., 418 F.2d 736 (2d Cir.1969).

says that her initial proposal is her firm and final offer. A negotiator who begins to use such an approach will likely be tested often in the early going, resulting in frequent trials or many broken deals. Once a negotiator begins using Boulwarism, she must never make concessions from her initial proposal without a persuasive justification; otherwise, future claims that her initial proposals are fair, firm and *final* will not be believed.

8. COMPETITIVE RESPONSES TO OTHER PARTY'S INITIAL PROPOSAL

The goal of competitive negotiation tactics is to undermine the other party's confidence in his evaluation of the negotiation situation. Therefore, the negotiator's visible responses to the other negotiator's initial proposal are extremely important.

Assume that Michael Van Meter's attorney, Maria, values her client's case at something in the $2.1 million range. Further, Maria wants to obtain the highest possible settlement for her client, and plans to use a predominantly competitive negotiation strategy. Much to her surprise and delight, Baltimore & Western makes an initial offer conceding liability and offering to pay $2.4 million to settle the case. How should Maria respond?

A larger than expected offer from Ashton, Baltimore & Western's attorney, indicates one of three possibilities to Maria. The first is that she has substantially underestimated the value of the case. Second, Ashton may be using a cooperative initial proposal, employing a reasonable and moderate initial bid based upon a modestly overestimated value of the case. Third, it is possible that Ashton intended to use a competitive tactic with an extremely low initial offer, but wildly overestimated the value of the case.

When the beginning lawyer actually receives a substantially-better-than-expected first proposal from the other negotiator, all her instincts drive her to respond favorably or enthusiastically. She says something like, "I think we're close to reaching an agreement" or "That sounds reasonable." At best, like Thomas Edison,[12] she responds with dumbfounded silence. These responses forfeit any possibility of realizing additional meaningful concessions from the other party because the negotiator communicates implicitly that the first offer is near, or even exceeds, her reservation point. Further, the conciliatory approach often makes the other lawyer realize that he has misjudged the case, and he may respond with belligerence.

How should the negotiator respond to the extremely favorable first offer? A basic choice must be made at this early point between pursuing cooperative or competitive tactics. If the initial offer from the other lawyer is already favorable to the client and the client desires either to maintain a favorable working relationship with the other party or to

12. *See supra* page 122.

conclude negotiations quickly, a cooperative response is probably warranted. This cooperative response should be generally favorable, expressing recognition and appreciation that the other party is approaching the negotiation realistically, but should stress the need for further bargaining. The indication that there is more bargaining ahead mitigates the possibility that the other negotiator will believe that he has undervalued his case and will respond defensively.

How should the negotiator respond if she intends to employ a competitive countermove in this situation? It may be time for an Oscar-winning performance. Regardless of how delighted the negotiator actually is with the offer, should she react decisively *against* the proposal, claiming it is wholly inadequate and asserting that opposing counsel either does not understand the case or regards her as a fool? This specific competitive negotiation tactic warrants further reflection on the ethical and moral aspects of the lawyer as competitive negotiator. Is it wrong to enact a professional role-play designed to convince the other negotiator that what your client in fact regards as a favorable offer is wholly outrageous and unacceptable?

This question can be addressed at several levels. The only reasonably certain conclusion is that such deception violates neither formal professional rules nor prevailing norms. As previously described, *Model Rule of Professional Conduct 4.1* provides that lawyers "shall not knowingly make a false statement of material fact or law to a third person";[13] however, the comment to the rule also indicates that "under generally accepted conventions in negotiation, certain types of statements ordinarily are not taken as statements of material fact."[14] The comment specifically provides that "a party's intentions as to an acceptable settlement of a claim,"[15] which implicitly includes statements about authority to settle a case, lie within the exception. Further, in actual practice, misrepresentations of bargaining authority by attorneys appear to occur frequently.

The underlying inherent ethical dilemma is that in distributive bargaining situations, achieving a result for the client that is more satisfactory than an agreement barely meeting his minimum requirements often requires deception, either by explicit statement or by omission, potentially at odds with at least the spirit of *Model Rule 4.1*. Yet the attorney's pursuit of zealous advocacy, coupled with her obligation to preserve her client's confidences—presumably including the client's reservation point—seems to sanction this behavior.[16] Within the parameters of the conduct allowed by professional rules and negotiation norms, personal ethical choices must be made. Is acting with outrage over an offer acceptable to your client consistent with your concept of yourself as a professional? As a person? If such conduct furthers your

---

13. MODEL RULES OF PROF'L CONDUCT R. 4.1(a) (2006).

14. *Id.* cmt. 2.

15. *Id.*

16. *See supra* page 74, n. 31 for a fuller discussion of these and related issues.

client's interests and is allowed by the profession's ethical code, can you refuse to use these tactics and be comfortable with yourself?

D. COOPERATIVE INITIAL PROPOSALS

1. AMOUNT OF OPENING OFFER OR DEMAND

Initial bargaining proposals that are a part of a cooperative strategy are designed to achieve the goals of that approach to negotiation: to reach an agreement that is fair and just for both parties and to develop a relationship based on trust with the other negotiator. Cooperative initial proposals, therefore, differ in two important regards from competitive initial proposals. First, the amount of the negotiator's initial demand (the extremity of her proposal) is more moderate and reasonable than an initial competitive proposal. Second, the negotiator employing a cooperative initial proposal justifies her opening bid by reference to objective standards.

According to proponents of cooperative tactics, the negotiator should begin bargaining, not with an extreme position, but rather with a more moderate opening bid that she regards as favorable to her client, yet barely acceptable to the other party.[17] In other words, the cooperative opening proposal should only exceed the negotiator's target point by a modest amount. On one hand, the initial proposal should be moderate enough to communicate clearly to the other party that the negotiator is trying to be reasonable and to establish a cooperative bargaining relationship. On the other hand, the initial proposal must contain enough of a cushion to allow the negotiator to make concessions so that she does not appear intractable in later phases of the negotiation.

The differences between competitive and cooperative initial bids cannot be readily quantified. More than anything else, the difference is in how the initial bids will be perceived by opposing counsel. As an example of the difference between the two approaches, consider again the initial demand on behalf of Michael Van Meter in his case against the Baltimore & Western Railroad. If Maria Santiago has concluded that from Michael's perspective a reasonable settlement value of the case is between $1.8 million and $2.2 million, a competitive opening demand might be in the range of $2.8 million or more. On the other hand, an opening cooperative demand is likely to be in the $2.2 million to $2.5 million range.

What are the advantages of the cooperative negotiator's moderate initial proposal? Experimental studies of opening moves in negotiation establish that early cooperative behaviors facilitate the development of trust and a mutually beneficial, cooperative relationship.[18] Further, tra-

---

17. Otomar J. Bartos, *Simple Model of Negotiation: A Sociological Point of View*, 21 J. CONFLICT RESOL. 561, 567–570 (1977), *reprinted in* THE NEGOTIATION PROCESS: THEO-

RIES AND APPLICATIONS 13, 19–24 (I. William Zartman ed., 1978).

18. *See* JEFFERY Z. RUBIN & BERT R. BROWN, THE SOCIAL PSYCHOLOGY OF BARGAINING AND NEGOTIATION 263–64 (1964). Rubin and

ditionally it has been assumed that an initial cooperative proposal minimizes the possibility that the bargaining will break off prematurely when, in fact, a mutually advantageous agreement can be reached. In his study of Phoenix attorneys, Gerald Williams found that competitive negotiators reached an impasse in 33 percent of their cases, compared with only sixteen percent for cooperative negotiators.[19]

A study by Russell Korobkin and Chris Guthrie, however, found that moderate first offers actually led to more negotiation breakdowns than did more extreme first proposals.[20] They attribute this counterintuitive result to two factors. First, the negotiator's initial proposal may anchor the other negotiator's expectations. When Maria initially demands $2.8 million as compensation for Michael's injuries, Baltimore & Western's evaluation of the case may shift, and it might expect to pay generously in order to avoid litigation. On the other hand, if Maria initially demands only $2.2 million and then fails to make significant subsequent concessions, Ashton becomes frustrated and angry and the negotiations break down. Similarly, Korobkin and Guthrie suggest that when the other negotiator ("B" for purposes of clarity) initially rejects the negotiator's ("A's") initial cooperative offer, it would create "cognitive dissonance"[21] to subsequently accept the same offer. Arguably it also might create cognitive dissonance for B to accept A's subsequent offer that is in the same general range as A's original proposal, that is, a subsequent proposal only slightly improved when viewed from B's perspective.

More extreme competitive negotiating proposals often produce better results in simulated negotiations. Before the novice negotiator accepts the notion that she needs to follow suit in order to avoid being disadvantaged, however, it is important to remember that a majority of attorneys use a cooperative approach that includes moderate initial proposals. Williams found that 65 percent of negotiating attorneys used a cooperative approach, and these attorneys were more likely to be evaluated as "effective" than were their competitive counterparts.[22]

2. JUSTIFICATIONS FOR THE INITIAL PROPOSAL

The cooperative initial proposal is justified by reference to objective criteria. Such justification serves to legitimize the initial proposal and to establish the basis for a fair and reasonable agreement between the parties. The sources of objective criteria are limited only by the negotiator's diligence and imagination. In a transactional negotiation, such as the licensing-agreement negotiation between Banting Medical Technologies and Dr. Volkov, the "going rate" for licensing fees for new medical technologies may be widely accepted. Certainly in more routine transactions, such as commercial lease negotiations, the fair market rate provides such a recognized standard. In lawsuit settlement negotiations,

Brown describe a number of studies reaching this conclusion.

19. GERALD R. WILLIAMS, LEGAL NEGOTIATION AND SETTLEMENT 51 (1983).

20. Korobkin & Guthrie, *supra* note 4, at 13.

21. *Id.* at 20.

22. WILLIAMS, *supra* note 19, at 19.

including the one involving Michael Van Meter and the Baltimore & Western Railroad, comparable verdicts from the same or similar jurisdictions provide an obvious reference point. In either of these two cases, and in many others, the opinion of an impartial expert with good credentials also may serve as a standard to legitimize an initial proposal.

In addition to focusing on objective standards, cooperative negotiators strive to prove the proposal's fairness and reasonableness. As such, they rely heavily on the facts of the transaction or dispute, and the applicable law. They avoid threatening or undermining the other party.

3.   COOPERATIVE RESPONSES TO THE OTHER PARTY'S INITIAL PROPOSAL

The negotiator who wishes to use cooperative tactics faces her most difficult situation when she realizes that the other party is engaging in competitive negotiation tactics. As previously discussed, the success of cooperative tactics depends entirely upon enticing the other party to reciprocate and to engage in similarly cooperative behavior.

How should the negotiator who wishes to behave cooperatively respond to what she recognizes as a competitive opening bid from the other negotiator? First, she should expose the other party's initial bid as an extreme position, either explicitly or more tactfully. If she explicitly tells her counterpart that she recognizes that he is demanding more than he ever expects to realize, she risks making him defensive. A more subtle approach is to question the other lawyer about the justifications for his demand. How did he arrive at this figure? Can he verify it by reference to specific objective criteria? In this way, the negotiator moves the bargaining toward a discussion of the merits. This approach, however, risks giving some *credence* to an unreasonable opening.

The question of whether the negotiator should respond to an extreme demand with a proposal of her own is a more difficult one. In the best of all possible situations, she hopes the questioning process discussed above will lead the other party to acknowledge that his initial proposal was extreme. If he does, a genuinely cooperative response from the negotiator is in order at this point. In the more likely event that the other party sticks with his extreme opening proposal, the negotiator who prefers to use cooperative tactics has three options. She may:

(1) respond with an equally extreme initial proposal so that the midpoint between the offers is in the range regarded by the negotiator as being fair and reasonable;

(2) refuse to respond to the extreme initial proposal until the other party displays reasonableness; or

(3) make a fair and reasonable offer.

The third approach is premised on the assumption that if the negotiator behaves cooperatively, the other negotiator will trust her and respond in kind. The negotiator who wants to use cooperative tactics probably can afford to be this trusting *once*, and only *early*, in the negotiation. If her confidence in her ability to make the other negotiator more cooperative proves to be unfounded, and the other negotiator does not make major concessions from his initial extreme proposal, the cooperative negotiator must STOP her cooperative behavior until she has evidence that the other negotiator is also prepared to cooperate.

The role of the negotiator who desires to use cooperative negotiation tactics is considerably easier when the other party begins the negotiation with a moderate and reasonable offer. Under these circumstances, the negotiator can acknowledge explicitly that she recognizes that the other party is being reasonable, and indicate that she hopes to respond in kind. When the other party makes a realistic initial bid, cooperative negotiation theorists suggest that the negotiator calculate her responding offer so that the midpoint between the two initial bids represents a fair and equitable outcome of the negotiation.[23]

E.   PROBLEM–SOLVING INITIAL PROPOSALS

1.   TIMING OF PROBLEM–SOLVING PROPOSALS

Before discussing the problem-solving approach to initial proposals, it is important to reiterate that the use of problem-solving tactics, including those involving initial proposals, often does not occur until later stages of the negotiation. Sometimes a negotiator is able to initiate a problem-solving approach to the negotiation from the earliest stages. In many other cases, however, the parties do not turn to problem-solving techniques until their initial competitive tactics yield mutual frustration. Therefore, even though the problem-solving approach for handling initial proposals is discussed at this early point in the text, a negotiator might not use problem-solving proposals until after a period of bargaining using predominantly competitive and cooperative tactics.

Problem-solving initial proposals almost inevitably follow a period of information exchange. In contrast, recall that competitive and cooperative initial proposals may come either before or after a phase of the negotiation characterized by the exchange of information. Information exchange, however, necessarily precedes problem-solving initial proposals because information about each party's needs usually must be shared before viable solutions can be formulated.

Thus, proposals under the problem-solving approach frequently occur only after the parties have negotiated for a greater length of time and have exchanged more information than is necessary for competitive or cooperative initial proposals. Fisher, Ury and Patton, leading proponents of the problem-solving tactics, caution negotiators to "avoid premature judgment."[24] The early articulation of bargaining positions, according to Fisher, Ury and Patton, endangers a collaborative working relationship between the parties. It can also lead to unnecessary rounds

---

23. Bartos, *supra* note 17, at 21.

24. Roger Fisher, William Ury & Bruce Patton, Getting to Yes: Negotiating Agreement Without Giving In 57–58 (2d ed.1991).

of proposals and counterproposals that may not meet the parties' needs because they are not based upon an understanding of their interests.

Prior to initiating problem-solving initial proposals, the negotiator should employ the full array of information-gathering techniques discussed in Chapter Five, "Information Bargaining," in order to determine the other party's underlying needs. Further, as discussed in that chapter, the negotiator must be willing to fully, accurately, and specifically describe her own client's needs in the negotiation. This disclosure of her client's interests serves two functions. First, the other negotiator requires an understanding of her client's needs so that he can effectively participate in the process of proposing and evaluating solutions that meet both parties' needs. Second, the lawyer's disclosure of her client's needs encourages the other negotiator to reciprocate.

2. PROBLEM–SOLVING RESPONSES TO POSITIONAL BARGAINING PROPOSALS

When a lawyer who desires to use problem-solving tactics negotiates with a counterpart who expects to bargain in a traditional fashion with opening demands and opening offers, she both faces a challenge and encounters an opportunity. The challenge, of course, is to transform the negotiation—without sounding either naive or condescending—into something other than positional bargaining with the traditional dance of offer and counteroffer, concession and threat. The opportunity is to gain insights into the other party's underlying interests.

Let us return to the negotiation between Katie Eisinger, the attorney representing Dr. Anton Volkov, and Jonathan Prevas, negotiating on behalf of Banting Medical Technologies, as they attempt to reach agreement on a technology-licensing contract. Recall that Dr. Volkov insists on a very large up-front royalty payment. Here is an example of how Jonathan, faced with this seemingly intractable problem, might respond to Katie's initial negotiating position:

1—Katie: Dr. Volkov insists that any agreement include at least a $1.5 million up-front royalty payment. The Viral Sharpshooter, after all, likely is a cure for some forms of cancer and all other viral illnesses.

2—Jonathan: So Volkov's very convinced of the long-term value of his discoveries. We also recognize the great potential of the Viral Sharpshooter technology. And Dr. Volkov expects to be fairly compensated. But he seems unusually committed to a very large up-front payment. Do you have any sense as to what is driving this? Would he really prefer a large up-front payment to some kind of a royalty agreement over time that would make him far wealthier if the Viral Sharpshooter is as good as he thinks it is?

3—Katie: Well, to tell you the truth, he really has a need to get his hands on a considerable sum of cash immediately. He wants to help his brother set up a business.

4—Jonathan: I see. Now things are beginning to make some sense. Is there anything else that is driving his focus on the up-front cash?

5—Katie: Sure. He's never been wealthy, and he's very risk adverse. He's concerned that some other drug or technology might come along that's even better than Viral Sharpshooter and render his discovery less valuable on a long term basis.

By repeatedly probing into the reasons behind Volkov's initial bargaining position, an up-front payment in excess of $1.5 million, Jonathan accomplishes two things. First, he gathers information about Volkov's underlying needs. Later, this will assist him in making proposals which will satisfy the legitimate interests of Volkov, as well as those of his own client. Second, Jonathan transforms the discussion into a consideration of the needs of both parties rather than an exchange of negotiating positions. His gentle "prodding" and use of "why" questions change the process into a problem-solving negotiation more effectively and subtly than would a mini-lecture on why problem-solving negotiation is superior to traditional negotiation approaches. Jonathan accelerates the change in the tenor of the negotiation when he engages in active listening and explicitly acknowledges the legitimacy of Volkov's interests in segment #2.

3. SEARCH MODELS

After exchanging information about the parties' requirements and aspirations, the lawyers using problem-solving tactics search for solutions that satisfy the underlying interests of their clients. This process may proceed in either of two ways. First, the negotiator may present a previously developed proposal to the other negotiator for consideration. Second, the lawyers, often together with their clients, may try to devise solutions that satisfy their respective interests.

This problem-solving process requires two steps:

(1) generation of potential solutions or proposals; and

(2) evaluation of such proposals.

Both the generation of possible solutions and their evaluation are informed by the facts which the negotiator has learned from her own client and from the other party.

Social scientists refer to the set of goals and other requirements, which the bargainer uses to generate and screen alternatives, as a *search model.*[25] A search model is used to evaluate known alternatives and to suggest additional approaches. A lawyer begins the negotiation with a search model reflecting the aspirations and requirements of her client, as well as the known and anticipated requirements of the other party. As she learns more about the other party's preferences, the search model is fine-tuned. Further, the negotiator adjusts the search model if she finds that no identifiable alternatives fit all the aspirations and requirements of the model as it currently exists.

A search model for the negotiation between Dr. Volkov and Banting Medical Technologies might contain the following requirements and aspirations:

Volkov's Goals

(1) Needs access in immediate future to substantial cash, estimated to be at least $1.2 million, to start his brother's fashion design business.

(2) Wants to be relieved of potential financial uncertainty resulting from competition from competing technologies.

(3) May be interested in changing his career position to allow him more flexibility than his current university position.

(4) Wants to be fairly compensated for a discovery that he believes has enormous profit potential.

Banting Medical Technologies' Goals

(1) Obtain the rights to the Viral Sharpshooter Technology!

(2) Avoid setting a precedent that would increase licensing fees for other new discoveries and technologies.

(3) Avoid bearing the entire financial burden for human testing of Viral Sharpshooter technology, particularly because there are no guarantees of successful testing.

(4) Avoid bearing the entire financial burden of FDA approval process, when such approval is not certain.

4. TYPES OF INTEGRATIVE AGREEMENTS

Regardless of whether or not the problem-solving negotiator consciously articulates a search model, she usually attempts to find a negotiated resolution that provides high joint benefit to both parties by satisfying their requirements and aspirations. Four basic types of integrative agreements are available for this purpose:

(1) *solutions which bridge* the parties' needs and satisfy both sets of underlying interests;

(2) solutions involving *logrolling*, or the trading of concessions on different issues;

(3) *cost-cutting* agreements that reduce the negative consequences imposed upon one party in making a concession necessary to satisfy the other party; and

25. *See, e.g.,* DEAN PRUITT, NEGOTIATION BEHAVIOR 167–68 (1981).

(4) *compensation* agreements that provide substitute compensation for the party making a concession required by the other party for an agreement.

The last three types of integrative agreements involve the exchange of concessions on various issues or other methods to compensate a party for making concessions. Because lawyers often use these tactics to resolve the last remaining—and generally most troublesome—issues in a negotiation, they are discussed fully in Chapter Eight, "Narrowing of Differences and Closure: Problem–Solving Tactics." They can, of course, be used earlier in the negotiation.

5. PRESENTATION OF BRIDGING PROPOSALS

The process of devising solutions that bridge the parties' interests is the heart of the problem-solving method. Chapter Three, "Negotiation Planning," addressed how the attorney and her client can work together in counseling sessions, particularly by using brainstorming techniques, to devise solutions providing high joint benefit. How should the proposals devised by the attorney and her client be handled during the negotiation?

When presenting problem-solving proposals to the other party, the negotiator can begin by acknowledging the legitimacy of the needs expressed by the other lawyer and by showing that her client's proposal addresses these needs. Active listening responses to the other party's expressed interests often are an effective transition to a discussion of the client's proposal. Consider Katie Eisinger's presentation of the problem-solving proposal that she and her client, Dr. Volkov, have decided to present to Banting Medical Technologies:

1—Katie: Your client believes that it cannot make an up-front licensing fee payment of more than $500,000. It never pays more than this because it does not want to create a precedent. Further, your client is concerned about bearing all the human-testing costs and FDA approval costs if it must pay a substantially larger sum without knowing whether the Viral Sharpshooter technology will ever be commercially available.

My client needs access to a large sum of money as soon as possible in order to help his brother. He wants to be fairly compensated if the Viral Sharpshooter turns out to be the wonder technology he believes it to be. He wants to be relieved of any uncertainties created by competing technologies. And he has some interest in having greater career flexibility.

I'm wondering whether we might work something out along the following lines:

First, Banting will make a lump sum payment of $1.5 million to Volkov, but we agree that the amount of this payment is strictly confidential and that if Volkov breaks the confidentiality clause, he would be subject to substantial financial penalties.

Second, before the lump sum payment is received, Volkov will obtain approvals from other sources to foot a significant share of the bill for both the human-testing costs and the expenses involved in FDA approval. He believes that NIH [National Institutes of Health] will provide funding for the human testing and that the university will provide a portion of the FDA approval costs, assuming that he, or he and the university, have a residual interest in the revenues generated by Viral Sharpshooter.

Third, Volkov will receive royalty payments based on the revenues generated by the sale of products and services resulting from the Viral Sharpshooter technology. These royalties would be at the customary rate, but Banting would receive a credit for the first $1.0 million of royalties owed because of the larger than usual up-front payment.

Fourth, we would like to explore with you the possibility that Volkov might work on a long-term basis with Banting as either an employee or a consultant. Volkov may be interested in having a less structured career as a researcher than he currently has at the university. We think that the Viral Sharpshooter technology will prove the value of Volkov's services to your client and that it likely is only the first of many exciting medical discoveries by Volkov.

These are the four basic principles from which we hope to negotiate an agreement that will serve the interests of both Volkov and Banting.

The process of justifying bridging proposals is somewhat different than justifying either competitive or cooperative proposals. The negotiator explains why the proposal meets the other party's needs. Furthermore, repeated active listening of the other party's needs as a part of the justification process, allows the other negotiator another chance to correct any misunderstanding of her client's needs. It also builds rapport because it provides a further testimonial that the other party's needs have been heard and understood.

What follows then is a cyclical process of reaction to the proposal and subsequent refinement of the proposal. This process may occur several times because the other party's reaction to the proposal often provides additional information about his needs and aspirations. This process of proposal—reaction—refined proposal, is a fundamental problem-solving method for coming closer to agreement. Accordingly, it is considered further in Chapter Eight, "Narrowing of Differences and Closure: Problem–Solving Tactics."

6.   DEVELOPMENT OF BRIDGING PROPOSALS

If the greatest fantasy of the negotiator using competitive tactics is for her negotiating counterpart to capitulate immediately to an outrageous initial demand, then the problem-solving negotiator's fondest dream is to have both negotiators engage in a brainstorming session. In this utopian situation, both parties, knowing first-hand all there is to know about the dispute under negotiation and their respective clients' preferences, sit down together and brainstorm. However, many attorneys are not familiar with brainstorming or other aspects of problem-solving bargaining. If the negotiator blatantly attempts to "educate" an attorney with decades of bargaining experience about a "different" way of negotiating, her efforts probably will not be greeted enthusiastically. Subtle approaches are usually more successful.

If the other attorney starts the negotiation with a negotiating position and appears headed toward traditional positional bargaining, the negotiator can respond by probing behind the articulated position to discover the other party's underlying interests. Recall how Jonathan inquired about the reasons for Dr. Volkov's insistence on a $1.5 million up-front, lump-sum licensing fee. If he is successful in encouraging the other negotiator to discuss his client's justifications for his initial proposal, this will lead naturally to an opportunity for Katie to explain her client's requirements and aspirations.

When introducing a solution-generation process into the bargaining, the negotiator usually should not explicitly identify it as "brainstorming" (or "solution generation," for that matter). If Jonathan believes it is advantageous for the two attorneys to engage in a joint session of identifying possible solutions instead of presenting those he and his client already have developed, he can introduce the solution-generation process by demonstrating an understanding of Volkov's goals. He also can reiterate his own client's needs and interests. He might then proceed as follows:

1—Jonathan: We both understand what each other's requirements and goals are for this negotiation. It doesn't make much sense for me to make a demand for bargaining purposes, knowing that your client can't accept it.

I'm wondering whether we couldn't cut the process short and instead work together to throw out some ideas that we might consider including in the licensing agreement. If you come up with

an idea, I'm not going to hold you or your client
to it if it turns out that it is not acceptable to
your client.

What are your thoughts on how we might satisfy
Dr. Volkov's need for considerable up-front cash
while at the same time not bankrupting my
client by having it pay large up-front licensing
fees, as well as additional testing and government approval costs, all with the possibility that
it will never yield anything commercially viable?

Very informally, Jonathan has suggested that the parties refrain from
exchanging bargaining positions, but instead consider a variety of solutions. He explicitly focuses attention on the underlying needs of the
parties. He attempts to separate the inventive phase of brainstorming
from the evaluative or judgmental stage by indicating that neither party
is bound by a proposal, thus avoiding premature judgment.

If the other negotiator begins the bargaining process by expecting
Jonathan to make an offer, he can transform the process into a joint
search for mutually beneficial solutions by tactfully refusing to engage in
positional bargaining:

2—Jonathan: Rather than begin with a specific list of provi-
              sions that we must have in the licensing agree-
              ment, let me tell you what my client really needs
              here. Banting's situation looks like this. . . .

This discussion of Banting's requirements and aspirations can then lead
Jonathan to question Katie about her client's needs and eventually to a
joint search for solutions, as previously described.

The problem-solving negotiation strategy proceeds directly to the
task of finding an agreement that satisfies both parties. Posturing is
comparatively absent from this approach. As a result, it is important to
reiterate that the timing of the introduction of problem-solving techniques into the negotiation must be right. Often, the frustration of failed
competitive tactics precedes meaningful problem-solving negotiation.

Chapter Seven

NARROWING OF DIFFERENCES AND CLOSURE: COMPETITIVE AND COOPERATIVE TACTICS

A. INTRODUCTION

Initial negotiation proposals are on the table. Each side attempts to learn more facts about the matter being negotiated and the other party's requirements and expectations. How do the parties move from initial proposals to agreement?

This chapter focuses on tactics the negotiator uses to negotiate issues that she perceives as predominantly distributive or "fixed pie" issues, that is, issues where she perceives that gains for her client require the other negotiator to yield something desired by his client.[1] The use of such tactics, either competitive or cooperative ones, is intended both to "narrow the differences" between the parties and to achieve "closure" on the resolution of these issues. Chapter Eight will focus on those problem-solving tactics that achieve parallel results when the negotiator perceives an issue as a predominantly integrative one. In short, these two chapters depart from the earlier organizational structure of the book because the sub-processes of narrowing the differences and closure, though analytically separate, are intertwined in practice. For the first time in this book, the chapters are divided by the dichotomy between bargaining issues, perceived on one hand as distributive and on the other hand as integrative, rather than by the sub-processes of narrowing differences and closure that occur in every negotiation.

Having said this, the book will continue to separately identify, for example, competitive tactics that are "narrowing of differences" tactics and those that are "closure tactics." Hence, part B of this chapter will describe competitive tactics for narrowing differences. Part C will consider cooperative tactics for narrowing differences. Part D and E then will address competitive and cooperative tactics for achieving closure.

---

1. *See supra* page 15.

The process of narrowing the differences between the parties on distributive issues, more than any other aspect of negotiation, resembles the traditional stereotype of "bargaining." Each lawyer uses tactics intended to induce the other negotiator to accept an agreement favorable to her client; usually the final terms are vastly different than those suggested by the original proposals. In addition, this phase often is time-consuming. In predominantly competitive negotiations, the process is characterized by arguments, threats and frustration—the symbols of traditional haggling. Eventually the expectations of the parties change as realism sets in. In short, narrowing the differences between the parties is the work of negotiation when negotiating in the distributive context.

It is important to reiterate that narrowing of differences is not a "stage" of negotiation mutually exclusive of information bargaining or new proposals. While the negotiators are narrowing their differences, they continue to gather information and generate new proposals.

The negotiator has two complementary goals during this narrowing of differences or convergence process. First, she seeks to induce the other negotiator to agree to terms that are favorable to her client. Regardless of the strategy employed by the negotiator, she possesses some leverage over the other party because the negotiating relationship is almost always a voluntary one. Although each party needs or wants something from the other, the lawyer retains the option of walking away from the negotiating table. Because this would frustrate the other party's hopes, it gives the lawyer some influence over the other party. She uses this influence by communicating her client's interests during the narrowing of differences phase—either directly by using arguments or indirectly by conceding on some issues and not on others.

As she participates in narrowing the differences between the parties, the negotiator's second goal is to determine what terms are acceptable to the other party. Information-gathering tactics obviously address this goal. At the same time, by observing the other party's modifications of his original proposals, the lawyer also learns about the other party's level of resistance to modifying his initial proposal and the relative importance he attaches to various issues. For example, the negotiator sometimes attempts to monitor her counterpart's concession behavior to determine if there is a pattern that suggests the other party's "bottom line."

B. COMPETITIVE TACTICS FOR NARROWING DIFFERENCES

When using competitive convergence tactics, the negotiator attempts to convince the other party that she will not enter into an agreement substantially less advantageous than her original proposals. Further, she seeks to persuade the other negotiator that his alternatives to a negotiated agreement are not as favorable as he believes. Taken together, these two messages are designed to convince the other negotiator that it is in his client's best interests to yield, that is, to "concede" more in negotiation than he originally believed necessary.

A *concession* is defined as any modification of a negotiator's bargaining proposal making it less advantageous to her client. Because the competitive negotiator believes that all gains for her client come at the other party's expense, she tries to force the other negotiator to concede. One way to do this is to convince the other negotiator that if there is to be an agreement, he must do most of the conceding. To achieve this end, the negotiator should show reluctance in making concessions—she should concede infrequently, and in small increments. These concession tactics are described below in the section entitled "Limiting the Negotiator's Own Concessions."

With the exception of limiting one's own concessions, perhaps the most important tactic to induce the other negotiator to make concessions is the *argument*, previously discussed as an information disclosure tactic in Chapter Five.[2] You will recall that we defined an argument as the invocation and reasoned elaboration of norms and their application to the subject matter of the negotiation. The competitive negotiator uses arguments to convince the other negotiator that his alternatives to a negotiated agreement are not as favorable as he previously thought and that therefore he should make concessions. Argument undermines his confidence in his own analysis of the bargaining situation.

The other primary method the negotiator uses to induce the other party to make substantial concessions is threats. To augment the effect of threats, the negotiator can use other competitive tactics including displays of anger, or a staged "walk-out," or premature termination of the negotiation.

1. THREATS

A *threat* is a conditional commitment by a negotiator to act in a way that appears detrimental to the other party unless the other party complies with a request. The most common type of negotiation threat is the threat to terminate the negotiation unless the other party makes specified concessions. The cooperative analog of the threat is the *promise*, a conditional commitment to act in a way that appears beneficial to the other party if the other party complies with a request. For example, a negotiator might agree to drop one demand if her counterpart would make significant concessions on another issue. Promises, and their relationship to exchanges of concessions, are discussed more fully in the next section on "Cooperative Tactics for Narrowing Differences."

Threats serve two functions in negotiation. First, and most importantly, threats induce the other negotiator to concede and enter into an agreement more favorable to the negotiator's client than his previous bargaining position suggested would be possible. Second, threats serve as a means of communicating the negotiator's own commitment to her

---

2. *See supra* pages 119–20.

bargaining position. If, for example, Katie Eisinger, representing Dr. Anton Volkov, threatens to break off negotiation with Jonathan Prevas, representing Banting Medical Technologies, unless Jonathan agrees to a minimum up-front, lump-sum payment of $3.0 million, Katie sends a strong message to Jonathan that the need for an immediate payment of a substantial amount of cash is an important issue to her client, Dr. Volkov.

Although implicit threats are present throughout negotiation, explicit threats should be used carefully and sparingly. Empirical studies suggest that while a negotiator's threats do lead to more concessions from the other negotiator, they also increase the degree of hostility between negotiators and the probability of negotiation breakdown and impasse.[3] Threats frequently elicit counter-threats. As a result, many negotiators use threats only when they cannot exert influence in other ways.

When the negotiator does decide to use a threat, she may be able to minimize these potential risks by stating the threat calmly and rationally, in a friendly style. Sometimes the negotiator can soften the threat by "blaming" the client or another party. For example, Katie might say, "I am really sorry, Jonathan, but Dr. Volkov has just told me that if you don't agree to a $3 million up-front payment this afternoon, I am to stop negotiating with you."

A threat may involve issues over which the parties are negotiating or matters extraneous to the negotiation. Possible threats involving issues within the negotiation include not only a threat to terminate the negotiation as a whole, but also a commitment not to make concessions on specified issues unless the other party complies with the negotiator's demand. An example of an external threat would be the announced intention of one business negotiating with another never to do business with the other again.[4]

Most often, the value of a threat is lost if it must be carried out. As an extreme example, consider the presence of American military personnel in Western Europe during the Cold War. Although those few personnel were clearly an insufficient force to defend against a full-scale Soviet invasion of Europe, the implicit threat was that a military attack on Western Europe would have been regarded as a military attack on the United States. Appropriate American responses, it was believed at the time, might have included the use of nuclear weapons. Had that threat ever been carried out, the threat would have failed in its intended purpose! A threat's value lies in increasing the probability that the other

---

3. JEFFERY Z. RUBIN & BERT R. BROWN, THE SOCIAL PSYCHOLOGY OF BARGAINING AND NEGOTIATION 278–87 (1975).

4. The lawyer is ethically prohibited from using many forms of extraneous threats. *See* CHARLES W. WOLFRAM, MODERN LEGAL ETHICS 714–19 (1986). For example, the lawyer in a personal injury negotiation who threatens to publicize photographs of

the defendant's embarrassing (but unrelated) marital infidelities commits criminal extortion. ALI MODEL PENAL CODE § 223.4(3) (Proposed Official Draft 1962). Threatening criminal prosecution in negotiation of a civil matter is similarly prohibited. *Ethical Guidelines for Settlement Negotiations*, ABA SEC. OF LITIG. § 4.3.2, committee note (2002).

negotiator will accede to a request, or in the Cold War example, that the Soviet Union would not invade Western Europe.

To be effective, threats must be credible, and the impact of carrying out the threat on the other party must be significant. If the other party does not believe in the reality of the threat, the threat fails. If the other party understands the reasons for the threat, he is more likely to view it as credible. Therefore threats are not credible when they are disproportionate to the issues at stake. The attorney who threatens to take her client's small claims action "all the way to the Supreme Court" generally is not believed unless she can demonstrate that the issue is one of great personal conviction for her or her client and that they have the time and resources to pursue it.

The most important factor affecting the credibility of a threat is the past record of the negotiator. If she has said twenty times before that she "must have" a specified sum of money or she "would break off negotiation and set the case for trial," and each time she has avoided trial and settled for a lesser amount, her twenty-first threat is not credible.

Similarly, the negotiator sometimes takes steps during the negotiation demonstrating her willingness to carry out threats. For example, a negotiator can openly prepare to carry out her threat. Suppose that Katie Eisinger, the attorney for Dr. Volkov, tells Jonathan Prevas, counsel for Banting Medical Technologies, that unless Banting agrees to a licensing agreement by May 1, she will terminate discussions and begin negotiations with a competing pharmaceutical company. Katie makes her threat more credible if she announces that she has scheduled a meeting shortly after the deadline with an executive responsible for licensing new technologies for a competing corporation.

The negotiator accomplishes the same result if she breaks down a major threat into a series of incremental threats, and then carries out several of the initial, incremental threats. Suppose Maria Santiago has threatened to break-off negotiation on behalf of her client Michael Van Meter and to try the case unless Baltimore & Western Railroad quickly agrees to her assessments of the liability issue and the amount of appropriate compensation for medical bills and lost wages. When counsel for Baltimore & Western does not respond to her demand, Maria could schedule the dates for the final depositions, the final pre-trial conference, and the trial.

Threats are also more credible if the negotiator suggests that she cannot back away from a commitment or undo a threat, as when her client has given either her or a third party binding instructions. Assume that just before leaving on a three-week trip to Antarctica where she would be out of communication, Rachel Goldberg, Banting's Vice–President for Research and Development, gives Jonathan Prevas binding instructions to break off negotiation with Dr. Volkov on May 1 unless Volkov has agreed to certain specified terms. Jonathan's threat to Volkov's attorney based upon these facts would be quite credible!

Threats often can be made more credible if blamed on the client's intransigence. "My client is adamant about it, Ashton," Maria Santiago tells counsel for the Baltimore & Western Railroad, "Unless you offer $1,950,000 by next Thursday, he wants me to set the case for trial as quickly as possible."

A negotiator also makes a threat more credible if she ties it to her own reputation or to her concern about setting a precedent. For example, Banting Medical Technologies might threaten to break off negotiations unless Volkov stops demanding an up-front, lump-sum royalty payment in excess of $1.5 million. To increase the credibility of this threat, Banting can stress that such a large up-front royalty payment would establish a dangerous precedent for negotiations with other scientists. In addition, the negotiator's own strong personal commitment can lend credibility to a threat, as in the case of the legal services attorney who is willing to appeal a small claims case all the way to the United States Supreme Court, if necessary, because of her strong belief that her client has been unjustly wronged.

2. BREAKING–OFF NEGOTIATION

One type of threat that is both common and extreme, the threat to break-off negotiations, deserves special attention. Sometimes this "threat" is accomplished when one of the negotiators walks out of a bargaining session. Her expectation is that the other negotiator will make concessions in order to entice her back to the bargaining table; she gambles on the other negotiator's willingness to make concessions to avoid a deadlock. Further, walking out tells her whether the other negotiator's apparent unwillingness to concede is firm, or whether it is a negotiating tactic. Walking-out may be risky behavior, however; the other party might elect not to resume negotiations again. Accordingly, walking-out as a concession-inducing tactic should be used only when the negotiator strongly believes that concessions will be forthcoming or when favorable alternatives to a negotiated agreement exist.

3. DISPLAYS OF ANGER—REAL OR FEIGNED

Real or feigned displays of anger sometimes accompany competitive arguments or threats. Negotiators frequently express anger, effectively suggesting to the other negotiator that a threat or a particular position should be taken seriously. Depending upon the psychological make-up of the other negotiator, the display of anger can sometimes intimidate him and induce concessions.

Anger, particularly real anger as compared with feigned anger, also has its risks in negotiation. For one thing, it is likely to elicit similar outbursts from the other party, thus contributing to a cycle of hostility and fear in the negotiation. Also, when genuinely angry, most people do not think as clearly as they do in calmer moments. When angry, negotiators are likely to make threats they will not carry out, thus decreasing their credibility. They may also disclose information or make other negotiating errors they would not make if they were in control of their emotions.

4. READING CONCESSION PATTERNS

The competitive tactics described above are intended to induce the other party to make concessions. The competitive negotiator's objective is to reach an agreement with the other negotiator that is as close as possible to the other's reservation point. The information-gathering tactics previously described in Chapter Five aid the negotiator in determining the other party's reservation point. The negotiator may find additional clues to the other party's reservation point by observing his concession pattern.

Suppose that Michael Van Meter's attorney, Maria Santiago, originally demanded $4.8 million in her complaint against the Baltimore & Western Railroad. Several months later, after pleadings and initial motions were filed, Maria offered to settle for $3.5 million "to avoid the risks of litigation." After fifteen months of discovery, Maria reduced her demand to $2.6 million, acknowledging that the depositions or her client and other witnesses were weaker than she had anticipated. With the beginning of serious bargaining, Maria's subsequent concessions went to $2.2 million, then to $2.0, then to $1.9, and, finally to $1.85 million. What is Michael Van Meter's reservation price? Probably $1.8 million or a figure very close to it. How does the negotiator know? Because the concessions fit into a pattern of decreasing magnitude, converging on a settlement figure of $1.8 million.

Concessions typically decrease as bargaining continues. Sometimes, by observing this pattern, it is possible to determine the other party's reservation price. However, some negotiators who are aware that it is possible to read concession patterns avoid revealing their true reservation points by creating a pattern of decreasing concessions around a false reservation point. For example, Santiago might sequentially concede to $3.8 million, $3.3 million, $3.2 million, and $3.15 million, with the intention of misleading her sophisticated counterpart—who has learned the tricks of the trade—into believing that his minimum disposition is $3.1 million.

5. LIMITING THE NEGOTIATOR'S OWN CONCESSIONS

The negotiator using competitive tactics not only seeks concessions by the other party, but also seeks to concede as little as possible herself. Her reluctance to concede serves another function: it is the single most important factor convincing the other party he must make more and larger concessions if an agreement is to be reached.

Strictly speaking, any concession is a cooperative negotiation tactic; only a refusal to concede is described accurately as a competitive tactic. Even negotiators using mostly competitive tactics, however, find it necessary to make concessions. Accordingly, this section focuses on competitive tactics for limiting the frequency and magnitude of concessions.

Most often, lawyers think of concessions in terms of dollar amounts. For example, Maria Santiago originally demanded $4.8 million in satisfaction of Van Meter's personal injury claims; later she "conceded" and indicated her willingness to accept $3.5 million. Concessions, however, do not necessarily involve dollar amounts. For example, if Katie Eisinger in her negotiation representing Dr. Volkov informs counsel for Banting Technologies that Volkov will accept royalty payments in lieu of a large, up-front cash payment, this is a negotiating "concession" that does not strictly involve a decrease in dollar amounts.

Two reasons support the competitive negotiator's reluctance to make concessions. The first is *position loss,* the abandonment of the pre-concession negotiating position that is more favorable to the negotiator and her client than her position after the concession. Because negotiating norms generally make it impossible to withdraw a concession once made, when the negotiator concedes, she loses any chance at an agreement based upon her earlier bargaining position that was more satisfactory to her client. Further, the negotiator "uses up" a concession, and cannot later trade that same concession for a reciprocal concession favoring her client. In addition to position loss, the second disadvantage in making concessions is *image loss.* The negotiator's concession often leads the other negotiator to believe that if he just "hangs tough," the negotiator will concede again. Accordingly, it may encourage him to engage in further competitive tactics.

Even the negotiator pursuing predominantly competitive tactics, however, recognizes the necessity of making concessions. The two most important reasons to make concessions are to:

(1) prevent premature termination of the negotiation or deadlock; and

(2) encourage the other to make reciprocal concessions.

In addition to preventing premature breakdowns in negotiation, timely concessions may also prevent either the client or the other party from becoming so "locked-in," or emotionally committed to a position, that appropriate concessions at a later point in the negotiation become impossible.

Concessions also have the advantages that have been discussed previously in the context of general cooperative tactics. Concessions are often necessary to preserve a good future working relationship between the parties. In addition, at times a negotiator who wants to demonstrate her reasonableness to a third party (such as a judge who encourages settlement or a mediator) concedes. Finally, concessions can speed the resolution of a negotiation. Sometimes when a negotiation is stalemated, or when the issue at stake does not warrant extended haggling, the negotiator who begins making concessions expedites the negotiation process.

The competitive approach to the necessary evil of making concessions is to concede as infrequently as possible, and in amounts as small as possible. Patience is a key for the competitive negotiator. The uncertainty that characterizes negotiation is frequently anxiety producing, particularly for inexperienced negotiators. When matched against a competitive negotiating counterpart, a negotiator usually ends up with a less advantageous agreement if she expresses a strong desire to settle early in the process. Consider, for example, the negotiation between Maria Santiago, Michael Van Meter's attorney, and Ashton Crutchfield, counsel for the Baltimore & Western Railroad. In the actual case upon which this hypothetical is loosely based, the defendant denied any liability and refused to pay anything other than "court costs" for a period of more than two years. Discovery continued and motions were heard, but still the defendant continued to "stonewall" it, even past the point of the pre-trial conference shortly before trial. Not until one week prior to trial did the defendant finally make an initial offer that was substantial in amount and begin serious bargaining. Personal injury cases frequently do settle literally on the courthouse steps. The attorney who attempts to bargain seriously too early in the process may disadvantage her client.

Similar testimonials to the virtues of patience are present in labor negotiation and international diplomacy. Labor agreements frequently settle after 72–hour marathon sessions; the negotiator who makes a reasonable offer well in advance of a strike deadline may disadvantage her client.[5] The 1978 Camp David Peace Accords entered into by Egypt and Israel were not agreed to until President Carter had "confined" President Sadat of Egypt and Prime Minister Begin of Israel at Camp David for a period of thirteen days.[6]

a. Justifying Concessions

The competitive strategy suggests that the negotiator accompany each concession with two explanations:

(1) the reasons why the negotiator is willing to concede and change her previously articulated position; and

(2) the reasons why the negotiator cannot and will not make a greater concession than the one articulated.

The importance of such explanations lies in their tendency to counteract image loss. As stated previously, one of the risks in making concessions is reinforcing the competitive tactics of the other negotiator by convincing him that additional concessions are forthcoming. Concessions may make the negotiator's previous bargaining position look arbitrary, and suggest that, once begun, concessions will continue indefinitely. An explanation of a concession dispels the notion that the concession

---

5. *See* RICHARD E. WALTON & ROBERT B. McKERSIE, A BEHAVIORAL THEORY OF LABOR NEGOTIATIONS 90–91 (1965). The trend in recent years has been for labor and man-agement to reach agreement earlier in the collective bargaining process.

6. *See* JIMMY CARTER, KEEPING FAITH: MEMOIRS OF A PRESIDENT 327–37 (1982).

resulted from the other negotiator's competitive tactics or his lack of concessions. The negotiator's proffered justification, explaining why this concession is the last, is designed to counteract the impression that one concession will lead to another because the negotiator has not "stuck to her guns."

Consider again the Michael Van Meter personal injury negotiation. Assume that the previous demand of Michael's attorney, Maria Santiago, was $3.5 million and that he now intends to lower her demand to $2.6 million:

1—Maria: As you know, Ashton, we've now completed fifty-four depositions in this case, and it's set for trial next month.

2—Ashton: It certainly looks like we'll be going to trial. You're still asking for $3.5 million in a case in which my client believes it faces little exposure.

3—Maria: I'm glad to hear that after all those depositions you recognize that your client does face at least *some* risk of liability. Discovery has given us both a pretty good idea of what is going to happen at trial. I think you'll agree that we have plenty of evidence of negligence on the part of the railroad—not trimming the shrubs, tree branches and weeds so that vehicular passengers could see a train coming—to get to the jury. I will admit, however, that there is some risk that the jury will reduce the damages because they might find that my client was also negligent in driving onto the railroad tracks. Michael says he stopped at the crossing and looked as carefully as he could. But your engineer claims that Michael did not stop. Because of the risk we face on that issue, I'm willing to attribute 25 percent of the fault to Michael and reduce my prior demand to 75 percent of $3.5 million, or $2,625,000.

4—Ashton: It's most generous of you to allocate 25 percent of the fault to your client who drove his truck out in front of a roaring locomotive.

5—Maria: I choose that figure because of a recent verdict in Ohio, with facts very similar to these, in which the jury allocated fault 75 percent to the railroad and 25 percent to the driver.

In this dialogue, Maria provides both a reason to concede and a reason to limit her concession. In segment number 3, Maria justifies her concession on the basis of the facts uncovered during discovery—that is, the factual dispute as to whether Michael did or did not "stop and look" before proceeding across the tracks. The engineer's testimony was new information to Maria, not available at the time she formulated her earlier demand. Later, in segment number 5, Maria provides a reason for the amount of her concession and why the concession is not larger. She discloses that the jury in a comparable case allocated the fault between the railroad and the driver on a 75 percent–25 percent basis. In other words, she makes an argument that her demand is justified by the facts of the instant case and its similarities with a recent verdict from another court.

Two other aspects of this dialogue are worth noting. First, Ashton's opening comment in segment number 2 that his client believes it "faces little exposure" may be a significant concession if Baltimore & Western's previous posture had been that this was a "no liability" case. In segment number 4, Ashton's comment that allocating 25 percent of fault to a plaintiff who drives his truck in front of a train is "generous" is both strategically competitive and also stylistically competitive, i.e., sarcastic. Ashton's competitive response, of course, is not necessarily indicative of how he might respond to Maria's concession later in the negotiation.

b. *Positional Commitment*

Patience in making concessions, and providing credible reasons why the negotiator cannot concede further, are both competitive tactics to express *commitment* to bargaining positions. Walton and McKersie, in their study of labor negotiation, define commitment as the taking of a bargaining position with some implicit or explicit pledge regarding a future course of action.[7] Threats, therefore, are one form of commitment, because they promise detrimental consequences unless the other negotiator responds as demanded. A second form of commitment is a *positional commitment* where the negotiator pledges an unalterable bargaining position and no more concessions.

Positional commitment is the quintessential competitive tactic. If the other party accepts the negotiator's positional commitment at face value, then the other party is limited to the options of accepting the negotiator's current proposal or forgoing an agreement. Professors Lax and Sebenius of the Harvard Business School go so far as to claim that any negotiation in a distributive context "can be 'won' by the side that first commits credibly and irreversibly to a preferred settlement."[8] Credible positional commitments, however, also carry a high risk of negotiation breakdown or stalemate. The negotiator should be careful when using positional commitments to avoid unintended negotiation breakdowns in cases where the client's interests suggest continued negotiation.

The negotiator can use the same methods to make positional commitments credible as she uses to make threats credible. For example, the negotiator or her client can take actions consistent with the positional

---

7. WALTON & MCKERSIE, *supra* note 5, at 82.

8. DAVID A. LAX & JAMES K. SEBENIUS, THE MANAGER AS NEGOTIATOR: BARGAINING FOR COOPERATION AND COMPETITIVE GAIN 124 (1986).

commitment, that is, she can visibly prepare for a negotiation break-down. She also should demonstrate that she is under minimal time pressure to conclude the negotiation, thus suggesting that she has no need to make concessions to resolve the negotiation quickly. For example, when negotiations seeking an end to the war in Vietnam began in Paris between diplomats from the United States and North Vietnam, the Vietnamese delegation reportedly rented a house with a two-year lease.

A negotiator can justify a positional commitment in much the same manner as she might justify a threat. In the first instance, she can blame the positional commitment on the intransigence of her client. In the alternative, she can buttress the credibility of the positional commitment by coupling it with reference to her situation as the client's bargaining agent. For example, she might say that if she conceded more than she has indicated, then the other party's next bargaining session would be with a different lawyer.

c. Avoiding Consecutive Concessions

That concessions will be reciprocated is a typical norm in many legal negotiations. After all, a negotiator's concession accomplishes nothing for her client unless it also brings the other party closer to an acceptable agreement. Therefore, the negotiator should always be wary of making consecutive concessions. A pattern of unreciprocated concessions could indicate that she needs to take a stronger stand to avoid being pushed around.

Some negotiators use the norm of reciprocated concessions to engage in a competitive negotiation tactic best described as *disingenuous consecutive concessions*.[9] For example, assume that Ashton Crutchfield, representing the Baltimore & Western Railroad, admits—after an extended period of discovery—that his client faces some exposure of liability, and he initially offers to pay $600,000 to settle Michael Van Meter's claims. Following the trial court's denial of his motion for summary judgment, he offers $650,000 and explains his concession on the basis of the denial of his motion. Subsequently, he concedes again to $675,000. At this point, he claims indignantly that he has made "three consecutive concessions" and has not received anything in return. Obviously, the magnitude of the later two concessions was minor, and he could just as easily have offered $675,000 instead of $600,000 in the first instance. Instead, he sought to use the "reciprocated concession norm" to force Maria to respond meaningfully to his last two concessions. The negotiator should not react to such a ploy and should focus on the cumulative magnitude of the concessions instead of solely on their frequency.

9. *See* CHARLES B. CRAVER, EFFECTIVE LEGAL NEGOTIATION AND SETTLEMENT 288–89 (5th ed. 2005).

C. COOPERATIVE TACTICS FOR NARROWING DIFFERENCES

1. CONCESSIONS BEGET CONCESSIONS

The negotiator using cooperative tactics views the concession as an affirmative tool, not just as a necessary evil. The primary cooperative tactic for encouraging the other party to concede is for the negotiator to make a concession herself, believing that her own concessions will lead to reciprocity. In fact, research suggests that the negotiator who makes concessions is more likely to elicit cooperation from the other party than the negotiator who uses competitive tactics.[10]

The tendency for the negotiator's concessions to beget concessions by the other party results from strong bargaining norms that concessions should be reciprocated. More generally, as previously discussed, most people are socialized to cooperate with those who cooperate with them. When one of their friends, co-workers or family members "makes a concession," most individuals are unlikely to see this as a sign of weakness to be exploited by using even more competitive tactics. It should not be surprising, therefore, that attorneys who have negotiated with each other throughout their careers make concessions, realistically believing that they will encourage the other lawyer to reciprocate. Once again, it is important to reiterate that Williams found that 65 percent of the attorneys described in his survey were "cooperative," and that "willing to move from original position" was one of the characteristics Williams used to categorize a negotiator as cooperative.[11]

2. PROMISES

The *promise* is the cooperative counterpart of the threat. A promise is an expressed intention to act in a certain way that appears beneficial to the interests of the other party.[12] Thus, it commits the negotiator to an affirmative or cooperative action, as contrasted with a threat which commits the negotiator to take detrimental action.

Most often the promise can be predicated on the other negotiator taking some action that would benefit the negotiator's own client. For example, Jonathan Prevas, representing Banting Medical Technologies, might promise "to look more closely at a larger up-front royalty payment if Volkov would both agree to keep such a payment confidential and would explore both university and NIH funding to finance some of the additional research required to prove the efficacy of the Viral Sharpshooter." Similarly, Ashton Crutchfield might promise to accept Maria Santiago's calculations on Michael Van Meter's economic damages—wage loss and medical expenses—if Santiago becomes more realistic regarding the percentage of fault attributable to her client. In this manner, the promise serves effectively as a means of initiating the reciprocal concession process; the negotiator promises to make a conces-

---

10. *See* DEAN G. PRUITT, NEGOTIATION BEHAVIOR, 59–60 (1982); RUBIN & BROWN, *supra* note 3, at 269–78. More than thirty studies reaching this conclusion are cited in these two texts.

11. GERALD R. WILLIAMS, LEGAL NEGOTIATION AND SETTLEMENT 18, 21 (1983).

12. RUBIN & BROWN, *supra* note 3, at 278.

sion on the condition that the other negotiator either concedes on a certain issue, reexamines his position, or takes other action favorable to the negotiator's client.

Empirical evidence supports the effectiveness of promises as negotiating tactics.[13] Studies show that negotiators use promises more frequently than they use threats in simulated negotiations. These same studies show that promises tend to result in immediate concessions by the other party. Further, their use increases the likelihood of reaching a mutually satisfactory agreement, while the use of threats decreases that likelihood. Finally, as would be expected, the use of promises, instead of threats, produces better interpersonal relationships between the negotiators.

3. ARGUMENT AS A COOPERATIVE TACTIC

The nature of argument as a negotiating tactic was previously discussed in Chapter Five.[14] The purpose of cooperative argument is to establish the basis for a fair and just agreement, generally using objective criteria or norms. Objective criteria used by the cooperative negotiator include those previously discussed: trial results in other cases, settlement results, fair market values, or principles like equal sharing. To transform the bargaining session into a discussion of what constitutes a fair and just agreement, Fisher, Ury, and Patton suggest asking the other negotiator to articulate the reasons why he thinks his negotiation proposal is a fair and just one.[15] Further, they suggest that the lawyer first seek an agreement with the other negotiator on a principled basis for deciding what constitutes a fair and just agreement before they apply such an agreed-upon standard to the specific issue at hand.

4. COOPERATIVE TACTICS TO PROTECT AGAINST COMPETITIVE EXPLOITATION

The risk inherent in making concessions and in using other cooperative tactics is that instead of reciprocating the lawyer's cooperation, the other negotiator will seek to exploit the negotiator's tactics through an even more competitive stance. This section describes a number of cooperative tactics that can be used to protect against competitive exploitation.

a. Limiting the Risks of Concessions

If the negotiator concedes and there is no reciprocal concession by the other party, the negotiator has impaired her client's interests without gain. How can the negotiator protect herself against the unreciprocated concession?

One method is for the negotiator to communicate flexibility on an issue without making a concession. This enables her to test the other

13. *See id.*, at 278–88; PRUITT, *supra* note 10, at 76–81.

14. *See supra* at pages 119–20.

15. *See* ROGER FISHER, WILLIAM URY & BRUCE PATTON, GETTING TO YES: NEGOTIATING AGREEMENT WITHOUT GIVING IN 88–92 (2d ed. 1991).

negotiator's response to her expressed flexibility before deciding whether to proceed with the concession. She hopes that her indication of a willingness to concede will induce the other negotiator either to begin with a concession or at least to offer a statement of flexibility similar to her own. For example, Maria Santiago might indicate that she would be willing to "look again at" the issue of her client's degree of fault in the crossing collision, if Ashton Crutchfield, representing Baltimore & Western, would do likewise.

Obviously, expressing flexibility is inconsistent with a posture of extreme commitment to the prior negotiating position. After the negotiator states her flexibility on an issue, she usually cannot convincingly assert that there will be no further concessions on that issue. Nevertheless, by merely stating flexibility rather than actually conceding, the negotiator experiences no position loss unless the other party reciprocates. At some point in the future, for example, Maria will still be able to trade a concession on her client's degree of fault in exchange for a concession from Ashton that benefits her client. At the same time, however, the negotiator who expresses flexibility affords the other negotiator an opportunity to break out of a competitive stalemate.

The second tactic that the negotiator can use to protect against the unreciprocated concession is the "disownable concession." Recall that negotiation norms establish rather clearly that concessions once made cannot be withdrawn. However, assume that an ambiguous communication from the negotiator to the other party appears to contain a concession. If the other negotiator responds by reciprocating the concession, the negotiator can affirm that the original ambiguous message did indeed contain a concession. On the other hand, if the other party does not respond cooperatively, the negotiator can argue an interpretation of the ambiguous message that denies that a concession was made.

Consider the following exchange between Maria Santiago, representing Michael Van Meter, and Ashton Crutchfield, counsel for the Baltimore & Western Railroad. Remember that Maria earlier referred to a similar case in Ohio in which fault had been assessed 75 percent to the railroad and 25 percent to the driver of the vehicle. Assume that prior to the following exchange, this Ohio verdict had been the only prior case regarding the parties' respective degrees of fault that the lawyers had discussed:

1—Ashton: The biggest obstacle to us settling seems to me to be your highly inflated value for pain and suffering damages. If you were willing to accept a value of $975,000 for pain and suffering, to be discounted by your client's percentage of fault, I think I could convince my client to resolve the division of fault issue consistent with the way it's been handled in similar cases in other jurisdictions.

2—Maria: I certainly can't accept your pain and suffering figure. Get serious. This is a young man who is now a paraplegic for the rest of his life. I'm going to have to stand with my demand for $1.8 million. I am encouraged, however, that you have agreed that your client's share of the fault will be assessed at 75 percent in accordance with the Ohio case.

3—Ashton: No, I'm sorry. You've misunderstood. I've uncovered settlements in two other virtually identical cases in California and Michigan. One assesses the railroad's fault at 30 percent and the other assesses it at 15 percent.

In segment number 1, Ashton obviously expresses his willingness to agree to the 75 percent–25 percent division of responsibility referred to earlier, if Maria agrees to a substantial concession on the amount of pain and suffering damages. Both parties understand tacitly the terms of the exchange of concessions being offered. Maria responds competitively, however, and refuses to make the concession, at the same time that she tries to capture the concession that Ashton offered. Instead, Ashton, in segment number 3, reacts by suggesting that Maria misunderstood him and that he was not willing to accept the 75 percent degree of responsibility, but was instead referring to additional cases from other jurisdictions. When his offer to exchange concessions was not accepted, Ashton "disowned" his original concession. He has sustained image loss—Maria now realizes that he may accept the 75 percent liability figure. On the other hand, Ashton has suffered no position loss and subsequently should be able to extract a concession from Maria in exchange for his agreement that his client will pay 75 percent of the damages.

A third cooperative tactic to reduce the risk of unreciprocated concessions is the use of "fractionated concessions."[16] Instead of making one large concession and awaiting the other negotiator's response, the negotiator divides the issue into a series of small concessions, where if any one is unreciprocated, there is little damage to the negotiator's position. One limited concession is made, and the negotiator awaits a response from the other negotiator. If he responds cooperatively, the negotiator then proceeds with the next in the series of concessions.

When the object of the negotiation is division of dollars between the parties, it is easy to see how fractionated concessions work. They also can be employed, however, on less quantifiable issues. Consider Banting Medical Technologies' demand to have Volkov's university pick up some of the costs of both the further research required for FDA approval, and the legal and other administrative expenses to be incurred in seeking FDA approval. Volkov's attorney might arrange for the university to pick up the tab for some of the further research costs, but might await a reciprocal concession from Banting before further proposing that the university fund the expenses associated with FDA approval.

16. Pruitt originated the use of this term. *See* Pruitt, *supra* note 10, at 99–100.

b. Negotiation Breaks to Limit Concessions

The use of negotiation breaks or "walk-outs" as a competitive tactic to induce the other party to make concessions was discussed previously in this chapter. Calling a temporary halt to negotiations also can be used "defensively" when a negotiator senses that the bargaining is not going well from the perspective of her client or that she is being otherwise "swept away." This can occur under several different circumstances:

    (1) she perceives an emotional shift in the climate of the negotiation against her client;

    (2) she is confronted with unexpected new information or negotiating positions from the other party;

    (3) her own negotiating tactics are not having the effects she anticipated; or

    (4) she is confused or tired.

A recess under any of these conditions often breaks the psychological momentum against the negotiator and gives her a chance to reassess her evaluation of the case and the posture of the negotiation. Coaches sometimes call time-outs in basketball games for similar purposes.

c. Responding to Extremely Competitive Tactics

All negotiators, particularly inexperienced ones and ones who attempt to use cooperative or problem-solving tactics, sometimes become targets for extremely competitive tactics from more traditional negotiators representing opposing parties.[17] These tactics include personal attacks, escalating demands, artificial deadlines and extreme threats. For example, how should Katie Eisinger respond when Jonathan Prevas informs her that Rachel Goldberg, Banting's Vice President for Research and Development, has instructed him to break off negotiations with Volkov unless an agreement is reached by February 1, when there appears to be no logical reason for such a deadline? First, Katie should ask "why" the seemingly artificial deadline is being established. If Jonathan is not able to articulate a credible reason, then her inquiry confirms her suspicion that the deadline is a competitive negotiating tactic and not a legitimate requirement. Second, Katie should let Jonathan know that she recognizes that he is using a competitive tactic:

    1—Katie: Jonathan, I have the sense that you're trying to pressure me into reaching an agreement quickly.

Third, Katie should make it clear to Jonathan that the tactic will not work:

    2—Katie: I just want to let you know that I've discussed this with my client and we've agreed that we will not

17. This section was influenced substantially by the teaching of my former colleague Don Peters of the University of Florida. *See also* FISHER, URY & PATTON, *supra* note 15, at 129–143 (suggesting how to respond to extremely competitive tactics).

rush into any agreement until we've had a chance
to evaluate other options and all the terms of the
agreement.

In this portion of her response, Katie tells Jonathan both that the tactic
will not be successful and, that if Jonathan continues to pursue the
tactic, he risks alienating Katie and her client. This dialogue may then
lead naturally into an explicit discussion of the negotiation process and
the actual time pressures under which the parties are bargaining.

D. COMPETITIVE TACTICS FOR ACHIEVING CLOSURE

The negotiation processes described in previous chapters are col-
lapsed occasionally into a two-minute conversation between prosecutor
and defense attorney in the courthouse halls. More often, the investigation, meetings, phone calls and exchange of correspondence last for
months, or even years. Ultimately, however, whether an agreement is
reached often comes down to what is said and done in a few minutes.

By this time, the negotiators usually have substantial information
about each other's requirements and expectations for an agreement. It is
theoretically possible that one negotiator may obtain everything from
the negotiated agreement that her client could ever have hoped for. Such
a result occasionally occurs if the lawyer has relentlessly pursued purely
competitive tactics, and the other negotiator lacks the bargaining power,
the negotiating ability or the will to adequately protect his client's
interests. Bridging solutions that wholly satisfy both parties' interests
may lead to an outcome similarly utopian from the client's perspective.
More likely, however, both parties will give up something in the final
stages of negotiation.

This part describes competitive tactics used to bring the negotiation
to a conclusion. The next part then analyzes various aspects of making
the final concession, a cooperative tactic critical during the final stages of
negotiation.

1. DEADLINES AND ULTIMATUMS

Frequently, negotiators become considerably more cooperative as
deadlines approach. Personal injury actions, much to the frustration of
judges and sometimes clients, often settle only at the last minute "on the
courthouse steps." As a deadline approaches, it puts pressure on the
parties to state positions as close to their reservation points as possible
in order to avoid a negotiation failure. Sometimes parties even are forced
to change their reservation points to reach an agreement. Further, the
use of competitive tactics decreases as the deadline approaches. Empirical research repeatedly demonstrates that time pressures increase the

likelihood of agreement and tend to reduce the aspirations of negotiators, the extremity of their demands, and the prevalence of bluffing.[18]

Why does so much agreement take place at the last possible moment? Basically, because the negotiator using predominantly competitive tactics sees bargaining as the proverbial game of "chicken." The longer the negotiator holds out in the face of possible negotiation breakdown, the more likely it is that the other negotiator will yield and come closer to her position. Also, if both negotiators use predominantly competitive tactics, information about the parties' true underlying interests will be exchanged slowly, grudgingly and incompletely throughout the bargaining process. As a result, the negotiator never knows what constitutes the best agreement she can obtain for her client.

At some point, however, the negotiator using competitive tactics believes that she has enough information about the other side's reservation point and that she is never going to get a better deal. At that point, she puts the other negotiator under a genuine or artificially imposed deadline to respond to an offer. Genuine deadlines include approaching trial dates, strike deadlines or deadlines imposed by third parties. As an example of a deadline created by a third party, consider the negotiation between a sub-contractor and a contractor who intends to bid on a government project. The deadline for bids for the government contract creates a somewhat earlier deadline for the contractor and sub-contractor to reach agreement. Artificial deadlines can be attributed to the insistence of the negotiator's client or the negotiator's expressed need to begin to pursue other options to an agreement if bargaining stalls. For example, Maria Santiago might establish a deadline in her negotiation with Baltimore & Western Railroad based upon her need to begin extensive trial preparations if agreement cannot be reached.

The setting of a *deadline* often is accompanied by a *"final offer"* or *ultimatum*. The negotiator should rarely designate the final position an "ultimatum" because yielding to an ultimatum involves loss of face. In order to be credible, final positions or ultimatums usually cannot be announced too early in the process. When the negotiator announces an ultimatum too quickly, she finds it difficult to convince the other negotiator that she has exhausted her attempts at compromise and that she has no further room to concede. Another reason for delaying any "final" offer is the other negotiator's increased motivation to achieve an agreement later in the negotiation when he already has invested considerable time and effort in the bargaining process.

In order to be effective, the ultimatum must be supported by reasons. By justifying the ultimatum, the negotiator makes it more credible and decreases any loss of face the other party will experience in yielding to the ultimatum. To avoid the ego threat to the other negotiator, the final position should be stated in a cooperative style. Sometimes it can be attributed to the negotiator's client: "This is absolutely the most that the railroad claims manager will allow me to offer," Ashton Crutchfield informs Maria Santiago. In other cases, the negotiator can

18. *See* RUBIN & BROWN, *supra* note 3, at 123.

offer the other party two or more choices, both of which serve her client's interests. Offering the other party a choice may mitigate the ego threat to the other party at the same time that either choice serves her client's interests.

2. CONSOLIDATION OF THE AGREEMENT

When a negotiator is ready to close the deal, she should repeat all the elements of the agreement in summary form. Like active listening for content, such summarization serves to check for mutual agreement or understanding on each issue. Often the attorneys reduce the agreement to writing in a summary form and initial it on the spot. In more complex cases or cases with multiple issues where it may not be possible to draft a memorandum of agreement immediately, it is advisable to follow an oral agreement promptly with either a letter summarizing the terms of the agreement or a brief memorandum stating the "agreement in principle." At a minimum, the lawyer should draft a memorandum to her file stating the terms of the agreement. Experience teaches many lawyers that "If it isn't in writing, it doesn't exist."

The negotiator should volunteer, where possible, to draft any written agreement to be signed by the parties. The language chosen by the lawyer in drafting is unlikely to be identical to the words her counterpart would use, particularly if the agreement is long and complicated, or when the bargaining has been competitive. This is not to suggest in any way that the drafting lawyer should modify the terms agreed upon, or add or delete any provision of the agreement. Such an artifice constitutes unprofessional conduct and would create considerable professional damage within the bargaining community.

Most often, however, minor details and exact language have not been specifically negotiated. Counsel for the other party actually may appreciate the attorney's willingness to draft the agreement. Some counsel representing other parties will not engage in hair-splitting if minor points, not expressly negotiated, are drafting in a manner favorable to the negotiator's client. Conversely, drafting the agreement also protects the negotiator against shading of provisions by the other lawyer. If the other lawyer does draft the agreement, the negotiator should always compare the agreement and her own notes of the oral agreement. Optimally, the negotiator has developed a negotiating record throughout the bargaining process by drafting a continuous stream of memoranda to the file covering her contacts with the other lawyer. She should not hesitate to insist upon corrections of any imperfections in the statement of the agreement or any shading of the terms.

Finally, the negotiator should refrain from suggesting to either the other negotiator or to a third party that she "won" the negotiation. Lawyers tend to negotiate with the same negotiators in future dealings. If the other negotiator hears that the lawyer thought she took advantage of him in a prior negotiation, it makes later negotiations with him considerably more difficult.

E. COOPERATIVE CLOSURE TACTICS

1. FINAL CONCESSIONS

As in other phases of the negotiation, cooperative tactics during the concluding stages do not consist of threats and ultimatums, but instead focus on initiating the reciprocal exchange of concessions. There are two variations of this basic tactic in the final stages of the negotiation. The first is for the negotiator to announce a final concession and invite reciprocation. In Maria Santiago's negotiation with Ashton Crutchfield, Maria might initiate an exchange of final concessions as follows:

> 1—Maria: We started a long way apart in these talks. It's been two years and we've taken fifty-four depositions. The case is set for next Tuesday, but I think we're close enough that we ought to be willing to settle our differences. Your last offer was $1.6 million, and my last demand was $1,950,000. I've talked with my client and we are willing to settle this thing for $1,850,000. But he's made it clear that he will go no further. If you can't accept $1,850,000, we'll go to trial.

A second method for initiating the final exchange of concessions is for Maria to tell Ashton that if he were willing to pay $1,850,000, she "thinks it would be acceptable to her client." Without actually making the concession, Maria tacitly communicates her client's willingness to accept a settlement of $1,850,000.

How large should the final concession be? As previously discussed, the magnitude of each consecutive concession decreases during the bargaining. Accordingly, one would expect a final concession to be small. A disproportionately large concession in the latest stages of the negotiation may suggest to the other negotiator that the lawyer has not reached her reservation point and probably can concede further. On the other hand, the final concession should arguably be larger than the concessions immediately preceding it in order to be a dramatic and symbolic gesture of closure.

A negotiator frequently proposes a final exchange of concessions by suggesting that the parties "split the difference." Empirical evidence suggests that negotiations tend to reach agreement near the midpoint between the parties' respective bargaining positions once two realistic offers are on the table.[19] However, the negotiator should not use "splitting the difference" as a justification for making a concession early in the negotiation process. At that early stage, concessions should always be justified on grounds related to the substance of the matter being negotiated so that the negotiation process does not become only a game of

---

19. Otomar J. Bartos, *Simple Model of Negotiation: A Sociological Point of View*, 21 J. CONFLICT RESOL. 561, 567–570 (1977), *reprinted in* THE NEGOTIATION PROCESS: THEORIES AND APPLICATIONS 13, 19–24 (I. William Zartman ed., 1978).

willpower yielding arbitrary results. In the final stages of negotiation, however, when the differences between the parties are modest, "splitting the difference" is an acceptable justification for resolving the remaining discrepancies. This assumes that the proposed agreement exceeds the client's reservation point and is agreed upon by the client.

The negotiator should be careful to be sure that the other lawyer has not manipulated the result of "splitting the difference" by his concession pattern during the last several rounds of bargaining. If, during these prior rounds, the lawyer has made concessions diminishing her client's level of satisfaction with the agreement substantially more than the other lawyer's concessions have reduced his client's satisfaction, then "splitting the difference" is no longer an equitable means of compromise.

2. CREATING CONSTRUCTIVE AMBIGUITIES

Traditionally, good lawyers are taught that a contractual agreement should anticipate every possible contingency and resolve them in an unambiguous manner. Unfortunately, disagreement about minor or peripheral points occasionally jeopardizes an agreement when all major issues have been resolved. One way to deal with this situation is "to agree to disagree" and to include in the agreement a "constructive ambiguity."[20] Ambiguous language on a peripheral point may enable each party to believe he has accomplished his objective. Frequently, the issue in question will never become an object of dispute between the parties. If it does, the parties to a transactional negotiation probably will have been working together under the agreement long enough to have established sufficient rapport to resolve minor disagreements as they arise. Sometimes it may be desirable to add an explicit provision to an agreement concerning disputes or general interpretation, providing for resolution either by arbitration or by a decision of some other specified third party. Occasionally the results of the negotiation include a "reopener agreement" indicating that upon the occurrence of certain conditions, specific provisions will be re-negotiated by the parties.

3. DETERMINING WHEN THE OTHER PARTY'S "FINAL" OFFER IS FINAL

To protect herself from exploitation by a negotiator using the competitive tactics of ultimatums and final offers, the negotiator needs to ascertain when an offer designated by the competitive negotiator as "final," really is *final*.

The credibility of the statement that an offer is "final" can be judged by many of the same factors that suggest the credibility of other threats and commitments. The negotiator should consider the language used by the other negotiator in stating the ultimatum. Was it in absolute terms, or were there qualifiers or conditional statements that may allow room for future bargaining? For example, a statement that "my client

---

20. *See* CHARLES B. CRAVER, *supra* note 9, at 213–14.

and I have decided this is the best we can do based upon all the information we have" indicates a willingness to change the final position if additional facts are forthcoming. The lawyer should analyze any non-verbal communications or paralinguistic vocalizations that she might have observed as the other negotiator delivered the ultimatum. Further, whether or not the "final" position appeared to be a logical culmination of extended bargaining or whether it occurred too early in the negotiation process is an important indicator of its actual finality. The negotiator should also practice "role reversal" to decide whether it makes sense from the other negotiator's perspective to offer a "take it or leave it" deal. Finally, did the ultimatum occur in the heat of battle? Was it an inadvertent reaction to the course of the negotiation or even the result of the lawyer's emotional involvement in the situation instead of a genuine final offer?

Even when the other negotiator claims that his offer is "final," he usually modifies his position or compromises to some extent before the negotiators conclude an agreement. How can the negotiator respond to a final offer that is unacceptable to her client when she believes that it is in both parties' interests to continue the negotiation?

If the negotiator believes that the other lawyer has legitimately reached her limits and is not engaged in a competitive bluffing tactic, she should use active listening to express understanding of the other negotiator's inability to negotiate further, as in the statement "You feel you've gone as far as you can." Then she can restate the other party's final offer in a way that makes it a firm position, but not a final one. By diffusing the tension inherent in "final offers," the negotiator opens the door to the use of several additional tactics. First, she can respond with her own concession, even if it does not match the other negotiator's final demand. Consider Ashton Crutchfield's response to Maria Santiago's "final demand" of $1,850,000:

> 1—Ashton: I understand that $1,850,000 is the best you can do. I knew we were close to loggerheads, so I took the same attitude in talking again with my client. My client indicated its willingness to agree to $1,750,000, but absolutely refused to pay more. We may be stalemated, but why don't you take the $1,750,000 figure back to your client?

Notice that Ashton links his final concession with an explicit request that Maria take the new offer back to her client.

Another approach is for the negotiator to express her understanding that this is a final offer, but then to continue to ask "Why?" If Ashton asks Maria "Why?" her position is a final one and Maria responds, Maria's answer continues the dialogue on the merits at a time when Maria had intended to present a "take it or leave it demand" and stop further discussion. In addition, it will be difficult for Maria to find a reasonable explanation for a willingness to accept $1,850,000, but to refuse adamantly to accept $1,750,000.

The negotiator also can deflect a final offer by responding with new information or by advancing a new perspective on information previously considered by the parties. If genuinely novel, such additional input arguably justifies reconsideration of a final position because it was not considered when the other lawyer and his client formulated their "final" position.

Yet another option for the negotiator facing "a final offer" is to respond to the final offer on a specific issue by deferring consideration of the issue until later in the negotiation. If the parties are able to agree upon other issues, it increases the pressure on both of them to compromise on the stalemated issue. Finally, the negotiator can respond to a final offer by suggesting that the negotiation be recessed until later. This competitive response communicates that one party or the other must change its evaluation of the situation before agreement can be reached. The recess may be accompanied by a suggestion that the lawyers talk with their clients.

4. REOPENING DEADLOCKED NEGOTIATIONS

When a negotiator seeks to reopen a negotiation that has broken down, the other lawyer often views her as being overly anxious to settle. To propose new discussions, therefore, risks image loss. The negotiator's willingness to resume negotiation, without a change in circumstances, often leads the other lawyer to believe that her earlier "toughness" that led to the breakdown was mere bluffing, and that she can be pressured into further substantial concessions. To counter this perception, where possible, a lawyer should justify the resumption of bargaining by offering new information, obtained through investigation or discovery, which may change the parties' evaluations of the situation. Often, however, the only change since the breakdown of the heated negotiation is that tempers have cooled. Under these conditions, the lawyer proposing the reopening of negotiation should forthrightly offer her opinion that the best interests of both parties would be served by resuming bargaining.

Chapter Eight

NARROWING OF DIFFERENCES AND CLOSURE: PROBLEM-SOLVING TACTICS

A. INTRODUCTION

It is important to reiterate at this point that problem-solving bargaining can "break out" at any point during the negotiation. On one hand, negotiators sometimes use problem-solving tactics with great success during the earliest stages of the negotiation. As previously suggested, however, in many other negotiations competitive phases of bargaining precede problem-solving phases. Frequently, problem-solving tactics are effectively initiated precisely when the parties are becoming most frustrated with the exchange of arguments, threats, and limited concessions that leave their bargaining positions far apart and make their differences seem insurmountable. Accordingly, it is sometimes at this "stage" of the negotiation that parties may begin to devise bridging solutions or to share information about their interests and needs more openly. If this occurs, the grouping of problem-solving tactics with competitive and cooperative tactics in this book may no longer be in tandem. In other words, after using arguments, threats and the other competitive tactics described in the pervious chapter, the negotiator may begin using the problem-solving methods of information gathering, analyzed in Chapter Five, or the problem-solving tactics for initial proposals, described in Chapter Six.

For negotiators using problem-solving tactics, the narrowing of differences occurs in a conceptually different manner than it does for negotiators using predominantly either competitive or cooperative tactics. Negotiators who employ problem-solving tactics intentionally avoid beginning with two polar positions and then converging on a compromise middle position. Instead, as previously discussed, problem-solving negotiators devise numerous potential "solutions" to the problems faced by their clients. These solutions are developed either by the lawyer and her client during negotiation-planning counseling conferences[1] or by the two negotiating attorneys during bargaining sessions.[2] Sometimes clients also participate in these sessions.

This chapter builds upon the analysis presented in earlier chapters of the problem-solving approaches to planning, information sharing and solution-generating processes. Recall that the negotiator may have pursued either of two problem-solving paths to arrive at this point. Either she now is presenting proposed bridging solutions previously generated by the negotiator and her client prior to the bargaining session, or she and her negotiating counterpart themselves already have engaged in a process of developing solutions that meet each of their clients' needs.

B. PROBLEM–SOLVING TACTICS FOR NARROWING DIFFERENCES

1. EVALUATION OF BRIDGING PROPOSALS

The narrowing of differences through a convergence of bargaining positions, characteristic of the competitive or the cooperative strategy, is replaced in the problem-solving strategy with (a process for deciding which proposal, among the many possibilities previously identified by the two negotiators or presented by one of the negotiators after brainstorming with her client, best meets the needs and expectations of the parties.)

During this process of evaluating *bridging solutions*, the negotiators should consider together the potential solutions previously developed and evaluate how well these solutions meet their respective needs. They should address the following issues as part of this evaluation:[3]

(1) How well does each solution meet the client's interests?

(2) How well does each solution meet the other party's best interests?

(3) Is each solution practical and feasible?

(4) Which solution best meets both parties' interests?

(5) Is there another alternative, or a modification of one of the original solutions, that does a better job of addressing both parties' interests?

---

1. *See supra* pages 58–62.

2. *See supra* pages 143–44.

3. Professor Menkel–Meadow, in her classic early article analyzing problem-solving negotiation, identified similar criteria for evaluating the quality of any proposed solution, which include, among others, the following six criteria:

1. Does the *bridging solution* address the client's needs and goals?

2. Does the *bridging solution* address the other party's needs and goals?

3. Does the proposal facilitate the desired relationship with the other party?

4. Have the negotiators explored all possible alternatives that might either make both parties better off, or one party better off with no adverse consequences to the other party?

5. Is the proposal feasible and realistic or will it create additional problems?

6. Is the solution fair and just?

Carrie Menkel–Meadow, *Toward Another View of Legal Negotiation: The Structure of Problem Solving*, 31 UCLA L. REV. 754, 760–61 (1984).

(6) Is the best solution preferable to each party's BATNA (Best Alternative to a Negotiated Agreement)?

The negotiators' evaluation of bridging proposals requires both additional information sharing between the parties and the use of arguments. Recall that prior to developing potential bridging solutions, the negotiators using problem-solving tactics shared information about their underlying interests. At this later point in the process, problem-solving negotiators exchange information again. They tell each other how well each of the proposed bridging solutions satisfies their respective clients' interests and which of the possible options their clients prefer.

The negotiators also use arguments to assist in evaluating bridging solutions. A negotiator might argue, for example, that one specific proposal fits her client's needs best. She might also identify for the other counsel the respective advantages and disadvantages of the various proposals as her client views them. Because the other negotiator previously has informed the lawyer of his client's needs and interests, the negotiator additionally is able to assess and argue how each of the proposals satisfies the other party's interests.

How would this evaluation process work in the negotiation between Dr. Volkov and Banting Medical Technologies? In order to keep this analysis manageable, this section will do something that a good problem-solving negotiator would never do: focus only on a single issue—the compensation that Volkov will receive for the licensing of the Viral Sharpshooter technology. Remember the brief solution-generating (brainstorming) session between Jonathan Prevas and Rachel Goldberg, Banting's Vice–President for Research and Development. Together they identified seven options to bridge the gap between Banting's reluctance to pay Volkov a large up-front royalty fee and Volkov's insistence on such a fee:[4]

(1) the payment of royalties to Volkov based on a percentage of the revenues earned from the technology;

(2) the payment to Volkov of additional fees if and when the Viral Sharpshooter Technology achieves certain benchmarks, such as FDA approval or achieving certain results in clinical trials;

(3) the inclusion of a confidentiality clause in the agreement that would protect Banting from creating a dangerous precedent that would cause future researchers to insist on larger fees;

(4) conditioning the payment of larger fees to Volkov on his ability to obtain government funding, perhaps through NIH, to reimburse the costs of necessary further testing, such as clinical trials;

4. *See supra* Chapter Three, *Negotiation Planning*, at 59–61.

(5) Conditioning the payment of larger fees to Volkov on his university providing free testing services or at least reducing their usual overhead charges;

(6) Additional compensation for Volkov through a lucrative long-term consulting contract with Banting; and

(7) A fundraising effort by Banting and Volkov targeted to family members of patients currently suffering from incurable forms of cancer.

Chances are that Jonathan and Rachel will not seriously consider engaging in a joint fundraising campaign focused on family members of cancer victims. It is unlikely that Banting has the institutional capacity to conduct such a campaign. Further, it would be an unseemly public relations disaster if the Viral Sharpshooter in fact becomes very profitable for Banting, and its development costs are borne by family members of cancer victims. Jonathan and Rachel, accordingly, will not introduce this option in their negotiations with Katie and Volkov. Similarly, once the parties begin to negotiate, they probably can make expeditious decisions regarding which of the other alternatives may be viable. For example, university policy may forbid the subsidization of research for drugs or medical technologies that already have been licensed to pharmaceutical manufacturers. Similarly, NIH grant requirements may require reimbursement of research expenditures in this context.

This leaves four options to be evaluated seriously by Katie and Jonathan in their next bargaining session:

(1) the payment of royalties to Volkov based on a percentage of the revenues earned from the technology;

(2) the payment to Volkov of additional fees if and when the Viral Sharpshooter Technology achieves certain benchmarks;

(3) the inclusion of a confidentiality clause; and

(4) a lucrative long-term consulting contract for Volkov.

Without knowing the full range of information available to the two negotiators and the preferences of their client, it is difficult to predict how the evaluation process might proceed from this point. It seems very likely, however, that the eventual agreement will include both some form of compensation for Volkov that is greatly in excess of Banting's usual, up-front lump-sum payment and a confidentiality clause protecting Banting from creating a precedent that might cause other researchers to insist on similar largesse. Banting's interests probably are best protected by a royalty agreement dependent upon sales revenues, but Katie might argue that her client's compensation for his research should not depend in part on Banting's success in marketing the new product or the potential commercial threat that might result from emerging competitive treatments. He might prefer further payments related only to achieving certain defined benchmarks. However, Banting may not be as generous if Volkov refuses to share the risk by agreeing to royalty payments dependent upon commercial success. It is possible that a lucrative consulting agreement would be advantageous to both parties, but it is also possible that Volkov has other plans that would create a conflict of interest or place prohibitive demands on his time.

At this stage of the problem-solving negotiation, the evaluation process should be a joint analysis, where the two lawyers try to decide what alternative meets the requirements and aspirations of both their clients. Although the lawyers may have begun the negotiation process with competitive tactics, no longer will threats and arguments resonate in the negotiation chambers. The lawyers, instead, must participate in a joint analytical process to find an agreement satisfactory to their clients' interests. In whatever manner the bargaining began, this is how many negotiations end.

2. REFINEMENT OF BRIDGING PROPOSALS: INCORPORATION

As described in Chapter Six, the development of bridging proposals during negotiation is a continuing and cyclical process.[5] As new information about the parties' preferences is shared, the proposals originally advanced are modified to reflect a better understanding of the parties' needs.

Two very different variations of this "proposal—response—refined proposal" cycle are described by social psychologist Dean Pruitt.[6] The first, *incorporation*, involves adding to the negotiator's own proposal some element or proposal made by the other party. Consider, for example, Katie Eisinger's problem-solving proposal regarding the compensation terms between Dr. Volkov and Banting Medical Technologies. Katie begins by suggesting the following proposal for compensating Dr. Volkov for the Viral Sharpshooter technology:

(1) Banting Technologies will pay Volkov a lump sum of $500,000 at the time that the parties execute the licensing agreement;

(2) Banting Technologies will pay Volkov an additional $7.5 million at the time of the completion of clinical trials showing specified results; and

(3) Banting Technologies will pay Volkov an additional $7.5 million at the time of FDA approval.

In evaluating this proposal from Banting's perspective, Jonathan Prevas might respond with two objections. First, the proposal does not protect Banting from creating a precedent that would cause other researchers whose technologies had been licensed by Banting either to be jealous or to try to renegotiate their deals. Second, while Volkov becomes rich, Banting bears all the risk that other competing cures for cancer might emerge.

---

5. *See supra* Chapter Six, "Initial Proposals," at pages 139–44.

6. *See* DEAN PRUITT, NEGOTIATION BEHAVIOR 169–86 (1981).

Katie, recognizing the reasonableness of these concerns, could then incorporate a modified version of Jonathan's suggestions into her original proposal. Her refined proposal might look like this:

Katie: We could add to my original proposal a confidentiality clause with the understanding that any breach of the confidentiality clause by Volkov would terminate Banting's further payment obligations.

My client and I also would consider allowing Banting to pay the royalties to Volkov over a period of years. That way, if we can identify the competing technologies that currently are in the pipeline, we would agree that if the FDA were to approve one or more of these other technologies, any remaining payments owed to my client would be reduced.

Katie has incorporated into her original proposal new provisions that specifically address Banting's articulated concerns.

3. REFINEMENT OF BRIDGING PROPOSALS: HEURISTIC TRIAL AND ERROR

Pruitt designates the second method for refining bridging solutions as *"heuristic trial and error."* Using this technique, the negotiator makes frequent variations in her own proposal that only gradually reduce her own client's level of satisfaction with the proposal. These changes do not necessarily respond to any explicit information from the other negotiator; on the contrary, they are often proposed without any idea as to how the other negotiator will react. Accordingly, heuristic trial and error is not a conscious, planned attempt to have the refined proposal meet the underlying interests of the other party. Instead, the negotiator only learns how well her proposal meets the other party's needs when the other negotiator reacts to each of the series of modifications of the original proposal.

The heuristic trial and error approach can be an important tool for the problem-solving negotiator when the other negotiator is unable or unwilling to communicate fully and accurately his client's interests, how well each negotiating proposal meets these interests, or his client's preferences among various proposals. Heuristic trial and error is particularly important in multiple-issue negotiation when the negotiator is unclear as to which of the issues is most important to the other party. Sometimes even the other party himself is not able to consciously rank or prioritize the importance of the issues. In these cases, his responses to a wide variety of proposals on a trial-and-error basis may be the best indicators of what issues are most important to him. For example, one variation of a proposal might include a concession on one issue, whereas a second variation might concede on a different issue. The other party's responses to these two variations implicitly, but reliably, communicate his preference.

C. PROBLEM–SOLVING CLOSURE TACTICS

1. AGREEMENT ON A BRIDGING SOLUTION

Prior chapters discussed the process of inventing bridging solutions that satisfy both parties' underlying interests. As described, this process can occur either between the attorneys during bargaining sessions, or between the lawyer and her client during counseling sessions before or during the negotiation process. In either case, the lawyers ultimately evaluate any proposed solutions from the perspectives of their respective clients during a bargaining session between the lawyers, perhaps attended by the clients as well. Closure in the bridging process occurs when the lawyers (and perhaps their clients) together evaluate the possible alternative bridging solutions and agree that one of the bridging solutions is preferable to the others because it best satisfies the clients' underlying interests. Bridging solutions that totally satisfy all of the aspirations and requirements of both parties, without compromise or diminished expectations, occasionally occur, but are quite rare.[7] In most cases, agreement on a bridging solution requires one or both of the parties to concede on peripheral issues or to have their initial expectations on more important issues frustrated to some extent.

2. LOGROLLING

The most common technique used to achieve final agreement in negotiation is the problem-solving tactic of logrolling, which has been previously described. To review briefly, *logrolling* occurs when the parties exchange concessions on different issues; each party concedes on the issue he cares least about, thus creating high joint benefit. Most negotiations involve multiple issues, and in final bargaining each negotiator frequently offers to concede on one issue in exchange for a concession on an issue more important to her client. For example, let us assume that Banting Medical Technologies and Dr. Volkov have agreed in principle that Volkov will receive both an up-front royalty payment and two subsequent payments when the benchmarks of successful clinical trials and FDA approval occur. Dr. Volkov has always been most interested in a large initial payment because of his desire to assist his brother in emigrating from Russia. Banting, on the other hand, is most concerned about avoiding both (1) a large lump-sum payment that would create a precedent with other scientists with whom it may negotiate and (2) paying too much if the Viral Sharpshooter technology does not prove to be a market success. Banting might agree to a larger up-front payment if the agreement includes both a confidentiality clause and a lesser overall amount of compensation to be reflected in lower subsequent payments.

Logrolling frequently can be used simultaneously with any of the other problem-solving closure tactics—bridging solutions, compensation

---

7. *See id.* at 157.

or cost-cutting. For instance, the previous example, you will recognize in a moment, combined logrolling with cost-compensation. Even when the negotiators resolve an issue using one of these other problem-solving tactics, the expectations of one party or the other frequently are frustrated to some extent. In a logrolling compromise, the party's acceptance of the agreement reached on a specific issue through the use of bridging solutions, compensation or cost-cutting, is conditioned upon a favorable resolution of another issue that has a higher priority for him. Any frustration resulting from the resolution of the first issue is outweighed by his enthusiasm for the advantageous resolution of the second issue.

3.   COST–CUTTING

In order for the lawyer and the other negotiator to reach an agreement meeting all the requirements of the lawyer's client, it is often necessary for the other party to make concessions that reduce his level of satisfaction with the agreement. To encourage such a concession, the negotiator may seek to reduce the costs or detriments experienced by the other party in making the concession. Pruitt refers to this process as "cost cutting."[8]

Cost-cutting is any method that reduces the disadvantages to the other party of agreeing to a proposal which benefits the negotiator's client. Two specific forms of cost-cutting, however, are common. The first addresses the other party's concern that if he concedes on an issue during the current negotiation, his concession will set a precedent for future dealings. For example, consider the resolution of the negotiation between Banting Medical Technologies and Dr. Volkov outlined in a previous paragraph. The confidentiality clause agreed to by Banting and Volkov is an example of cost-cutting: it addressed Banting's concern that the larger than usual up-front payment would create a precedent for future bargaining with other medical researchers for their discoveries and also create morale problems with those researchers with whom it already has licensing agreements.

The second common method of cost-cutting is to find a way to reduce the image loss, or slighting of ego, that either the other lawyer or his client may experience when making a concession. Frequently, the other lawyer experiences a sense of diminished status when making a critical concession. For example, if Maria Santiago is a young attorney and she makes a large concession at the end of the negotiation with Ashton Crutchfield, she might perceive that Ashton or others would view her as a less worthy negotiator, in other words, she fears a loss of professional esteem. To mitigate the ego damage, Ashton might comment that at the beginning of negotiation when she had demanded $3.5 million, Maria was not aware of the strong evidence undermining Michael Van Meter's case. Through this comment, Ashton suggests that, in his eyes, neither Maria's initial high demand nor the subsequent large concession resulted from her inexperience. Ashton might also suggest

8.   *Id.* at 142–48.

that Maria and he probably will negotiate some other matter in the future and on that occasion, "It will be [his] turn" to make the final major concession.

4. COMPENSATION

As previously described, *compensation* is a problem-solving tactic which indemnifies the other party for making concessions.[9] In exchange for a concession that her client requires for an agreement, the negotiator provides the other party something in return. Logrolling is a form of compensation in which the consideration for the concession is a concession on a different issue. As another example of compensation, consider the negotiation between Dr. Volkov and Banting Medical Technologies, Inc. In exchange for conceding to a reduced lump-sum royalty payment to Volkov, Banting Medical Technologies might agree to provide Dr. Volkov with valuable laboratory space or laboratory equipment. Even though the lab space and equipment were not among the items originally scheduled to be negotiated, Banting may find it more advantageous to supply them as a means of "compensating" Volkov for a reduced royalty payment, than it would be to agree to higher royalty payments that would create problems now and in the future with other researchers.

D. ACHIEVING CLOSURE ON LEARNING ABOUT THE NEGOTIATION PROCESS

Closure marks the last of the negotiation processes. It is possible that in multiple-issue negotiation closure may be achieved on one issue while other issues remain in stages characterized by "narrowing of differences" tactics or even information gathering tactics. Despite the unevenness of issue development in a particular negotiation, this discussion of closure completes this book's analysis of the basic negotiation process between lawyers representing two parties. Chapter 9 will describe the added complexities of multiple-party negotiation and a few new tactics primarily suited for use in these negotiations.

This is an appropriate point, however, to stress that every negotiator uses tactics from each of the three negotiating strategies in virtually every negotiation. The negotiator who uses only competitive tactics and never concedes, for example, will find that all of her negotiations terminate prematurely without agreement. Conversely, the cooperative negotiator who never holds the line and never threatens either implicitly or explicitly to terminate negotiation, does not negotiate—she only capitulates to demands. The negotiator who always seeks to find bridging solutions and who fails to realize the distributive nature of many issues will soon learn that all negotiators must compromise.

People go through life using a mixture of competitive, cooperative and problem-solving tactics in day-to-day human relationships. If you now consciously recognize some of your own behaviors as negotiation

---

9. *Id.* at 148–53.

tactics, then this text has succeeded. Such recognition allows you to make deliberate choices regarding tactical decisions in legal negotiation. None of us has perfect instincts for choosing the most effective tactics in every legal negotiation. Conscious analysis helps.

Chapter Nine

MULTIPLE–PARTY NEGOTIATION

A. INTRODUCTION

The previous chapters have focused upon negotiation as an interaction between two participants. Many negotiations, however, involve more than two parties. For example, multiple defendants increasingly are joined in civil litigation. Or consider a construction dispute between the owner of a building and the general contractor. Ultimately, the negotiation may involve attorneys representing architects, engineers, subcontractors and various other parties' sureties. Similarly, labor negotiations frequently include multiple unions and bargaining units, and in corporate bankruptcy reorganizations, many creditors usually negotiate. Even decisions of public agencies, such as where to locate a hazardous waste disposal site, typically involve protracted negotiations among a number of interest groups.

In the arena of international diplomacy, an extreme example of multiple-party negotiation has been the continuing negotiations under the umbrella of the United Nations Framework Convention on Climate Change (FCCC).[1] In 1990, the UN General Assembly facilitated an intergovernmental negotiation that resulted in the drafting of the FCCC, which subsequently was ratified by 188 parties, including the United States. Years of prolonged, complicated, and intense negotiations under the FCCC led to the adoption of the Kyoto Protocol, which became effective in February 2005 after its ratification by 168 parties.[2]

The analysis of the negotiation process described in previous chapters generally applies to multiple-party negotiation. In such negotiations, as in two-party bargaining, the participants choose among *competitive*, *cooperative*, and *problem-solving* tactics. Multiple-party negotiation, how-

---

1. *See* United Nations Framework Convention on Climate Change (1992), *available at* http://unfccc.int/resource/docs/convkp/conveng.pdf (last visited April 18, 2007). *See generally* John H. Knox, *The International Legal Framework for Address-*

ing Climate Change, 12 PENN ST. ENVTL. L. REV. 135 (2004).

2. *See* Kyoto Protocol (1998), *available at* http://unfccc.int/resource/docs/convkp/kpeng.pdf (last visited April 18, 2007). As of

ever, is a more complex process than two-party negotiation. As the number of negotiating parties increases, frequently so do the number of issues to be resolved and the time it takes to reach an agreement.

Even in the planning stages, the increasing complexity of multiple-party negotiation substantially affects the process. The client's alternatives to a negotiated agreement among all the parties include the possibility of reaching agreements with some, but not all, of the negotiating partners. Conversely, often the number of possible alternatives to a negotiated agreement available to the other parties is increased by the prospect of some group of these parties reaching an agreement among themselves that excludes the negotiator's client. Therefore, an analysis of bargaining power in multiple-party negotiations must include consideration of the client's ability to reach agreements and form coalitions with a subset of the parties, and the other parties' abilities to do the same.

The lawyer chooses between two basic approaches when negotiating with multiple parties. The first is to intentionally seek to build coalitions or bargaining alliances between her client and other negotiating parties, and then to bargain on behalf of the coalition with the remaining parties. This approach to multiple-party negotiation follows naturally from the *positional* conception of negotiation inherent in the competitive and cooperative strategies, notwithstanding that negotiators can employ problem-solving, as well as competitive and cooperative, tactics in both forming coalitions and when negotiating with other coalitions or parties. This process is analyzed in the next section of this chapter. The second approach is for the representatives of all the parties to negotiate together in an attempt to identify a proposal or package of proposals that satisfies all the parties' underlying interests. This approach obviously is related closely to the problem-solving strategy.

Just as the use of competitive tactics does not preclude the use of problem-solving tactics at another point in the negotiation, the tactics outlined in this chapter are not mutually exclusive. For example, a coalition formed among the developed, more industrialized nations in climate-control negotiations might also prepare a "single text" for presentation to all other nations as a part of an ongoing negotiation. Further, it is important to reiterate that all the tactics described in previous chapters can be used in multiple-party negotiation.

B. COALITION FORMATION

1. AN OVERVIEW OF COALITIONS AND NEGOTIATION

The primary characteristic of multiple-party negotiation is the formation of bargaining coalitions among some or all of the negotiation partners.[3] A *coalition* is the joining of power or resources of two or more

---

June 2007, the ratifying parties did not include the United States.

3. *See* HOWARD RAIFFA, NEGOTIATION ANALYSIS: THE SCIENCE AND ART OF COLLABORATIVE

DECISION MAKING 430–49 (2002); JEFFERY Z. RUBIN & BERT R. BROWN, THE SOCIAL PSYCHOLO-

parties so that they have greater ability to determine the content of the negotiated agreement.

In most legal negotiations, bargaining alliances emerge sooner or later. When entering into such coalitions, the parties typically agree upon what each needs to receive in order to be satisfied with a negotiated agreement. Therefore, the process of entering into a coalition with another party is much like any other negotiation between two parties. The negotiation to form a coalition includes the use of problem-solving, cooperative and competitive tactics. This coalition then proceeds to negotiate with other coalitions or with another individual party that has not yet joined a coalition. In these negotiations, the negotiators once again use competitive, cooperative and problem-solving tactics. In short, multiple-party negotiation is perceived as a series of two-party negotiations.

The bargaining among coalition members includes elements of the *counseling process* as well as those of the negotiation process. When each party to the coalition is representing its own interests in the intra-party bargaining among members of the coalition, the parties use traditional negotiation tactics. When, however, the members of the coalition together consider what bargaining positions and tactics to use in negotiation with other coalitions or lone parties, this process resembles the pre-negotiation planning process between the attorney and client described in Chapter Three. Obviously, the two processes intertwine.

2. A THEORETICAL PERSPECTIVE ON COALITION FORMATION

Most research regarding coalitions focuses on the variable of power and its effect on coalition formation.[4] This research suggests that coalitions tend to form when parties perceive that they lack the bargaining leverage necessary to obtain the results they desire without such alliances.

Somewhat surprisingly, the research finds that when there are three negotiating parties, the two less powerful parties tend to form a coalition instead of either of them joining forces with the stronger party.[5] Each of the weaker parties apparently fears exploitation by a more powerful coalition partner. A party's decision to join a coalition thus is influenced not only by the potential coalition's prospects for success in the negotiation, but also by how it will fare in the "intra-coalition" bargaining, when the benefits to be "won" by the coalition in the negotiation are

gy of Bargaining and Negotiation 64–79 (1975); Henk A. Wilke, *Coalition Formation From A Socio-Psychological Perspective, in* Coalition Formation 115–72 (Henk A. Wilke ed., 1985). *See also* Hubert M. Blalock & Paul H. Wilken, Intergroup Processes: A Micro–Macro Perspective 394–96, 405–08 (1979); James P. Kahan & Amnon Rapoport, Theories of Coalition Formation (1984); Charles E. Miller, *Coalition Formation in Characteristic Function Games: Competitive Tests of Three Theories*, 16 J. of Experimental Soc. Psychol. 61–76 (1980).

4. *See, e.g.*, Blalock & Wilken, *supra* note 3, at 394–95, 405–08; Rubin & Brown, *supra* note 3, at 64–74.

5. *See, e.g.*, Rubin & Brown, *supra* note 3, at 73–74.

divided. On one hand, the ideal coalition partner is strong enough to add the bargaining leverage required to succeed in the negotiation. On the other hand, the prospective partner should be weak enough to allow the negotiator to dominate the bargaining among coalition members. The spoils of a coalition's negotiation "victory" are likely to be shared in a manner proportional to the perceived bargaining power of the respective coalition members.

Social scientists' analysis of coalitions in multiple-party negotiation suggests that under two conditions, coalitions usually will not be formed.[6] First, coalitions do not form when it is useless to do so because one party would still possess overwhelming bargaining power even after coalition formation. Second, a party with strong bargaining power may actively attempt to prevent coalitions from forming among other negotiators by establishing a counter-coalition with one of the weaker parties or by instigating divisiveness or contention among these parties.

A party's attractiveness as a coalition partner is influenced not only by its bargaining power, but also by its perceived status and the bargaining ability of its lawyer or other negotiator. In addition, the party's reputation for success in past negotiations and its track record for honoring its past commitments to its coalition partners often play a role.

3. APPLICATION TO LEGAL NEGOTIATION

How does the theoretical work of scholars regarding coalition analysis apply to multiple-party legal negotiation? This section applies coalition analysis to two legal negotiations: the first is a litigation example and the second is a transactional negotiation.

Consider hypothetically a medical malpractice case filed on behalf of the estate of Lee Buccarelli. Lee died during an operation, allegedly because of a reaction to the anesthetic. The executor of Lee's estate has filed suit against the anesthesiologist, the attending surgeon and the hospital. During discovery, plaintiff's attorney learns that the patient's death probably resulted from an excessive dose of anesthetic caused by a malfunctioning valve in a piece of equipment manufactured by Medical Devices, Inc. Accordingly, Medical Devices is joined as a defendant.[7]

Prior to discovery, the defendants in Lee's lawsuit likely view themselves as belonging to a bargaining coalition with the plaintiff standing alone on the other side of the case. As in most cases, the defendants here begin with common interests in denying liability and in minimizing the amount of damages to be paid to the victim. Further, the attorneys representing the various health care providers may have worked with each other in the past; they also probably share a certain

---

6. *Id.* at 71–73.

7. For purposes of this negotiation hypothetical, I am ignoring any preemptive effect of the Medical Device Amendments of

1976, Pub. L. No. 94–295, 90 Stat. 539 (codified at 21 U.S.C. §§ 360c–360k (2000)). *See, e.g.,* Medtronic, Inc. v. Lohr, 518 U. S. 470, 475 (1996).

ideological and psychological perspective when malpractice claimants sue their clients.

As the lawsuit progresses, however, this initially defined alignment of the parties changes. The anesthesiologist and the surgeon both possess knowledge about the operating room incident helpful to the plaintiff's attorney in establishing a case against Medical Devices, Inc. or even against the hospital. Conversely, the plaintiff's attorney has the bargaining power to grant each of the physicians what they desire—a quick release and exit from the lawsuit without substantial payment. Therefore, favorable conditions exist for the building of a coalition between the estate of the plaintiff and either of the two defendant physicians. In exchange for their testimony and cooperation against Medical Devices—the product manufacturer—or against the hospital, the physicians obtain dismissals from the litigation.

How might the attorneys representing Medical Devices, Inc. or the hospital prevent the formation of this coalition? As suggested by coalition theory, counsel for these defendants might attempt to form a "counter-coalition" focused on either denial of liability or minimization of the plaintiff's damages. Similarly, these attorneys might seek to instigate divisiveness or contention between the plaintiff and the two physicians; for example, in communicating with the physicians' attorneys, counsel for Medical Devices might stress the lack of merit of the plaintiff's case as a whole.

A second example of coalition bargaining occurs in the transactional negotiation between the management and the various creditors of a hypothetical corporation, the "Omigosh Mfg. Co."[8] Omigosh is insolvent and seeks to prevent involuntary liquidation in bankruptcy by reaching an agreement with its creditors to continue the business. The various creditors and owners all stand to lose—most of them substantially—if the business is sold for liquidation value. If Omigosh is to avoid such a fate, however, the creditors must give up some of their rights, perhaps agreeing to defer payment of obligations owed to them or even to loan new money to the debtor-corporation.

The negotiation is chaired by an attorney representing Omigosh and includes attorneys representing (1) the shareholders who own the corporation and who recently advanced personal funds to enable the corporation to meet its payroll, (2) the Certain Insurance Company that is owed $4 million on a fifteen-year note secured by a first mortgage on all the corporation's real estate, plant and equipment, and (3) the Unsure Financial Corporation, the short-term lender whose $6 million revolving line-of-credit is secured by a lien on accounts receivables and inventory. Further, a single attorney represents the more than 300 unsecured creditors, mostly "trade" creditors who supply parts, supplies and essen-

---

8. This example is taken from the transcript of a fascinating mock creditors' meeting enacted at the August 2, 1983 meeting of the Commercial Financial Services Committee of the Section on Corporation, Banking and Business Law of the American Bar Association and reprinted in Maury B. Poscover, *The Business in Trouble—A Workout Without Bankruptcy*, 39 Bus. Law. 1041 (1984).

tial raw materials, and who are owed a total of $2.75 million. Finally, a tax consultant hired by management attends the meeting and advises the lawyers present concerning both a multi-million dollar tax refund that may be owed the corporation and overdue payroll taxes. Not represented in this creditors' meeting is an injured judgment debtor who recently obtained a $3 million products-liability verdict against Omigosh, which the company's attorneys believe will be upheld on appeal, and various labor unions representing the company's employees.

Negotiation in the Omigosh case proceeds in a manner typical of bargaining among creditors in this situation. Despite its weak financial condition, Omigosh has considerable bargaining power, because the creditors' alternatives to a negotiated agreement are so unattractive. During the creditors' meeting, two secured creditors, Unsure and Certain, form a coalition. Unsure, the accounts receivable and inventory lender, indicates its willingness to extend further credit provided that it is given a second lien on the company's fixed assets. Certain, unwilling to extend additional funds itself, agrees to allow Unsure to take a second lien on the real estate, plants, and equipment that are subject to Certain's first mortgage, so long as Unsure agrees not to initiate foreclosure proceedings. By entering into this agreement, Unsure has improved its priority in regard to the fixed assets when compared with the interests of all other creditors. The two secured creditors, Unsure and Certain, thus form a bargaining coalition in opposition to the interests of the unsecured creditors who also are capable of bargaining as a unit with Omigosh management. In the intra-coalition bargaining between Unsure and Certain, it is Certain who has the stronger bargaining position as a result of its fully secured status. As predicted by coalition theory, it is Unsure, therefore, who concedes and agrees to advance additional funds.

This coalition of Certain and Unsure then proceeds to negotiate with the company for other new priorities and an increased voice in company management. Ultimately, Certain agrees to defer collection of principal repayment on its loan from Omigosh in exchange for receiving both increased rights to monitor the business and the personal guarantees of the principal shareholders that they will stand by the corporation's debts. Together the two secured creditors have more bargaining leverage than either one would have alone, and more than enough to extract concessions from Omigosh and its shareholders. Eventually, the unsecured creditors, with little bargaining power, join the agreement in exchange for modest concessions. Parties not represented at the creditors' meeting, most notably the labor unions and the product liability judgment creditor, receive no concessions, but still are probably better off than if the company had been liquidated.

C. STRUCTURING MULTIPLE–PARTY NEGOTIATION

In some ways, the two-party negotiation dyad is a relatively uncomplicated social interaction. As more and more parties become involved in bargaining, however, the issue of structure or organization during the bargaining process becomes more important. For instance, in purely logistical terms, how do 188 nations negotiate an agreement addressing climate change? How is an agreement reached to handle hundreds of large personal injury claims among more than sixteen liability insurers and thirty-four asbestos manufacturers in intertwined insurance coverage disputes that involve shifting insurance coverages over a fifty year period?[9] If all the negotiators in such a "mega-negotiation" simply extrapolate from ordinary negotiation tactics, the process probably is doomed to end in confusion or stalemate. Scores of separate initial proposals, counterproposals, and reactions to proposals in the form of arguments, threats and concessions—without any imposed structure— are unlikely to produce agreement.

Particularly when the number of participants becomes very large, multiple-party negotiation requires consciously designed negotiation structures unnecessary in the two-party context. At some point, negotiation among 188 nations or 50 insurance carriers and asbestos manufacturers resembles a legislature more than it does the more traditional negotiation dyad. These large negotiations require agreement on procedures, almost a set of parliamentary rules of order for conducting the negotiation process. Multiple-party negotiators usually benefit as well from the presence of a chairperson or other similar facilitator to guide the deliberations.[10]

Even in multiple-party negotiations involving smaller groups, structure often is required. The participants in these negotiations usually should agree on an agenda and specify a process for reaching agreement. Often, it is desirable to designate one person to serve as a facilitator of the negotiation. This individual can be either a *mediator*—a neutral third party—or one of the negotiators herself. The use of *mediators* as neutral third-party facilitators is even more helpful in multiple-party negotiation than it is in two-party negotiation because the mediator has the ability to structure the negotiation process involving many parties that otherwise might descend into chaos. Further, mediators facilitate the use of problem-solving tactics, and the complexity of multiple-party negotiation usually necessitates the use of such tactics. Mediation and its effect on the negotiation process are discussed more fully in Chapter Twelve.

When a mediator is not available, one of the negotiators sometimes serves as a chairperson or facilitator of negotiation discussions. In most cases, the individual chosen should have moderate views, understand the conflicting interests of the different parties, and often represent a party with only a minor role in the negotiation. In other cases, the respect

9. From October 1982 through June 1985, Dean Henry Wellington of the Yale Law School facilitated negotiations among asbestos manufacturers, liability insurers and plaintiffs' attorneys. The resulting agreement, the Wellington Plan, established a voluntary nonprofit asbestos-claims facili-ty for settling and arbitrating asbestosis claims while preserving the claimant's right to a jury trial. *See* PAUL BRODEUR, OUTRAGEOUS MISCONDUCT 293, 335–36 (1985).

10. *See* RAIFFA, *supra* note 3, at 484–87.

shared by the parties for a particular lawyer or other negotiator makes
her an appropriate choice as facilitator. For example, even though the
attorney for Omigosh had more than a minor interest in negotiating the
inter-creditors' agreement, he was an obvious choice to facilitate the
discussion because of his role as a "stakeholder" and his impartiality
among the interests of the various creditors.

D. SINGLE NEGOTIATION TEXT

Another technique for structuring multiple-party negotiations, the
so-called *"single negotiation text,"* deserves special attention. The single
negotiation text is a problem-solving negotiation procedure of particular
value in multiple-party negotiations.[11] In this process, one of the negotiating parties or its lawyer, or a neutral third party, drafts a proposed
agreement and asks the other negotiators for their suggestions and
criticisms. At this point, the other negotiators are not asked to accept
the proposal or to evaluate its overall desirability, but only to make
comments and suggestions. After receiving specific suggestions and criticisms from the other negotiators, the original author redrafts the proposal, taking into account the feedback she has received and incorporating
the other parties' suggestions. She then submits the revised draft to the
parties. The process of soliciting criticism and redrafting begins again,
and may recur three or four times—or even twenty or thirty times.

No single negotiator usually perceives the single negotiation text as
becoming a better document at every step of the process. It is more likely
that a negotiator finds that one round of modifications to the text results
in a substantial improvement from her client's perspective—sometimes
at the expense of other parties—but that the next set of changes benefits
other parties, perhaps to her own client's detriment. Because the negotiators all desire to reach agreement, however, they probably tolerate
changes that modestly diminish their own clients' level of satisfaction as
the process moves along. Eventually the drafter believes that the current
draft does the best possible job of addressing the parties' interests, and
she submits it to the parties for their possible acceptance.

The single negotiation text, of course, can be used even in two-party
negotiation. When multiple parties negotiate, however, some type of a
focal point is required, and thus the single negotiation text is particularly important in this context.

Probably the most famous use of the single negotiation text occurred
during the negotiation between President Sadat of Egypt and Prime
Minister Begin of Israel at Camp David during 1978.[12] Representatives of
the United States, after listening to the Egyptian and Israeli delegations,
prepared an initial single negotiation text, which then went through

11. *See* ROGER FISHER, WILLIAM URY & BRUCE PATTON, GETTING TO YES: NEGOTIATING AGREEMENT WITHOUT GIVING IN 112–16 (2d ed. 1991); DAVID A. LAX & JAMES K. SEBENIUS, THE MANAGER AS NEGOTIATOR: BARGAINING FOR COOP- ERATION AND COMPETITIVE GAIN 176–78 (1986); RAIFFA, *supra* note 3, at 320–26.

12. FISHER, URY & PATTON, *supra* note 11, at 116.

twenty-three more drafts during the next thirteen days. At that point, the American facilitators believed that no further improvement was possible, and they recommended adoption of the text. Both Egypt and Israel agreed.

The use of the single negotiation text, however, is not limited to international diplomacy. Often committee chairpersons circulate a draft of a proposal or report to members of the committee and invite their feedback either prior to a subsequent meeting or during the meeting itself. After receiving the comments of other committee members, the chair or committee staff makes revisions. Consider also the example of a state legislature driven to address a perceived medical malpractice crisis by public outcry over dramatically increased medical malpractice premiums.[13] The professional staff of a state study commission that has been investigating the malpractice crisis, working together with legislative counsel, offers a comprehensive "draft" reform proposal. This initial draft legislation is widely circulated among key legislators, the governor's office, and representatives of various interest groups including physicians, hospitals, lawyers, insurance companies and consumer groups. As in other single negotiation text process, changes are made as a result of feedback, and the process is repeated. In most instances in the political arena, it is not possible to achieve the support of all the affected interest groups; some end up opposing the legislation. Eventually, however, after many drafts and modifications, the proposal attracts support from enough of the key legislators and interest groups, many of whose suggestions have been incorporated into the draft legislation by now, to be enacted into law.

The single negotiation text process is most effective if the individual drafting the proposal, soliciting criticism, and redrafting the agreement, is a mediator or other third party. Under these circumstances, the initial proposal is likely to be an honest attempt to reconcile the conflicting parties' interests, and not a document drafted to manipulate the negotiating process. Moreover, when a neutral mediator drafts the initial proposal, the negotiators often are more comfortable offering honest criticisms and suggestions. It is understood by the participants that no one, not even the author, is committed to the initial draft.

The single negotiation text procedure does not require the negotiator to make any concessions until the final stage of the process, when she is asked to accept the final version of the text. Instead, during the earlier phases of the process, she is asked only for her input, suggestions, and criticisms. With each successive draft, the negotiator is able to effectively communicate her client's priorities. The client's reactions to various provisions of the draft agreement reflect acquiescence on some issues and continued resistance on others. This is accomplished, howev-

13. The process described here reflects my personal experience as Associate Director of the State of Florida's Academic Task Force for Review of the Liability and Insurance Systems, a study commission created by the state legislature of Florida in 1986 to investigate why liability insurance sometimes was either unaffordable or unavailable and to report back with recommendations for changes in the State's laws.

er, without any image loss; the negotiator's response or lack of response to any particular provision of the single negotiation text does not communicate to the other negotiators that her bargaining resolve is being weakened or that their competitive bargaining tactics are working.

The single negotiation text can be used as a means of structuring complex multiple-party negotiations, even when a neutral facilitator is not available and one of the negotiators drafts the text. Under these circumstances, the negotiators should choose one among them whom they perceive to be capable of acting somewhat impartially and appreciating the other negotiators' interests. During the single negotiation text procedure, the other negotiators should evaluate carefully if the draft proposal, prepared by their negotiating counterpart, is a good faith attempt to provide a reasonable basis from which to begin bargaining, or whether it is so one-sided that it is intentionally drafted to gain a substantial initial negotiating advantage.

Just as the negotiator drafting a single negotiation text sometimes seeks to use the process to gain an unfair competitive advantage, the other participants also may seek to manipulate the process. Negotiators, when criticizing the single negotiation text and making suggestions, sometimes intentionally overstate their requirements or objections to a draft. In other words, the negotiator employs a form of the false demand tactic, believing that her subsequent acquiescence on issues she previously criticized, but of little real concern to her, will result in her negotiating counterparts' reciprocal flexibility on issues that are important to her. Like all competitive tactics, however, this game-playing can backfire. The chances of negotiation stalemate and breakdown are greater in multi-party negotiation because of the complexities of achieving consensus among many parties. In addition, in multi-party negotiations the competitive negotiator also risks the possibility that the other parties will reach an agreement that excludes her.

The single negotiation text is only one of several problem-solving tactics particularly well suited for use in multiple-party negotiations. The frequently precarious nature of reaching agreement in multiple-party negotiations means that competitive negotiating tactics, such as extreme proposals, bluffing, and information concealment, usually result in frustration and stalemate, at least in those negotiations where the parties do not readily divide into two bargaining coalitions. Therefore, from the negotiator's perspective, the most important difference between bargaining in the multiple-party context and bargaining in the simpler two-party context remains the increased importance of using various problem-solving tactics to determine whether there is a zone of agreement that satisfies the underlying interests of the many participants.

Chapter Ten

NEGOTIATION COUNSELING

A. INTRODUCTION

Legal negotiation is representative negotiation. It involves not only a relationship between the two negotiating attorneys, but also relationships between each lawyer and her respective client. In order to achieve the best possible negotiated agreement, the lawyer's ability as a counselor is at least as important as her negotiation skills. If the lawyer's effectiveness as a negotiator is measured by the extent to which the negotiated agreement serves the client's interests, the lawyer's ability to understand those interests is critical.

Counseling can be defined as the interaction between the lawyer and the client as they decide how to achieve the client's best interests. Chapter Three, "Negotiation Planning," described the planning process preceding negotiation as a joint one between the attorney and her client. Thus, the first opportunity in the negotiation process for client counseling occurs when the attorney and client prepare for the negotiation.

Whether to pursue or forgo the option of negotiating with a particular party is the most important decision during the initial client-counseling session. Dr. Volkov, for example, might decide not to negotiate with Banting Medical Technologies, but instead to substitute negotiation with another manufacturer of medical devices or pharmaceutical company. Similarly, Michael Van Meter might choose a path other than settlement. He might forgo the claim entirely if Maria's evaluation of the case against Baltimore & Washington Railroad indicates only a slim chance of recovery. In a different situation, Michael might feel so much anger toward the defendant that he would vehemently oppose any settlement talks and insist on a trial as soon as possible.

As suggested in Chapter Three, other decisions are made during the client-counseling conference prior to negotiation. The attorney and client decide the content of initial proposals and settle on which of the client's more important interests should be stressed during the negotiation. Optimally, the attorney and client discuss possible negotiating tactics and evaluate their effectiveness in achieving agreement and their impact on the client's ongoing relationship with the other party.

At the other end of the negotiation process, when the attorney concludes that she has received the best possible deal that this negotiation can produce, she and the client then engage in the "final" client-counseling conference. During this conference, they together decide whether to accept the negotiated agreement or pursue other alternatives such as litigation or negotiation with other parties.

Client counseling does not end with the beginning of negotiation, however, only to be resumed after the bargaining is completed. Instead, client-counseling conferences usually are interspersed throughout the negotiation process. The lawyer should confer often with her client during the course of the negotiation and report to him on proposals advanced by the other party and new information gained during the bargaining process. In fact, *Model Rule of Professional Conduct 1.4* requires such updating.[1] New information gleaned from the negotiating process itself and the negotiating behavior of the other attorney often cause the attorney and her client to change their assessment of how to achieve the client's best interests.

The next part of this chapter considers the conflict between client-centered advocacy and the tendency of many attorneys to dominate the client-counseling process. Part C of this chapter then discusses the client-counseling conference following the completion of the negotiations, when the client must choose between the negotiated agreement and other alternatives. Finally, Part D analyzes client-counseling conferences that occur during the ongoing negotiation itself. I analyze client counseling that follows negotiation before consideration of counseling sessions during negotiation, because the post-negotiation counseling sessions present the structure of client counseling in its simplest and purest form. The content and structure of counseling conferences during the negotiation itself are more varied. Further, these counseling sessions involve a greater mixture of issues related to both the substance of the negotiation proposals and the negotiation process itself.

Note that this clear distinction between the client-counseling conference that occurs after negotiation and client-counseling sessions during

---

1. *Model Rule of Professional Conduct 1.4* provides:

(a) A lawyer shall:

(1) promptly inform the client of any decision or circumstance with respect to which the client's informed consent, as defined in Rule 1.0(e), is required by these Rules;

(2) reasonably consult with the client about the means by which the client's objectives are to be accomplished;

(3) keep the client reasonably informed about the status of the matter;

(4) promptly comply with reasonable requests for information; and

(5) consult with the client about any relevant limitation on the lawyer's conduct when the lawyer knows that the client expects assistance not permitted by the Rules of Professional Conduct or other law.

(b) A lawyer shall explain a matter to the extent reasonably necessary to permit the client to make informed decisions regarding the representation.

MODEL RULES OF PROF'L CONDUCT R. 1.4 (2006).

negotiation is oversimplified in at least two ways. First, in many negotiations the client gives the attorney authority to accept a proposal containing certain terms before the attorneys in fact have reached agreement on such a proposal. In these cases, there is no "post-negotiation" client-counseling session in which the client must make a "yes or no" decision on an agreement reached by the attorneys. Thus, the most significant client-counseling session in these situations is the one during negotiation when the client gives his attorney authority to make a specific proposal or to accept a certain offer from the other party. In other words, the structure of client-counseling sessions during negotiation changes substantially depending upon what type of bargaining authority the client grants his attorney.

The second oversimplification underlying the notion of a separate and distinct client-counseling conference following negotiation is the illusion that the attorney and client always will know when the negotiation is finished. If the client grants his attorney authority to enter into an agreement on given terms, then it is always possible that the other party will accept those terms during the next round of negotiation. Accordingly, a conference perceived by the attorney and client to be an intra-negotiation counseling session may in fact be the final counseling session when a *de facto* decision to accept a negotiated agreement is made. Conversely, the attorney and client may believe at the time that a counseling conference is the "final" counseling conference, only to find that it is followed by additional rounds of bargaining. As previously discussed,[2] although the other negotiator may claim that he can concede no further in a negotiation, he often finds a way to reopen a stalemated negotiation following the negotiator's rejection of his final offer. A client-counseling conference in which the negotiator's client decides to reject the negotiated agreement, therefore, may turn out to be only an intra-negotiation counseling conference.

In any of these client-counseling contexts, decision-making is the focus. Should Dr. Volkov begin negotiations with Banting Medical Technologies? What proposals should be made to the other party? Which of the client's interests are most important? Which negotiating tactics should be used? Should the negotiated agreement be rejected or accepted?

A negotiated agreement that maximizes the satisfaction of the client depends as much upon understanding the client's interests—and in assuring that the agreement meets these interests—as they do on the lawyer's negotiation skills. Because of this, and because client counseling takes on a few interesting wrinkles in the negotiation context that may not be present in client-counseling situations not involving negotiation, counseling is presented as an integral part of this text.[3]

---

2. *See supra* pages 166–68.

3. The decision whether to address the vagaries of client counseling in a legal negotiation text is a difficult one. A single chapter on client counseling does justice to neither the importance nor the difficulty of effective client counseling. Separate law school courses and distinct law school texts

B. THE LAWYER'S TENDENCY TO DOMINATE NEGOTIATION COUNSELING

The *Model Rules of Professional Conduct* explicitly provide that the decision to accept a negotiated agreement is to be made by the client, not the lawyer.[4] Further, under the *Model Rules*, lawyers are required to consult with clients about the means of their representation.[5] There is nothing surprising about these professional norms. The essence of the lawyer's role is to represent the client's interests. In the context of negotiation, the quality of the lawyer's role as a hired professional negotiator should be judged only by how well the agreement serves such interests.

Client counseling is fundamentally a process of identifying all available alternatives, considering the advantages and disadvantages of each alternative, and reaching a decision that maximizes the client's interests. It is an interactive process between attorney and client. Only the client knows his own underlying interests and how he weighs the importance of various issues. Accordingly, only he can make the decision to accept or reject a negotiated agreement. On the other hand, the lawyer contributes her legal and practical expertise to the client's decision-making process. Her expertise is supplemented by the information and insights she gleans from the negotiation itself.

Unfortunately, lawyers sometimes exceed their proper roles of informing and facilitating the client's decision-making process. They dominate counseling conferences in ways that contravene the lawyer's appropriate professional role and jeopardize the chances for a negotiated agreement that actually serves the client's underlying interests. Many attorneys in the past *told* their clients to accept or reject settlement offers, and some probably continue to do so today. This arrogant and erroneous conception of the lawyer's professional role often results from the belief that the lawyer knows better than the client what is in the client's best interests. Clients often willingly abet this domination because they are reluctant to take responsibility for their own decisions.

Frequently, the lawyer undermines the client's decision-making process with greater subtlety. For example, at the beginning of the

are devoted exclusively to client counseling. *See, e.g.,* DAVID A. BINDER, PAUL BERGMAN & SUSAN C. PRICE, LAWYERS AS COUNSELORS: A CLIENT-CENTERED APPROACH (1991). To omit discussion of the counseling process in a negotiation text, however, runs the risk that some law students and lawyers who study legal negotiation will not study legal counseling. Such an omission is critical given the importance of client counseling to effective negotiation. The basic structure of the client-counseling session, outlined in this chapter with a few embellishments, is derived from the client-centered counseling

model presented by Professors Binder, Bergman and Price in their leading text.

4. MODEL RULES OF PROF'L CONDUCT R. 1.2(a) (2006) ("A lawyer shall abide by a client's decision whether to settle a matter.").

5. *Id.* ("[A] lawyer shall abide by a client's decisions concerning the objectives of representation and, as required by Rule 1.4, shall consult with the client as to the means by which they are to be pursued.").

litigation, the lawyer might paint a grim picture of the prospects at trial. Maria Santiago tells Michael that based upon her considerable experience, the jury is almost certain to find that he was comparatively negligent and reduce his damages appreciably, and that the question of the railroad's negligence is a "real gamble." When the Baltimore & Western Railroad makes an offer to settle Michael's case—any offer— Maria is in the position of presenting the offer as a minor miracle, pulled out of the hat by a terrific lawyer-negotiator. From the lawyer's self-interested perspective, the manipulation produces a great result. Her client is ecstatic with her representation. From the client's perspective, however, the situation may be tragic. The manner in which Maria has presented the offer to her client has enabled her to substantially engineer her client's acceptance of the offer. Michael probably decides to accept the offer without knowing that he may have a substantial chance of doing much better at trial. Client-centered advocacy requires unbiased and accurate information about each of the available alternatives.

Even lawyers who believe that the client should make the final settlement decision often experience the urge to dominate the client's decision-making process. The lawyer may sense that she knows more about the litigation or the transaction than does the client, and she is in a better position to make a decision. She also understands the negotiation process better than the client. Therefore, she believes that she is in a better position to decide what to include in a negotiation proposal because she knows what the other party is likely to accept or reject.

Participating in the negotiation process often psychologically encourages the lawyer to seize control of the client-counseling process. On one hand, it is the lawyer who actively competes in the negotiation process. It is difficult for most lawyers to report back to clients after an ego-involving negotiation session, only to have their clients tell them that they wish to pursue a different proposal or negotiation strategy. The lawyer naturally wants the client to accept the fruits of her negotiating efforts. In other cases, ironically, the lawyer's anxiety about her inability to control the uncertainties of the negotiation process compels her to establish control wherever she can—such as over her client during counseling sessions.

Choices regarding the substance of a negotiated agreement and negotiation tactics must be the client's if the agreement is to effectively serve his interests—attorney Maria Santiago goes on to represent another client; Michael Van Meter remains a paraplegic. If Maria believes there is an eighty percent chance of realizing a verdict in excess of $2.4 million dollars, a utilitarian calculation therefore suggests that any offer less than $1,920,000 should be rejected. Is Michael "wrong" to decide to accept an offer of $1.5 million? Is anyone else really in Michael's position to choose between a certain $1.5 million and a good chance—but still a chance—of a verdict in excess of $2.4 million? Also, could Maria's desire to try the case be influenced by extraneous factors such as the valuable publicity she would receive if she wins a multi-million dollar verdict for her client?

The counseling model outlined here is designed to allow the client the greatest possible autonomy in accepting or rejecting a negotiated agreement and in making other decisions that affect the negotiation process. There are limits, however, to the impact that any counseling model or structure can have on the allocation of decision-making authority between the attorney and the clients. It is more important for you to appreciate the importance of client-centered advocacy and the tendencies that push lawyers to dominate their clients than it is for you to adopt any particular structure for counseling sessions. Does the lawyer best serve her client's interests by communicating frequently with her client, contributing her expertise and experience to the collaborative relationship and seeking agreements that stress the client's articulated interests? Or is the lawyer's proper professional role to decide what is best for the clients she serves, pursue such agreements during the negotiation, and then give clear unambiguous "advice" to the client as to what that person should do?

C. CLIENT COUNSELING FOLLOWING NEGOTIATION

1. TIMING OF THE DECISIVE CLIENT COUNSELING SESSION

Following the negotiation process or late in the bargaining, the attorney and her client confer about the choice between the negotiated agreement and other options. In reality, this primary decision-making conference may occur in a variety of contexts:

(1) the attorneys already have reached a tentative agreement that the client must decide whether to accept and ratify;

(2) the client has received a final offer from the other party that he must accept or reject;

(3) the attorney has advised her client regarding the best possible agreement; or

(4) the attorney and the client are considering the terms of one last final offer in an effort to reach an agreement.

Only in the first context has the negotiation actually concluded. In the third and fourth situations, it is not even clear that an agreement can be reached or what the exact terms of such an agreement would be. Nevertheless, in most negotiations—particularly those involving multiple bargaining sessions between the attorneys—the client often makes the critical choice between a negotiated agreement and other alternatives in a counseling session that occurs before the end of the bargaining. After a few bargaining sessions, the attorney usually can predict the major terms of an eventual agreement with sufficient clarity to present the client with the choice between an agreement on those terms and the other available alternatives. Unless the attorney poses this choice to her client before proposing a "final offer" to the other negotiator, she leaves herself vulnerable to the awkward possibility that she will make a final proposal, the other negotiator will accept it, and then her client will disavow the agreement.

2. DIFFERENCES BETWEEN CLIENT COUNSELING IN THE DISPUTE RESOLUTION AND TRANSACTIONAL CONTEXTS

The exact structure of the client counseling session depends upon the nature of the ongoing relationship between the attorney and the client and the posture of the negotiation, i.e., is it completed or only nearing the critical phase? The format of the counseling conference also likely is different in a *dispute resolution* or litigation case from that in a business or other *transactional* negotiation. In a litigated case, the counseling session following the negotiation usually involves a choice between two clearly delineated alternatives: an agreement, the terms of which either already have been negotiated or will be concluded in the near future, and the probable outcome of a trial.

Critical counseling sessions in *transactional* negotiations often occur at an earlier point when the terms of an agreement are less solidified. At a stage in the negotiation substantially in advance of the resolution of all issues, Dr. Volkov and Banting Medical Technologies probably both decide that they are going to enter an agreement with each other on terms to be negotiated. Volkov does not wait until agreement with Banting Medical Technologies is reached on all minor details before evaluating how well an acceptance of the royalty agreement satisfies his interests when compared with other alternatives, such as negotiating with other companies. Once the parties reach agreement on the major issues, or at least perceive that an agreement eventually will be reached, Volkov and Banting Medical Technologies, in effect, decide to pursue negotiation with the other party to the exclusion of other such alternatives. Occasionally such a negotiation breaks down, but it is not realistic—after an initial commitment to negotiate with a certain party is reached—to view the negotiation as just another alternative. It represents the client's presumptive decision about how he will proceed unless he is surprised by subsequent events during the negotiation. To put it another way, most clients do not proceed with parallel negotiations with all available potential partners on an equal footing and then pick and choose which agreement is best.

This description of transactional negotiation suggests that in most situations there will be, in fact, two critical client-counseling sessions. The first usually occurs early in the negotiation after minimal contact with possible transaction partners. The probable terms of agreement on major issues to be negotiated can be tentatively, if somewhat inaccurately, predicted. At this point, the client decides with which of the potential partners he wishes to negotiate. This initial counseling conference includes consideration of the advantages of a deal with any of the potential negotiation partners and predictions of the eventual terms of an agreement with each of them.

Once the client decides to pursue negotiation with a particular party, and the negotiation has proceeded—interspersed with intra-negotiation counseling sessions between lawyer and client—there will be another important client-counseling conference at or near the conclusion of the negotiation. At this point, the client is asked to consider the detailed provisions of the agreement that has been negotiated and to accept or reject them. If the client finds some terms unacceptable, his alternative in most instances is not to reject the entire agreement, throw it in the wastebasket, and begin negotiation with another party. Instead, he is likely to return to the bargaining table with the same party and inform him of the unacceptability of specific provisions.

3. STRUCTURE OF CLIENT–COUNSELING CONFERENCES

In any of these contexts, the client-counseling conference follows essentially the same structure. The attorney and client together undertake a cost-benefit analysis to compare the various alternatives available to the client. To what extent does the negotiated agreement meet the client's interests? How would the client's level of satisfaction that would result from accepting the agreement compare with his probable satisfaction if he chose one of the other options instead? This process requires the attorney to outline the terms of the negotiated agreement, identify the client's alternative courses of action, consider with the client how each alternative addresses the client's interests, and solicit a decision from the client.

Often it is appropriate for the lawyer to begin a counseling conference with a *preparatory explanation* describing for the client what she expects will occur during the session. Suppose Maria Santiago has concluded her bargaining on behalf of Michael Van Meter with Ashton Crutchfield, the attorney for the Baltimore & Western Railroad. She has received an offer of $1,650,000 that has been described by Ashton as "final." Maria, in fact, believes it is a final offer. She probably should begin the counseling session with a brief explanation of the purposes of the meeting and how she intends to conduct the conference. For example, Michael might expect, as many clients do, that Maria will "tell" him whether he should accept or reject the offer. Assuming Maria is committed to client-centered advocacy, one purpose of the preparatory explanation is to counteract the client's notion that the attorney and not the client should make the decision. Accordingly, Maria might begin with the following preparatory explanation:

1—Maria: As you know, Michael, we're scheduled to take your case to trial next Tuesday. I have talked again with Ashton Crutchfield, Baltimore & Western's attorney, and he has made one last offer to settle this case. I thought we should talk about that before we talk about the possibility of your testifying next week. Does that make sense to you?

2—Michael: Sure. Does this mean we won't be going to trial?

3—Maria: That's possible. It will be up to you. Here's what I suggest we do. Let's try to list the choices available to you: going to trial, settling—there may be others. We can consider together how each possibility meets your interests or fails to address your interests. Then you will need to make a decision on how we will proceed.

Maria's preparatory explanation tells Michael that he needs to make his own decision and outlines a structure for the counseling session consisting of three parts: identification of alternatives, consideration of how well each alternative meets the client's interests, and making a decision.

The post-negotiation counseling conference should not be the first time that the lawyer and client have considered all available alternatives. Counseling is an ongoing process that begins prior to the negotiation. During the pre-negotiation counseling session described in Chapter Three, "Negotiation Planning," the lawyer and client necessarily identify the alternatives available to the client when they determine the client's Best Alternative to a Negotiated Agreement (BATNA). From the client's feedback during that negotiation planning session, the lawyer knows which alternatives the client considered most viable or attractive at that stage. Additional alternatives might have been suggested during the negotiation or may have become apparent from other sources since the bargaining began.

In identifying options for consideration by the client, the lawyer should list the alternatives discussed prior to negotiation and any others that he has become aware of during the intervening time period. During this initial *listing of alternatives* phase of the counseling session, the lawyer usually neither should describe in detail the alternatives nor indicate her personal preference among the various options. Either form of embellishment by the lawyer may exert too much influence on the client's decision-making process. It is appropriate, however, for the lawyer to summarize any conclusions that she and her client reached during the negotiation planning session regarding the viability of potential options. It is not usually advantageous to re-open a discussion of an option that the client rejected previously during the planning conference. Before discarding an option, however, the lawyer should check briefly to assure that the client continues to regard an alternative as unacceptable and that his earlier evaluation has not been changed by the negotiation process or other events occurring in the meantime.

In the case of Michael Van Meter's lawsuit against the railroad, the two readily apparent alternatives are (1) to accept a settlement in the amount of $1,650,000 or (2) to proceed to trial during the next week. There may be others, however. For example, depending upon Maria Santiago's past experience in dealing with opposing counsel Ashton Crutchfield and with the judge hearing the case, she might suggest as an option that she seek a further continuance, or postponement of the trial, on the premise that the negotiation is not actually concluded and an agreement still could be reached with a little more time. Another possibility might be for the parties to agree that Baltimore & Western is seventy percent "at fault." The parties then would agree to litigate only the amount of damages, and Baltimore & Western would pay seventy percent of the jury's damage-verdict.

Once the lawyer and client agree upon a list of alternatives to consider, they evaluate the extent to which each alternative meets the client's underlying interests. The consequences of each alternative include not only how the option affects the client's legal and economic interests, but also how it affects the client's social and psychological interests. The lawyer, because of her expertise, takes primary responsibility for predicting the legal consequences of the client's decision. For example, Maria Santiago would predict the probable results of taking Michael's case to trial. Predicting trial outcomes is a difficult process involving assessing the facts, the law, the credibility of witnesses, and how the judge will exercise his discretion. We previously considered predicting trial outcomes in Chapter Three, "Negotiation Planning."[6] The uncertainties of the trial process mean that the lawyer treads a delicate line between making trial outcome guarantees with an unrealistic degree of confidence, and failing to offer the client any useful prediction at all by telling him that trial "is always a gamble."

Both the lawyer and the client may contribute substantially to an evaluation of the economic consequences of an alternative. For example, Dr. Volkov and his attorney Katie Eisinger together would evaluate the most recent proposal from Banting Medical Technologies calling for a large up-front royalty payment to Volkov conditioned on both a confidentiality clause and an agreement that either the National Institutes of Health or Volkov's university would pay at least $1.5 million of expenses involved in the clinical testing of the Viral Sharpshooter. Volkov probably knows more than Eisinger about the feasibility of such an approach, at least unless Eisinger has considerable experience representing scientists in similar negotiations.

The *social* or *psychological* consequences of a negotiation proposal are usually best identified by the client. For example, Banting Medical Technologies' relationships with other scientists with whom it has licensing agreements might be impaired if Banting yielded to Volkov's request for a substantially higher up-front royalty payment and did not insist on a confidentiality clause. This is a social consequence of a proposed alternative, and Banting's professionals are probably in a better position to evaluate it than the attorney. An example of a psychological consequence of an alternative is the great anxiety that Michael Van Meter anticipates regarding cross-examination if he elects to go to trial. Although the client usually makes most of the contributions to the discussion of social and psychological factors, the lawyer can guide the inquiry

6. *See supra* Chapter Three, "Negotiation Planning," at 54.

by raising specific questions about concerns that other clients have had when faced with similar choices. However, the lawyer also should ask her client open-ended questions about the advantages or disadvantages of each option or how he feels about settling or proceeding to trial. Unless she asks such open-ended questions, her client's responses to her narrowly focused questions may never reveal additional considerations not specifically identified by the lawyer.

Once again, any discussions conducted by the lawyer and her client prior to negotiation make the post-negotiation counseling conference easier. During the earlier session, the lawyer and her client should have discussed the client's interests as a part of the negotiation planning process. Because the lawyer has gained an awareness of the client's underlying interests during the earlier session, she conducts the post-negotiation conference more effectively by referring back to the client's previously articulated interests. Of course, new facts gleaned from the negotiation process itself, or from other sources in the meantime, will affect the evaluation of how well each alternative meets the client's underlying needs. For example, after she learns about Ashton Crutchfield's evaluation of the probable trial outcome and some suggestion of his trial strategy, Maria Santiago can offer a better explanation of the trial alternative. In addition, even without new factual disclosures, the client may evaluate other issues in a new and different light. For example, as trial approaches, Michael may be more aware of his own anxiety associated with trial than he was two years earlier when negotiation began.

The amount of information available to the lawyer and her client in assessing the consequences of the negotiation alternative obviously depends upon how far the negotiation has proceeded. The specific consequences of a negotiated agreement can be detailed more effectively after the attorneys agree on a draft document that requires only the clients' ratification. When a counseling session occurs much earlier in the negotiation process, the lawyer can only describe the current negotiation proposals offered by the other side and her estimates as to the terms of an eventual agreement. Nevertheless, it is often at this earlier juncture that the critical decision is reached to pursue actively a negotiated agreement with a particular business partner. To be sure, the client can always reject the negotiated agreement once the negotiating lawyers agree to its terms. Neither the attorney nor her client is well served, however, by a string of negotiations that proceed for a substantial period of time and then break down. Dr. Volkov does not want to pay a series of lawyers to negotiate on parallel tracks for a lengthy period of time with every other pharmaceutical, medical device, or genomic firm. Instead, he probably decides at some point fairly early in the negotiation process to bargain with Banting to the exclusion of other corporations. He obviously makes this decision prior to the time when he knows all the terms of its eventual licensing agreement with Banting.

At some stage in the negotiation process, the client chooses between the available alternatives—including the negotiated agreement and other options—after considering how each option serves his interests. The client, and not the attorney, is in the best position to make this choice. Only the client knows the depth of the anxiety that he feels when faced with going to trial and how to weigh this fear in his decision-making process. Further, individuals possess varying levels of risk adverseness—some will gamble on a greater award at trial, others prefer a smaller, but more certain, payment, even if a strictly utilitarian calculation suggests a more lucrative probable trial outcome. Thus, proper understanding of the lawyer's role as a professional—and commitment to client autonomy—means that only the client should make the choice between a negotiated agreement and the other alternatives. However, the lawyer can—and should—bring her own expertise and experience to bear in assisting the client in making an informed decision.

Once the lawyer and client have identified the alternatives and considered the consequences of each one, the client reaches a decision. In her role in the client's decision-making, the lawyer assists him by summarizing the possible options and the consequences of each option. Sometimes she can do this best by listing the consequences of each option on paper. The client may require additional time, perhaps overnight, to think about his decision.

Clients frequently ask their lawyers if they should accept a negotiated agreement or pursue other options. In many cases, such a request poses no ethical dilemma for the lawyer. If the client is a sophisticated businessperson who customarily makes his own decisions without hesitation, then he probably is simply requesting additional input before making his own decision. In some cases, a client simply turns over an entire matter to an attorney. Examples of this practice include a business which turns over a series of collection actions to an attorney, or a large commercial real estate developer who asks an attorney to acquire several parcels of property at the best available price. In these cases, the attorney should not hesitate to make a recommendation to the client regarding the advisability of a negotiated agreement.

More troublesome is a request for advice on whether a negotiated agreement should be accepted or rejected from a client who is not a "regular player" in the legal system. Many people still believe that an attorney should make their decisions for them because of the attorney's supposedly greater experience in legal and worldly matters. If the attorney responds to the client's request for a recommendation, the client often finds it difficult to make his own decision regarding what is best for his own interests—given his particular value system and level of risk adverseness—in the face of potentially conflicting advice from his lawyer. Under these circumstances, the lawyer should refrain from making a recommendation and instead reiterate the reasons why it is important for the client to make his own decision.[7]

---

7. Under some circumstances, the attorney should advise her client in writing of the alternatives available to him and the consequences of accepting each alternative. This letter should clearly state that it is the client's decision whether to accept or reject

Suppose Michael Van Meter feels unable to decide whether to accept or reject the $1,650,000 settlement offer from Baltimore & Western Railroad, and asks Maria Santiago what he should do. Consider the following response from Maria:

1—Maria: I know you are finding this a difficult decision. The stakes are very high. You think that you're entitled to more than the $1,650,000 without the risks that you would face at trial. After all, they were negligent.

2—Michael: You got that right.

3—Maria: The trouble is, I don't know what the right decision for you is. I can help you out by giving you some predictions about what's going to happen at trial. We can review the various consequences about going to trial and not going to trial. But I can't make your decision for you. You're the one who has to live with it. It sounds a little cold-hearted, but I'll go on to another case. There's a risk in going to trial, and I don't know how much risk you're willing to take. I also don't know how bad you're going to feel if you settle for less than you think you're entitled to. Would it be helpful to you if we go over the advantages and the disadvantages of settling one more time?

Maria answered Michael's request for a recommendation in segment number 1 with an active listening response concerning the difficulty of making a decision and Michael's sense that he is entitled to better and more clear-cut choices than he has. In the third segment, Maria then explains again why Michael should make the decision instead of her. She offers to assist him by reviewing the alternatives and the consequences of each alternative again. Most of the time, this explanation—perhaps repeated more than once—leads the client to assume responsibility for his own decision.

The lawyer should be more active in offering advice to the client when the client's decision to accept or reject a negotiated agreement is inconsistent with the client's previously articulated interests. For example, if Michael Van Meter had informed Maria Santiago during the negotiation planning session that his reservation price was $1.8 million and that he could not possibly accept less, and he is now prepared to

any settlement offer. Besides confirming that the client understands his choices, this procedure protects the lawyer from a subsequent claim that she did not accurately inform him of the alternatives or coerced him into making his choice. For example, a defendant who pleads guilty sometimes later alleges that counsel did not accurately inform him about his choices. Therefore, he argues, his plea violates due process because he received ineffective assistance of counsel. *See, e.g.,* Hill v. Lockhart, 474 U.S. 52, 60 (1985) (permitting a defendant to claim ineffective assistance of counsel when not adequately informed of plea bargain alternatives, but ultimately rejecting defendant's claim as non-prejudicial error).

accept Baltimore & Western's offer of $1,650,000, Maria should call this discrepancy to Michael's attention. Although there is often an explanation for this change in position, it is important for the lawyer to highlight this inconsistency and inquire about its causes.

D. CLIENT COUNSELING CONFERENCES DURING NEGOTIATION

If the lawyer is to negotiate an agreement that serves her client's interests and is to facilitate client-centered advocacy, client counseling sessions prior to the negotiation and at the conclusion of the bargaining are not sufficient. The lawyer should confer frequently with the client during the bargaining itself, preferably after each contact with the other lawyer. Frequent client contacts between negotiation sessions facilitate both negotiation results that maximize the interests of the client and client-centered advocacy. Often these client conferences may be brief—in some instances, either a telephone or an exchange of e-mail or written correspondence may suffice.

During these intra-negotiation counseling sessions, the lawyer should report on the progress of the negotiation and solicit input from the client on what steps to take during the next bargaining session. This level of consultation is suggested by *Model Rule of Professional Conduct 1.4*, which requires the lawyer both to keep the client reasonably informed on an ongoing basis and to provide the necessary information for the client to make an informed decision about whether to accept or reject a settlement offer.[8]

In reporting to her client on the progress of the negotiation, the lawyer should discuss the proposals that have been made by both negotiators during the bargaining. She also should inform the client about any new information obtained from the other side that was previously unknown to the client. Particularly in transactional negotiations where discovery is not available, much of the client's information about the matter being negotiated will come from the bargaining itself. The negotiator also learns something about how the other party views a potential business relationship with her client and what the probable terms of the arrangement will be. During the initial stages of many negotiations, the client only vaguely understands how the other party sees the situation and has incomplete information about the facts. The lawyer, therefore, needs to correct any earlier errors in assessing the other party, as well as to relay any new information that emerges during the negotiation.

After the lawyer has reported to her client, she should seek input from the client on several issues:

 (1) decisions as to whether proposed agreements on specific issues are acceptable to the client;

---

   8. MODEL RULES OF PROF'L CONDUCT R. 1.4 (2006).

(2) the client's relative preference among the various issues being negotiated;

(3) approval of various proposals or concessions which the lawyer recommends as part of the negotiating process;

(4) changes in the client's reservation point or evaluation of her Best Alternative to a Negotiated Agreement as a result of new information received; and

(5) any changes in negotiating tactics or strategy and their potential implications for the client's ongoing relationship with the other party.

Most negotiations are multiple-issue negotiations, and the client seldom approves agreement on all issues in a single counseling session. More likely, agreements on various issues are reached at different stages of the negotiation process. Early in their negotiations, Katie Eisinger, as counsel for Dr. Volkov, informs Jonathan Prevas, representing Banting, of the importance to Volkov of a substantial up-front royalty payment. Jonathan responds that this is a problem for Banting because of its concern about setting a precedent. The parties might agree in principle to a confidentiality clause without, in this first negotiation, agreeing to the amount of the initial payment. Similarly, Eisinger probably indicates to Prevas that while her client expects to be rewarded handsomely if Viral Sharpshooter does in fact prove to be a cure for some forms of cancer and other viral illnesses, Volkov does not want his compensation subject to the vagaries of the marketplace. Thus, both negotiators might leave this initial session recognizing that some of Volkov's compensation would be deferred beyond the initial licensing fee, but that a royalty structure is probably not acceptable.

Each attorney then would meet with their respective clients, share what was said during the initial negotiation session, and seek to generate possible solutions that would be mutually agreeable. During the next meeting between counsel, the general structure of the licensing fee agreement might be agreed upon, but without specific agreement on dollar amounts. In addition, new issues might be raised, such as "Could some of the costs of clinical testing be reimbursed by Volkov's university or even by NIH or other funding sources?" Counsel then would consult with their respective clients regarding possible dollar amounts for each phase of compensation for the licensing of Viral Sharpshooter, and also regarding the newly raised issues. At the next negotiation session, counsel might agree to a draft agreement, subject to their clients' approval of the specifics.

More often than not, particularly in less weighty negotiations, not all of these negotiating transactions will take place in face-to-face meetings. Some of these issues might be considered in brief telephone calls or through the exchange of e-mail messages. Written or e-mail messages have the advantages of preserving a precise record of the exchange of proposals. One would imagine that such written words tend to be more carefully considered and more precise than the back-and-forth of oral conversations. They often are, but experience suggests that confusion or differing understandings of proposals may persist undiscovered in such remote exchanges, in contrast to face-to-face meetings or even telephone conversations, where the negotiators more readily would identify the ambiguity and resolve it. Further, in an e-mail exchange, the skilled negotiator forfeits her ability to read voice inflections and non-verbal communications that may tell her something about the other negotiator's tactics.[9] Sometimes this causes the negotiator to erroneously read a certain "tone of voice" into the other lawyer's e-mail message, which may cause the bargaining to break down. Unless the negotiators are careful, the customary spontaneity in drafting e-mail messages may mean that e-mail communication combines the worst of both worlds:

(1) The negotiators lack the ability to detect confusion and correct ambiguities that are generally recognized and corrected in face-to-face conversations; and

(2) The negotiators' lack of care and precision in drafting e-mail messages may lead to ambiguities generally not present in written communication.

Regardless of the method of communication, at each step of a bargaining process, where the lawyer-negotiators reach agreements on specific issues at different times, the client should approve the agreement on each significant specific issue. Perhaps the technical requirements of *Model Rule of Professional Conduct 1.2* would be satisfied by a blanket ratification of the entire agreement by the client following negotiations. Such an "up or down" decision by the client, however, is less likely to yield an agreement that serves the client's underlying interests to the greatest possible extent.

As the issues become more clearly defined during the negotiation, the lawyer also should inquire as to the relative degree of importance the client attaches to each issue. Recall that one problem-solving tactic, logrolling, consists of conceding on some issues in exchange for the other party's concessions on other issues. If logrolling is to result in an agreement that maximizes the client's level of satisfaction, then the lawyer needs to be acutely aware of how much the client values each issue. Katie Eisinger, for example, needs to know whether a large upfront payment is so important to Dr. Volkov that he would be prepared to accept a total licensing fee package that would be less lucrative for him in order to obtain the larger initial payment. Prior to the negotiation, the client typically "wants it all" and cannot tell his lawyer which issues he is willing to concede and trade for concessions on other issues. These decisions often must wait until the client learns during the negotiation process itself how highly the other party values each issue. In other words, the client's willingness to concede on a particular issue is

---

9. *See supra* pages 106–11 for a discussion of the importance of reading nonverbal communication during negotiation. At the same time, the negotiator must be careful not to mistake *friendly style* for *cooperative* or *problem-solving tactics. See supra* pages 18–22.

influenced by the concessions that he may be able to extract from the other party in exchange for his own concession.

The lawyer and client also should consider what proposals or concessions the lawyer should make during the next round of bargaining. Often it is advantageous for the lawyer to make a proposal knowing that if the other negotiator accepts it, then the parties have reached a binding agreement on that particular issue. This requires the lawyer to have authority to bind her client on a specific issue prior to bargaining on that issue. The lawyer's request for this authority from her client should be preceded by a discussion of the advantages and disadvantages to the client of the agreement that would result if the proposal is accepted by the other party. In other words, if the lawyer intends to make a proposal that conceivably could lead to an agreement that binds her client, her proposal should be preceded by the complete counseling process described in the previous section.

If the lawyer learns facts during bargaining that are significantly different from the information previously available, the lawyer and client should reconsider the possible use of problem-solving tactics. With greater understanding of the other party's specific interests, they may be able to use brainstorming or other solution-generating techniques to devise proposals that meet both parties' underlying interests. Further, the new information may suggest additional forms of compensation for the other party in exchange for his making concessions that the client needs in order to reach agreement. Finally, greater understanding of the other party's interests may suggest additional opportunities for employing cost-cutting techniques, that is, new methods of reducing the other party's costs in making necessary concessions.

The client's perception of his alternatives to a negotiated agreement and his reservation price also may change as the lawyer and client receive new input during the negotiation itself. For example, during the bargaining, Maria Santiago offers Michael her assessments of the probable trial outcome in his case, as well as her opinion of the credibility of the expert witnesses who will be testifying for Baltimore & Western. Her arguments on these points may yield new information for Michael that affects his own assessment of the probable trial outcome. He and Maria may decide together that the prospects for trial are not as rosy as they once perceived. Accordingly, Michael may well change his reservation point.

Finally, the lawyer and client, during the counseling conferences interspersed between bargaining sessions, should discuss potential changes in their negotiation tactics or strategy. As discussed in Chapter Two, "Choosing Effective Negotiation Tactics," the other negotiator's strategy is a primary factor to be considered in choosing effective negotiation tactics. For example, if the other negotiator is using predominantly competitive tactics early in the negotiation, this probably suggests that the negotiator should respond with competitive tactics unless she has reason to believe that her own more collaborative tactics would be reciprocated. Any change to more competitive tactics during the bargaining process after the negotiator has begun with collaborative tactics, however, risks impairing the client's ongoing relationship with the other party. Accordingly, when the lawyer decides that her negotiation strategy needs to be substantially altered, the lawyer and client should consider this decision jointly.

The alternation of bargaining sessions and counseling conferences may repeat itself any number of times during the negotiation. The most important recommendation for the lawyer is that she should regularly confer with the client during the negotiation process. These conferences enable the lawyer to negotiate the best possible agreement for the client by using all information available to the client and by continually monitoring the client's perceptions of his interests. In addition, continuing contact between the client and his lawyer usually results in greater client satisfaction with the lawyer's representation.

Chapter Eleven

NEGOTIATOR IDENTITY AND NEGOTIATION CONTEXT: THE EFFECTS OF CULTURE, GENDER, AND RACE

A. INTRODUCTION

The recognition that negotiation behaviors can be analyzed and taught should not obscure the reality that each negotiator remains, first and foremost, a human being. When the negotiator heads into a bargaining session, she does not leave behind her personality, her identity or her past experiences in interacting with other people.

When the President of the United States or the Secretary of State negotiates with a foreign leader, it is safe to assume that he or she has the benefit of an exhaustive psychological evaluation of her counterpart, drawing upon that leader's past interactions with other human beings. Rarely, if ever, as a negotiating lawyer, will you have such a luxury. However, often you will bargain with someone with whom you have negotiated before, and from those past experiences, you will have some idea about how he will react to competitive, cooperative, or problem-solving tactics. Obviously, negotiating with an attorney with whom you have negotiated fifty times previously is different from negotiating with someone for the first time.

Suppose, however, that you have not been exposed to the person with whom you are negotiating. Are there any shortcuts to figuring out how he or she will react in the negotiation context? The vast amount of research and writing available on the topic of gender and negotiation, nationality and negotiation, and even race or religion and negotiation certainly suggests that these are topics worth exploring. These issues closely parallel another issue about which even more has been written and debated: will individuals with certain identities and backgrounds react differently as jurors? Recall the classic 1936 article "Attorney for the Defense" in which Clarence Darrow advised:

If a Presbyterian enters the jury box and carefully rolls up his umbrella, and calmly and critically sits down, let him go. He is cold as the grave; he knows right from wrong, although he seldom finds anything right.[1]

On the other hand, I once remember hearing the great trial practice guru Irving Younger tell an audience that if he were representing a defendant in a criminal case, he obviously would not select the grey-suited banker as a juror—unless, of course, the banker also wore a Mickey Mouse wrist-watch. Though I do not know whether, in fact, a juror who wears a Mickey Mouse wristwatch really is more likely to favor a criminal defendant, I think Younger's broader point was to suggest that predicting people's behavior as jurors on the basis of easily identifiable stereotypes is likely to be a hazardous enterprise. The same caution should apply when trying to predict a negotiator's behavior on the basis of gender, culture, or race.

With that critical caveat in mind, in this chapter I explore four main issues that I regard as separate and distinct:

(1)   Are there differences in how negotiators are likely to respond to other negotiators based on the other negotiator's gender or race?[2]

(2)   Are there differences, in the aggregate, in how men and women negotiate? Are there any differences in negotiation behavior based on racial background?[3] These issues are sensitive ones, and the research results are inconsistent.

(3)   How is the negotiation process affected when the other negotiator is of a different nationality or comes from a different culture?[4]

(4)   Finally, are there negotiation sub-cultures within the American legal profession?[5] Do New York City lawyers tend to negotiate the same way as small town lawyers? Are personal injury lawyers likely to negotiate differently from corporate lawyers?

B.   DOES THE OTHER NEGOTIATOR RESPOND DIFFERENTLY DEPENDING UPON THE NEGOTIATOR'S RACE AND/OR GENDER?

In a powerful study published in 1991, Ian Ayres found that automobile salespeople negotiated differently with prospective purchasers based on their race and gender.[6] White males, white females, black males, and black females were trained as "testers," instructed to negotiate and otherwise react as identically as possible when negotiating the purchase

1.   Clarence S. Darrow, *Attorney for the Defense*, ESQUIRE, May 1936, at 37.

2.   *See infra* Part B.

3.   Both topics are explored in Part C.

4.   *See infra* Part D.

5.   *See infra* Part E.

6.   Ian Ayres, *Fair Driving: Gender and Race Discrimination in Retail Car Negotiations*, 104 HARV. L. REV. 817, 819 (1991).

of a car. Despite the similarity of these negotiators' own behavior, Ayres observed:

> The tests reveal that white males receive significantly better prices than blacks and women.... [W]hite women had to pay forty percent higher markups than white men; black men had to pay more than twice the markup, and black women had to pay more than three times the markup of white male testers.[7]

Ayres further found that what he termed "animus," or in this context, ill will directed against a consumer of a different gender or race, could not explain this disparate treatment because "each class of testers received its best treatment from salespeople of a different race and gender and, in many cases, the worst treatment from salespeople of the same race and gender."[8] Instead, Ayres found that sales personnel, regardless of their gender or race, believed that they were simply maximizing their profit margins ("revenue-based statistical discrimination"). Using the terminology of this book, they perceived it would be more difficult to exploit white males by using competitive tactics than it was females and African–Americans.[9] Ayres reasoned that dealers probably tended to believe that white males had a wider array of alternatives to a negotiated agreement with a particular dealer, because the dealers stereotypically perceived that white males had a greater ability to take time away from both employment and family obligations in order to research prices at multiple dealerships. He also cited surveys indicating that a much higher percentage of white auto consumers than African–Americans realized that the dealer's sticker-price was negotiable.

On one hand, Ayres' evidence that women and African–Americans pay more than white males proves a form of race and gender-based discrimination that ultimately rests on the stereotypical beliefs of sales personnel that white males will tend to bargain more effectively than will consumers of other races and/or genders. When negotiating with white males, dealers apparently perceived that their own competitive exploitative tactics were less likely to succeed than when negotiating with others. At the same time, the extent to which Ayres' findings apply to the world of negotiation among lawyers is less clear. Regardless of the race or gender of the negotiating attorney, her status as a well-educated member of an elite professional group, the bar, hopefully lessens, even if it does not entirely eliminate, some of the more blatant sexist and racist assumptions found to exist in the Ayres study.

Similarly, other studies suggest that people expect males to use more competitive tactics in negotiation. Wesley C. King, Edward W. Miles and Jane Kniska, for example, have found that subjects playing a variation of the Prisoner's Dilemma Game, when confronted with an unknown opponent using competitive tactics, were three-times more likely to guess that the opponent was male than female.[10] Similarly, K.

---

7. *Id.* at 817.
8. *Id.* at 847.
9. *Id.* at 847–50.

10. Wesley C. King, Edward W. Miles & Jane Kniska, *Boys Will Be Boys (and Girls Will Be Girls): The Attribution of Gender*

Matheson reported that when an unknown opponent in a computer simulation used a so-called "firm, but fair" set of negotiating tactics, subjects classified the strategy used against them as "competitive" when they were led to believe that the opponent was male, but "cooperative" when the simulation suggested that the opponent was female.[11] In their 2003 book *Women Don't Ask: Negotiation and the Gender Divide*, Linda Babcock and Sara Laschever write, "Men are thought to be assertive, dominant, decisive, ambitious and self-oriented, whereas women are thought to be warm, expressive, nurturing, emotional, and friendly."[12]

One hopes that such stereotypical assumptions about negotiation behavior based on gender (and race) lessen as time passes. Nevertheless, awareness of such assumptions may enable the negotiator, regardless of race or gender, to better understand how her negotiating counterpart is inclined to view her—a set of assumptions that may affect the negotiating counterpart's tactics. Obviously, if confronted with blatantly sexist or racist negotiating behavior, the negotiator may decide to call the other negotiator on such behavior and treat it like any other inappropriately hostile negotiating tactic,[13] or in an appropriate case, to report such behavior to opposing counsel's supervisor, disciplinary counsel, or the court.

C. DOES THE GENDER OR RACE OF THE NEGOTIATOR IN FACT AFFECT NEGOTIATION TACTICS?

1. GENDER

Regardless of perceptions, are there in fact differences in the way that women and men negotiate? Perhaps no other aspect of negotiation behavior has been researched and written about as much as the role of gender. Indeed, the attention focused on problem-solving bargaining during the past generation occurred simultaneously with an increasing appreciation that women tend to view the world through a different lens than do men. The work of Carol Gilligan, who studied the differences in the development of moral reasoning in boys and girls, in particular, may have had a role in encouraging the proliferation of problem-solving tactics.[14] Professor Carrie Menkel–Meadow, an important early proponent of what I have called problem-solving tactics, acknowledged the possibility of such a connection:

> In reading an earlier draft of this Article, my late colleague Donald Hagman remarked that the problem-solving conception

Role Stereotypes in a Gaming Situation, 25 SEX ROLES 607, 607–23 (1991).

11. Kimberly Matheson, *Social Cues in Computer–Mediated Negotiations: Gender Makes a Difference*, 7 COMPUTERS IN HUMAN BEHAVIOR 137, 137–45 (1991).

12. LINDA BABCOCK & SARA LASCHEVER, WOMEN DON'T ASK: NEGOTIATION AND THE GENDER DIVIDE 62 (2003).

13. *See supra* pages 161–62.

14. *See* CAROL GILLIGAN, IN A DIFFERENT VOICE: PSYCHOLOGICAL THEORY AND WOMEN'S DEVELOPMENT 2–3 & 25–32 (1982).

of negotiation described herein was the product of a feminist conception of dispute resolution and transaction planning. To the extent that some of the elements of problem solving, such as trying to satisfy the needs of all parties and addressing the relational aspects of negotiation, seem to represent women's concerns, this is so. Women are more likely to emphasize the relational and interpersonal aspects of moral decision-making, while men are more likely to reason with universal, abstract principles that are hierarchically arranged.[15]

The empirical evidence regarding whether men and women negotiate differently conflicts. A "meta-analysis" of 62 studies of the relationship between gender and competitive behaviors in negotiation, completed in 1998, suggested "that women are more cooperative bargainers than men, but that the difference was very slight."[16] Specifically, the analysis concluded that "gender accounted for less than 1% of the variance . . . in negotiator competitiveness."[17] Summarizing earlier studies, the authors observed:

> [T]he most noteworthy characteristic of this literature may be the inconsistency of the findings. Contrary to expectations, a considerable number of studies have found women to be more competitive, and less cooperative bargainers than men. Meanwhile, several other studies have reached the opposite conclusion finding men to be more competitive than women.[18]

It is likely that if differences in negotiation behavior do remain today, they are considerably less than even a few years ago when those negotiating had been raised as children at a time when there was a greater degree of gender stereotyping.

2. RACE

If the impact of gender on negotiations may be difficult for some to discuss, the issue of the impact of race on bargaining likely is even more difficult to talk about. Yet the Ayres study commands our attention. Similarly, long-time legal negotiation expert Charles Craver reports that the students he has taught over a twenty-five year period expect white students to use competitive tactics more than their African–American, Asian–American, and Latino peers.[19] Despite these expectations, Craver

---

15. Carrie Menkel–Meadow, *Toward Another View of Legal Negotiation: The Structure of Problem Solving*, 31 UCLA L. REV. 754, 763 n.28 (1984). Menkel-Meadow qualified her observation by continuing:

> Gilligan points out that her observations about gender are empirically based but that elements of both modes may be found in both genders. On the other hand, many scholars presently studying negotiation and offering problem-solving-like insights, such as Fisher and Ury, do not seem to have conceived of or observed negotiation processes with a feminist conscious-

ness. Furthermore, data on gender differences in negotiation motivation and behavior are as yet inconclusive.

Id.

16. Amy E. Walters, Alice F. Stuhlmacher & Lia L. Meyer, *Gender and Negotiator Competitiveness: A Meta–Analysis*, 76 ORGANIZATIONAL BEHAV. & HUM. DECISION PROCESSES 1, 20 (1998).

17. *Id.*

18. *Id.* at 4.

19. CHARLES B. CRAVER, EFFECTIVE LEGAL NEGOTIATION AND SETTLEMENT 389 (5th ed. 2005).

has found that race has no statistically significant impact on negotiation results.[20] A number of studies suggest that negotiators bargain with members of their own race more cooperatively than they do with those of another race.[21] A few studies have shown differences in negotiating behavior based on race. One study, for example, suggested that African–Americans tend to speak with greater verbal aggressiveness than whites during negotiations, perhaps reflecting a tendency to adopt what has been referred to in this text as an adversarial *style*.[22] Older studies had reported that African–Americans are more likely into use cooperative *tactics*.[23]

D. NATIONALITY AND NEGOTIATION

By now you realize that negotiation is a complex and nuanced process of communication interlaced with habit and ritual. How does the negotiator read the interplay of the other negotiator's offers, concessions, and nonverbal communications? Obviously such a "reading" of the other negotiator is extraordinarily culture-dependent. Learning another verbal or written language, in comparison, is likely to be easier than learning to read the subtle clues that a negotiator from another country sends to the discerning and culturally fluent observer regarding whether he is willing to compromise. In their book *Cross-Cultural Business Negotiations*, Donald W. Hendon, Rebecca Angeles Hendon and Paul Herbig advise:

> Culture impacts negotiation ... by conditioning one's perception of reality; by blocking out information inconsistent or unfamiliar with culturally grounded assumptions; by projecting meaning onto the other party's words and actions; and by impelling the ethnocentric observer to an incorrect attribution of motive.[24]

The issue of how the negotiation changes when the other negotiator is of a different nationality effectively breaks down into two questions:

(1) Are there cultural norms of which an American attorney should be aware when negotiating with someone from a different country? and

(2) Do negotiating behaviors tend to vary according to the nationality or cultural background of the negotiators?

If you are negotiating in a foreign country with a native of that country, an important part of your preparation for the negotiation will be to investigate the answers to these questions. Any concise, introducto-

20. Charles B. Craver, *Race and Negotiation Performance*, DISP. RESOL. MAG., Fall 2001, at 22.

21. *See* JEFFREY Z. RUBIN & BERT R. BROWN, THE SOCIAL PSYCHOLOGY OF BARGAINING AND NEGOTIATION 163 (1975).

22. Martin N. Davidson & Leonard Greenhalgh, *The Role of Emotion in Negoti-*ation: The Impact of Anger and Race, 7 RESEARCH ON NEGOTIATION IN ORGANIZATIONS 5 (1999). *See supra* pages 18–22.

23. *See* RUBIN & BROWN, *supra* note 21, at 163–65.

24. DONALD W. HENDON, REBECCA ANGELES HENDON & PAUL HERBIG, CROSS-CULTURAL BUSINESS NEGOTIATIONS 18 (1996).

ry negotiation text, such as this one, that tries to catalogue what you need to know in order to negotiate with someone from China, India, Saudi Arabia, Brazil, Germany, Mexico, or any of another 180 nations— each with important cultural differences—at best is doomed to failure and at worst may be offensive in its attempts to translate complex cultural attitudes into the written equivalent of sound-bites. Accordingly, this text merely seeks to provide examples of some cultural differences that you should be aware of when negotiating with someone of a different nationality.

First, the American negotiator should be educated about the social and cultural practices of negotiators from other nations and cultures, particularly when bargaining on their turf. Any attempt to negotiate with a friendly style[25] may be quickly derailed by insensitive cultural gaffes. Popular negotiation texts, for examples, include such admonitions as "Since it is considered extremely rude to display the bottom of one's foot to another in Saudi Arabia, foreigners should never sit with the soles of their shoes exposed to others."[26] A text on international negotiation advises:

> The American business negotiator who arrives in China hoping to establish rapport by presenting his host with a gift of a fine clock creates a problem before negotiations begin. Clocks are inappropriate gifts in China because they are associated with death.[27]

These are but a couple of examples of the virtually unlimited list of "do's and don'ts" for social interactions in foreign countries. For the negotiating American lawyer, the bottom line is simple to articulate, but often challenging to implement: be culturally competent.

The American lawyer also needs to research and understand cultural protocols that are specific to the negotiating process. For example, Japanese negotiators reportedly prefer to engage in *nemawashi,* or informal talks, prior to beginning negotiations.[28] Once the actual negotiations begin, a Japanese company likely is represented at the negotiating table first by a low-ranking official who is responsible in his company for the subject of the negotiations, followed later by middle-ranking managers, and finally by a senior executive. Only the final negotiator has authority to bind the Japanese company. Unless the American bargainer understands this, she likely may become angry and dismayed when the Japanese senior executive reneges or backs away from what she perceived as a concession by the first Japanese negotiator.

Nationality also affects the likelihood that the negotiator will employ competitive, as opposed to cooperative or problem-solving tactics. Michele J. Gelfand and Sophia Christakopoulou, for example, have found that American negotiators, raised in a more individualistic culture, are

25. *See supra* pages 18–22.

26. *See* CRAVER, *supra* note 19, at 470.

27. HENDON, HENDON & HERBIG, *supra* note 24, at 27.

28. *See* Damian Zhang & Kenji Kuroda, *Beware of Japanese Negotiation Style: How to Negotiate with Japanese Companies,* 10 NW. J. INT'L L. & BUS. 195, 197–99 (1989).

more inclined to use competitive tactics than negotiators from Greece, a collectivistic culture.[29] American negotiators made more extreme initial proposals, conceded less, and were more likely to threaten counsel with whom they were negotiating.

Hendon, Hendon and Herbig report that negotiators from China, as well as from other Asian cultures, tend to focus more than American negotiators on the importance of building and developing a long-term business relationship, often a "single source" relationship.[30] The Chinese negotiator often focuses on gathering information during earlier stages of the negotiation. Patience is regarded as key. Once the Chinese negotiator makes a proposal, he probably regards it as a fair proposal. The other side may find it difficult to induce concessions.[31] In contrast, according to Hendon, Hendon and Herbig, negotiators from Saudi Arabia tend to begin with extreme initial positions and then concede more willingly than perhaps do negotiators from other cultures.[32] This pattern, of course, reflects a tendency to change during the negotiation from competitive to cooperative tactics. Again, the purpose of these contrasting examples is not to provide a reliable guide for how to negotiate with someone from either China or Saudi Arabia. Instead, these examples are intended only to illustrate the importance of checking with those who previously have negotiated in a different nation before you begin bargaining yourself.

E. DIFFERENT NEGOTIATION CULTURES WITHIN THE UNITED STATES

The variance in cultural negotiating norms from one country to another raises important parallel issues even for the American lawyer negotiating solely in the domestic context. The bargaining community within the American legal community consists of many overlapping but discrete bargaining communities. The Los Angeles lawyer who negotiates licensing contracts on behalf of entertainers probably never interacts with the personal injury attorney from rural West Virginia. Do lawyers in urban areas of California tend to negotiate in the same manner as those in rural areas of the South or Midwest? Are they equally as likely to use competitive tactics or are there differences in their bargaining behavior? Similarly, are personal injury lawyers equally as likely to negotiate using competitive tactics as commercial lawyers?

First, as a general rule, attorneys negotiating within an urban environment are more likely, everything else being equal, to use competi-

29. Michele J. Gelfand & Sophia Christakopoulou, *Culture and Negotiator Cognition: Judgment Accuracy and Negotiation Processes in Individualistic and Collectivistic Cultures*, 79 Organizational Behav. and Human Decision Processes 248, 261–62 (1999).

30. Hendon, Hendon & Herbig, *supra* note 24, at 33–34 & 86–87.

31. This reluctance by the Chinese negotiator to make concession is similar to the tactic known in the United States as "Boulwarism." *See supra* pages 130–32.

32. Hendon, Hendon & Herbig, *supra* note 24, at 40.

tive tactics than are their peers in rural environments.[33] This result is not surprising. Attorneys who deal with each other on a regular basis have an incentive to develop accommodative working relationships with each other, thus suggesting the use of cooperative or problem-solving tactics.[34] Obviously, small town lawyers are more likely to negotiate with their peers on a regular basis than attorneys in large urban centers, at least unless the city lawyers are also part of a small, highly specialized legal fraternity.

Second, there are differences in negotiation behavior among attorneys practicing in different substantive specialties. For example, the filing of a lawsuit in a commercial dispute prior to bargaining between the attorneys often is regarded as unduly competitive, while sometimes the willingness of a personal injury attorney to negotiate prior to filing a lawsuit is regarded as an ineffectively cooperative sign of weakness.[35] Just as it is important for the lawyer practicing in the international arena to be knowledgeable about the negotiation norms of the other counsel's nationality, it is critical as well for the lawyer within the United States to be familiar with the negotiation norms of both the geographical area and the substantive specialty in which she is practicing.

While negotiation norms should be understood and taken into account in determining the lawyer's own tactics, it is important to highlight that nothing about the lawyer's own identity or the culture or context in which she functions should dictate her own tactical choices. Negotiation tactics are not genetically encoded. They are learned behaviors that the negotiator should analyze and specifically choose to advance her client's interests.

33. *See* GERALD R. WILLIAMS, LEGAL NEGOTIATION AND SETTLEMENT 81–82 (1983).

34. *See supra* pages 40–44.

35. *See* Donald G. Gifford, *A Context–Based Theory of Strategy in Legal Negotiation*, 46 OHIO ST. L. J. 41, 68 (1985).

Chapter Twelve

ALTERNATIVE DISPUTE RESOLUTION AND NEGOTIATION

The past generation has witnessed the burgeoning use of alternative dispute resolution processes.[1] Most often, these processes are viewed as "alternatives" to litigation and therefore analyzed through a litigation-lens. Viewed from this perspective, the casual observer is confronted with a hodge-podge of terms—mediation, arbitration, early neutral evaluation, mini-trials, summary jury trials, med-arb, arb-med, etc. and etc.—and the need to sort out the peculiar characteristics of each mysterious term. Viewed from the starting point of the study of negotiation, however, these processes all make sense. With the exception of binding arbitration (a trimmed-down version of the full-blown trial process), each of these alternative dispute resolution (ADR) processes can be unmasked as a means of facilitating negotiation through the help of a neutral third party.

Viewed collectively, then, how do ADR processes facilitate negotiation? The logical place to begin answering this question is to review why it is that settlement talks break down, why transactional negotiations fail to consummate a deal, or, even when negotiations succeed, why they take far too long. Most attorneys, regardless of which party they represent, would tell you that negotiations often fail because "opposing" counsel or his client overvalues the case and expects too much. Many negotiating attorneys also would admit that their own clients often begin negotiations with unrealistic expectations. In the litigation context, counsel might further explain that additional discovery and the court's rulings on preliminary motions must occur before a case can be accurate-

---

1. This expanded use of mediation, arbitration and other forms of alternative dispute resolution however, should not overshadow the long history of alternative methods for resolving disputes in this country, *see* JEROLD S. AUERBACH, JUSTICE WITHOUT LAW? RESOLVING DISPUTES WITHOUT LAWYERS (1983), particularly in the fields of labor, *see* ALAN M. RUBEN, FRANK ELKOURI & EDNA A. ELKOURI, HOW ARBITRATION WORKS 2–3 (6th ed. 1985); Nolan & Adams, *American Labor Arbitration: The Early Years*, 35 U. FLA. L. REV. 373 (1983), and commercial arbitration. *See* Soia Mentschikoff, *Commercial Arbitration*, 61 COLUM. L. REV. 846, 854–855 (1961).

ly valued. A few might also acknowledge that negotiations sometimes fail because they had not yet evaluated their cases because there were weeks to go before a scheduled trial date.

Most of the alternative dispute resolution processes described in this chapter operate by overcoming these impediments to negotiation. Consider, for example, an early neutral evaluation proceeding in which the parties informally present summaries of their cases to a neutral evaluator who then issues a non-binding judgment. Although not dispositive of the claim, the evaluator's decision serves as a focal point for further negotiations. Her evaluation suggests to the lawyer's own client and to the other party that they will not receive a substantially different result if the case is subsequently heard by a judge or jury, thus causing both parties to view the claim more realistically. Further, by forcing both parties to prepare for a hearing, the early neutral evaluation procedure reduces the likelihood that the lack of prompt case evaluation by either lawyer is preventing settlement.

A generation ago, proponents of ADR processes often promoted the use of such processes on the grounds that ADR would clear crowded court dockets and save both significant litigation resources and time by expediting the prompt and efficient negotiation of claims. It is not clear whether these goals have been achieved. Roselle L. Wissler, for example, has compiled and analyzed a number of studies of court-annexed mediation processes and, according to her, most studies showed no reduction in the transaction costs of dispute processing.[2] Similarly, attorneys participating in a study of an early neutral evaluation process in the federal district court of the Northern District of California divided approximately equally when asked whether the process resulted in cost savings.[3]

On the other hand, participants in alternative dispute resolution processes do perceive other advantages. Proponents of ADR claim that such ADR approaches are superior to litigation as a "process" and can be more flexible and responsive in resolving disputes. In fact, according to Wissler's compilation of surveys, a majority of those participating in court-annexed mediations regard the process as fair, appreciate both the opportunity to be heard and their opportunity for input in determining the remedy, and sense that they have had some control over the proceedings.[4]

The next part of this chapter describes *mediation*, perhaps the most important of the alternative dispute resolution processes. Mediation consists of a rather broad array of negotiation facilitation techniques.

2. Roselle L. Wissler, *The Effectiveness of Court–Connected Dispute Resolution in Civil Cases*, 22 CONFLICT. RESOL. Q. 55, 67–68 (2004); Deborah R. Hensler, *Our Courts, Ourselves: How the Alternative Dispute Resolution Movement is Re-shaping Our legal System*, 108 PENN. ST. L. REV. 165, 194 (2003). A majority of these studies did show a decrease in dispute-processing time.

3. Joshua D. Rosenberg & H. Jay Folberg, *Alternative Dispute Resolution: An Empirical Analysis*, 46 STAN. L. REV. 1487, 1488 (1994).

4. *See* Wissler, *supra* note 2, at 11; Rosenberg & Folberg, *supra* note 3, at 1488.

The remainder of the chapter describes other alternative dispute resolution techniques, including binding arbitration, final offer arbitration, court-annexed or other non-binding arbitration, summary jury trials and mini-trials. In contrast to the diversity of mediation techniques, most of these specific dispute resolution processes (with the exception of binding arbitration) rely on a non-binding substantive evaluation of the case by a neutral third party to assist the negotiators in reaching agreement.

A. MEDIATION

1. INTRODUCTION

Any number of dispute resolution processes has been called "mediation." For more than a generation, family and divorce mediation programs, mediation programs designed to avert the filing of criminal complaints in minor disputes, and mediation programs in small claims courts have operated as an integral part of the justice system. At the same time, mediation increasingly has been used on a more selective basis to resolve major public interest, environmental and corporate disputes, including the antitrust action against Microsoft.[5]

Most often mediation is of the so-called "court-annexed" variety. Here mediation is available as part of the dispute resolution process offered by the courts on either a voluntary or a mandatory basis. In some instances, all cases of a certain type must be mediated.[6] In other instances, individual judges may be authorized to require mediation of particular cases.[7]

Much to the consternation of professional mediators, the term "mediation" often is used loosely to describe virtually any negotiation assistance from a neutral third-party that does not result in a binding decision from him. Highly-skilled professional mediators have been known to bristle at the suggestion that the experienced lawyer who comes into small claims courts and simply tells the lawyers for the parties what he thinks the case is worth is functioning as a "mediator." In Section 3 below, I present a model of how a professional mediator might conduct a sophisticated mediation. At the same time, in the context of this book, mediation can be defined relatively broadly to include any efforts of a neutral party to facilitate the use by the negotiators of *problem-solving* and *cooperative* negotiation tactics. Many

---

5. *See e.g.*, Eric D. Green, *The Role of the Judge in the Twenty–First Century: Re-examining Mediator and Judicial Roles in Large, Complex Litigation: Lessons from Microsoft and Other Megacases*, 86 B.U. L. Rev. 1171, 1179–1191 (2006) (providing second mediator's account of Microsoft mediation); Jonathan W. Reitman, *The Allagash: A Case Study of a Successful Environmental Mediation*, Mediate.com (2003), *available at* http://www.mediate.com/articles/reitmanJ. cfm (last visited May 10, 2007) (describing the use of mediation to end a forty year standoff over management of the Allagash Wilderness Waterway in Maine).

6. *See e.g.*, Cal. Civ. Proc. Code § 1141.11(a) (1983) (requiring mediation of most civil cases with less than $50,000 in controversy); Fl. Stat. § 44.102 (West 2003) (requiring court to refer civil cases, with specified exceptions, to mediation when requested by a party).

7. *See e.g.*, Texas Civ. prac. & Rem. Code §§ 154.021–023 (2005).

of the techniques described in this section as tools of the mediator, such as active listening, brainstorming, and cost cutting, already have been considered as tactics employed by the negotiators themselves.

Just as negotiators often do not successfully engage in joint problem-solving until after an unproductive competitive phase of negotiation, parties often do not begin mediating until they acknowledge mutual frustration. When a party merely expresses a willingness to mediate, this should be recognized as a problem-solving tactic inviting reciprocal problem-solving or cooperative behaviors by the other party. On the other hand, a competitive negotiator sometimes views a willingness to mediate as a sign of weakness.[8]

2. THE FUNCTIONS OF A MEDIATOR

Virtually any technique used by a neutral third party to facilitate negotiation can be regarded as mediation. Most mediation techniques, however, fulfill one or more of the following goals:

(1) facilitating communication between the negotiating parties;

(2) improving the attitudes of the parties toward each other;

(3) educating the parties or their attorneys about the negotiation process;

(4) injecting a dose of reality when one party is viewing his situation in an unrealistically favorable light; or

(5) generating new proposals the parties have not identified.

The goals of improving communication between the parties and improving the attitudes of the parties toward each other are intertwined. The willingness of parties to share information with each other, and to engage in cooperative or problem-solving tactics, often is understandably constrained by the negotiator's realization that she will weaken her position unless the other party reciprocates her collaborative moves. Cooperation and problem solving require trust, and generally the parties in a lawsuit or other dispute are mistrustful and feel angry toward each other.

The mediator attempts to create an ambience conducive to cooperative and problem-solving tactics.[9] The mere presence of the mediator

---

8. In most labor mediations, the potential implications of a willingness to mediate as a cooperative tactic are avoided because mediation is mandated as part of the grievance process. *See generally* ELKOURI & ELKOURI, *supra* note 1, at 153–211.

9. Some forms of mediation profess even higher aspirations. The "transformative approach" to mediation seeks to undo what its proponents call "the negative cycle of weakness and self-absorption" that often results from interpersonal conflict by "empowering" the parties involved in the dispute and shifting their focus "from self-

centeredness to responsiveness to other" ("recognition"). *See* ROBERT A. BARUCH BUSH & JOSEPH P. FOLGER, THE PROMISE OF MEDIATION: THE TRANSFORMATIVE APPROACH TO MEDIATION 55 (2d ed. 2005). The United States Postal Service adopted transformative mediation as an alternative to its regular Equal Employment Opportunity complaint process, and early reports indicated considerable perceived success in achieving both empowerment and recognition objectives. *See* Jonathan F. Anderson & Lisa Bingham, *Upstream Effects from Mediation of Work-*

often affects the behavior of the negotiators. They become less likely to use verbal abuse or extremely competitive tactics in the presence of someone perceived to have influence over the outcome of the negotiation. Further, mediators frequently use active listening to convince the parties that someone has listened to their versions of the dispute and has understood their concerns. Active listening contributes to the negotiators' trust in the mediator. Their sense that someone is listening to them increases their willingness to explore new alternatives. Mediators also encourage each party to vent his underlying anger or fear, often without the other party present, so that these hidden emotions do not subtly undermine the party's ability to pursue a negotiated agreement that serves his best interests.

The mediator facilitates the information disclosure by the parties necessary for cooperative or problem-solving tactics to work. She can monitor the information-sharing process to assure that it is not one-sided, and can pressure a negotiator who is concealing information into reciprocating the other party's information disclosure. Once a party agrees to mediate, there is considerable pressure on him to answer a specific question from a mediator. Often the mediator asks questions of one of the parties in a *caucus* or a private meeting that excludes the other party. The mediator can agree not to share the information with the other party or share it only when the other party reveals similar information.

As a professional specializing in the negotiation process, the mediator also educates the parties about negotiation. One party may be overly competitive, thus inviting retaliatory competitive tactics, ill will, or even negotiation stalemate or breakdown. Another party might be too cooperative, subjecting himself to exploitation. The mediator can suggest cooperative or problem-solving tactics where appropriate, or even urge a slower concession pattern if the negotiator concedes too rapidly and may be left with no room to maneuver in the final stages of bargaining. The mediator's function as an educator is particularly valuable in facilitating problem-solving negotiation tactics. Restated briefly, these are encouraging the parties to discuss underlying interests, generating multiple solutions and facilitating the use of logrolling, cost-cutting and compensation techniques.

Under some circumstances, the mediator makes suggestions regarding the substance of the negotiated agreement, as well as the negotiation process.[10] For example, when the mediator has listened to the parties and

place Disputes: Some Preliminary Evidence from the USPS, 48 LAB. L.J. 601 (1997).

10. A difficult ethical question is whether or not the mediator should intervene substantively to prevent a negotiator from "giving away the family farm" and conceding more than is necessary to reach an agreement. In other words, is the mediator's ethical obligation solely one of *impartiality* or does the mediator also have a role in monitoring the *fairness* of the agreement? *See* Leonard L. Riskin, *Understanding Mediators' Orientations, Strategies, and Techniques: A Guide for the Perplexed*, 1 HARV. NEGOT. L. REV. 7, 24–32, 34–38 (1996). *Compare* Lela P. Love, *The Top Ten Reasons Why Mediators Should Not Evaluate*, 24 FLA. ST. U. L. REV. 937 (1998), *with* James Stark, *The Ethics of Mediation, Evaluation: Some Troublesome Questions and Tentative*

understood their interests, she may be in a position herself to suggest consideration of proposals or ideas that the parties have not identified. Usually the mediator offers her own proposals only as a last resort, preferring that the parties themselves identify possible resolutions. Even when she advances her own proposal, the mediator is often most effective when one of the negotiators believes that the suggestion was "her idea." Similarly, if one party has unrealistic expectations regarding either the negotiation process, or the trial or other alternative to a negotiated agreement, the mediator can offer her own realistic assessment. Finally, the mediator protects a party less experienced in the bargaining process by urging patience in making concessions, instilling poise, and occasionally blunting the fury of extremely competitive tactics from the other negotiator.

In any of these roles—suggesting her own proposals, injecting a dose of reality or protecting a weaker negotiator—the mediator risks becoming too involved in the substance of the agreement instead of serving only as a facilitator. For some parties, the mediator's influence on their decisions will be considerable. If the mediator intrudes excessively into the substantive content of the negotiated agreement, she virtually becomes an adjudicator and not a mediator. The final agreement may not serve the interests of the parties, and either side may resent the agreement because of his sense that it was imposed upon him.

3. THE MEDIATION PROCESS

The mediation session typically begins with the mediator introducing herself to the parties and their attorneys. This step is more than a formality, because the parties' trust in the mediator is essential to achieving a successful resolution. A brief opening statement by the mediator outlines the procedures to be followed during the mediation process, the mediator's role, and what is expected of the parties. The mediator should stress that the process is a voluntary one, that a dissatisfied party can walk away from the mediation at any point, and that the mediator has no power to impose an agreement. She also should stress her impartiality, including her lack of prior relationships with either party.

The mediator then should describe the procedures she intends to follow, including opening statements by both parties and possibly caucuses in which the mediator will meet individually and confidentially with one of the parties. An early explanation of the caucus procedure is important so that the party not included in the caucus understands its purpose and does not believe that the mediator and the other party are "conspiring," or that the caucus procedure jeopardizes the mediator's impartiality. Finally, the mediator should informally provide behavioral guidelines suggesting how the parties should treat each other during the mediation process.

Proposals, From An Evaluative Lawyer Mediator, 38 S. Tex. L. Rev. 769 (1997), *and* Lawrence Susskind & Connie Ozawa, *Medi-* *ated Negotiation in the Public Sector*, 27 Am. Behav. Scientist 255, 267–68 (1983).

Each party participating in the mediation has an opportunity to present an opening statement, including its version of the dispute and a description of its underlying interests. Obviously, this opening presentation often serves as an opportunity to vent frustration and gives the client the sense that someone hears his grievance. The opening statement also reduces misunderstandings between the parties, allows each party to learn about the other's actual interests, and identifies those areas where a genuine factual disagreement exists.

The mediator performs a variety of subtle functions during opening presentations. She asks questions to elicit further information about topics she believes are important or that may suggest a commonality of interests between the parties. She "active listens" to build rapport and to sympathize, without casting value judgments on the strong emotions often expressed in opening statements. She restates the parties' descriptions of historical facts and their interests, in order to clarify them. Often she paraphrases, in more neutral terms, pejorative or value-laden language so that the statements do not create anger or defensiveness. She prevents interruptions by the other party ring the presentation and verbal attacks by either participant.

The next, and probably most important, phase of the mediation process is analogous to the "narrowing of differences" component of the negotiation process described in Chapter Seven. During this stage of mediation, the mediator encourages and facilitates the use of both cooperative and problem-solving negotiation tactics. I first will describe the mediator's role in encouraging cooperative tactics; then, I will address the mediator's facilitation of problem-solving tactics.

The mediator uses a variety of approaches to encourage the parties to make concessions or use other cooperative negotiation tactics, depending upon what factors are inhibiting these approaches. In some cases, one of the negotiators refuses to concede because she believes that if she continues to use competitive tactics, the other party eventually will make most of the concessions. Here the mediator performs as an "agent of reality," offering the competitive negotiator a more realistic estimate of the other party's reservation point and the likely content of the final agreement.

In other negotiations, a lawyer or her client fears that concessions will lead to image loss, that is, her concessions will be seen as a sign of weakness and will encourage renewed competitive tactics by the other party instead of reciprocation. The mediator can mitigate image loss under these circumstances in any of several ways. Most important, she can use a series of private meetings or caucuses with the parties and their lawyers to transmit concessions between them in ways that avoid image loss. For example, during the mediator's session with Michael Van Meter and Maria Santiago, they might communicate to the mediator a willingness to settle for $1,850,000, even if they would not be willing to directly convey the same information to Ashton Crutchfield, the lawyer representing the Baltimore & Western Railroad, in an open negotiation session. They fear that if during a bargaining session they openly express this concession, Ashton would see it as a sign of weakness and he would refuse to concede further. In a subsequent caucus with Ashton and the railroad claims manager, however, the mediator might present the $1,850,000 figure as her own estimate of where an agreement with Michael is possible. Because it is never attributed to Michael or his attorney, this "disguised" concession produces neither image loss nor any loss of room to maneuver within the bargaining range if Baltimore & Western rejects it. Conversely, where the mediator becomes convinced during a caucus that one party sincerely has reached its limits and can concede no further, this information also can be communicated to the other party. The other party then knows it must make concessions to avoid negotiation stalemate or breakdown.

Some lawyers and clients obviously will not tell the mediator their true bottom line, certainly not at the beginning of the mediation process. When the mediator makes it clearly understood that indications of its reservation point are not to be shared with the other party, however, it is likely that parties will be more open and flexible with a mediator than with the other party in the negotiation. As one mediator once told me, "Both parties lie, but they lie less to the mediator." Further, as the mediator gains the trust of the lawyer and her client during the negotiation and succeeds in delivering concessions and other indications of flexibility from the other party—who had been unyielding prior to the mediator's involvement—the lawyer and client are more likely to be flexible and to reveal their true interests.

The mediator also facilitates cooperative tactics by assisting negotiators in releasing themselves from positional commitments they have made during the bargaining process. Ordinarily, if a lawyer has stated that her client "could not possibly accept a settlement of $100,000," she sustains a substantial image loss or loss of credibility if she then concedes to such a figure, even if her client's best interests indicate that such a concession is warranted. On some occasions, particularly late in the negotiation, the mediator's direct suggestion that a party retreat from an earlier positional commitment may be all that is required. In other cases, the mediator assists in developing a rationale for why the commitment no longer applies to current circumstances. For example, recall Israel's commitment that the Sinai could not be returned to Egyptian sovereignty because of Israel's security concerns about having the Egyptian Army positioned in the Sinai within striking distance of Israel. The suggestion of the American mediators that the Sinai be returned to Egypt, but remain demilitarized, released Israel from its earlier negotiating commitment to retain sovereignty over the Sinai.

Finally, the mediator herself may make a substantive proposal that she knows satisfies both parties' requirements for an agreement. Little or no image loss occurs when a party "concedes" to the proposal of the neutral facilitator. However, the mediator should advance her own proposal with reluctance and only during the last stages of mediation. If the parties reject such a proposal, both the mediator's credibility and her image as an impartial facilitator are impaired.

In many negotiations, the most important role for the mediator is to facilitate the use of problem-solving negotiation tactics. Many of the problem-solving tactics described elsewhere in this text—brainstorming, the use of the single negotiation text, logrolling, compensation and cost-cutting—may not be familiar to many lawyers. The mediator's role and experience make her particularly qualified to educate the negotiators about these procedures.

A well-qualified mediator has had special training and experience in encouraging parties to reveal their underlying interests, in facilitating the identification of alternative solutions, and in evaluating each of these alternatives. In addition to her expertise, the mediator's neutrality makes it easier for her to conduct a brainstorming or other solution-generating session, because her leadership during the process does not threaten any of the other participants. Mediators also can suggest, either during negotiation sessions or during private caucuses, appropriate specific applications of the logrolling, cost-cutting and compensation techniques. The mediator's better understanding of both the parties' interests and the relative importance of various issues to each of them makes her particularly able to guide the logrolling process.

The role of the mediator as a facilitator of problem-solving tactics is particularly valuable in multiple-party negotiations. As previously described, the complexity of these negotiations often makes it difficult to reach agreement through the exchange of concessions, thereby increasing the importance of problem-solving tactics. Further, as discussed in Chapter Nine, the mediator is uniquely capable of using the single negotiation text as a problem-solving tool. When a mediator drafts the text, the parties are more likely to view it as a neutral document. The mediator does not face the same conflict as the negotiator preparing a single negotiation text. The negotiator must choose between a balanced text that clearly indicates her willingness to make concessions or a text that is so favorable to her client that the other parties will not view it as a credible starting point for serious bargaining. The mediator also can serve the role of chairperson or facilitator in multiple party negotiations and thus provides the necessary structure for these complex interpersonal interactions.

In the concluding phases of the negotiation process, the mediator often restates agreements reached between the parties. As agreement is achieved on individual issues, the mediator's summary both assures that the resolution is understood by all parties and also spurs the negotiators in their efforts to resolve remaining issues. Mediators frequently are involved in drafting the written agreement with the parties' attorneys.

4. THE APPROPRIATE USE OF MEDIATION

Though mediation of some types of cases may be mandatory in some court systems, the lawyer often has considerable discretion as to whether to seek mediation of her case. Should she suggest that the judge require mediation? In other instances, in either the litigation process or as part of transactional negotiation, the parties themselves may decide to engage in an entirely voluntary private mediation.

When should the lawyer encourage her client and the other negotiating parties to employ a mediator? It is impossible to define categories or rules for determining what cases should be mediated. Generally, mediation is appropriate when both parties share high aspirations and therefore are reluctant to concede, but continue to believe that a negotiated agreement is preferable to the other alternatives. Often the parties only understand the need for mediation late in the negotiation process. By this time, they recognize that their competitive tactics are not succeeding, and their mutual frustration makes it difficult for them to employ problem-solving or cooperative tactics without outside intervention. Specifically, mediation is suggested when the negotiators recognize that the negotiation context offers integrative potential that they have failed to develop. Mediation can also be fruitful in a predominantly distributive negotiation context if the lawyer's client or the other party has unrealistic expectations.

Usually, the lawyer has a role in selecting the mediator. No decision is as important to the client pursuing a satisfactory negotiated agreement except perhaps the initial decision regarding which mediator to retain. A poorly trained or inexperienced mediator may pressure a client into an agreement that does not meet her interests and may miss opportunities for substantially better agreements. Unfortunately, the range of abilities of those in the expanding profession of mediation varies widely. It is incumbent upon the lawyer to check carefully the experience, training, and references of the mediator.

B. ARBITRATION

1. BINDING ARBITRATION

Arbitration is a process in which the disputants submit a controversy to a neutral party, or sometimes a panel of neutral parties, to hear arguments, consider evidence, and render a decision. The arbitration decision may be either binding or non-binding on the parties. Binding arbitration is functionally a substitute form of adjudication by a third party, replacing adjudication by a court. On the other hand, non-binding arbitration requires the parties to agree to the award for it to be dispositive. Therefore, it is not a substitute form of adjudication, but rather a facilitator of negotiated agreement. Referring to both the binding and non-binding types of this process as "arbitration" is misleading and confusing. It will be apparent during further consideration of alternative dispute resolution processes that non-binding arbitration functions more like mediation, early neutral evaluation, summary jury trials or mini-trials, than it does like binding arbitration. These kinds of dispute resolution techniques facilitate negotiation, and unlike binding arbitration, do not involve a binding decision by a third party. Accordingly, non-binding arbitration will be discussed in the next part of this chapter, alongside early neutral evaluation and other processes with a closer similarity to non-binding arbitration than is shared between the two so-called "arbitration" processes.

Most often, parties voluntarily agree to binding arbitration as a dispute resolution mechanism either as part of a contractual provision governing disputes that might happen in the future or after the dispute has occurred. For many decades, binding arbitration has been used extensively in grievance proceedings and other labor disputes.[11] More recently, arbitration has proliferated, as it has become the typical practice when disputes arise in any number of commercial settings, such as construction contracts[12] and contracts between securities brokers and their clients[13] that require the parties to submit any disputes between them to arbitration. The Federal Arbitration Act[14] or similar state arbitration laws[15] typically govern the resulting arbitration proceedings. Finally, globalization tremendously increases the demand for arbitration. Business partners from different continents seek to avoid conflict resolution in a potentially hostile legal environment, as well as protracted litigation proceedings in a distant court, by placing arbitration clauses in their commercial agreements.[16]

The voluntary nature of most binding arbitration enables the parties to stipulate to the procedural and evidentiary rules used during arbitration and the process for selecting the arbitrator. Because the parties usually control the selection of the arbitrator, they are able to choose someone with the substantive expertise necessary to understand their dispute. Arbitration proceedings usually are more informal than court hearings and the rules of evidence are applied flexibly. Discovery prior to the hearing is usually minimal.[17] In simple cases, the arbitrator renders his decision orally at the conclusion of the hearing, but most often the arbitrator issues his decision in writing, accompanied by a short written opinion, only after he has had adequate opportunity to review the written documents and other testimony presented at the hearing.

11. Arbitrations between employers and unions are governed by § 301 of the National Labor Relations (Taft–Hartley) Act. 29 U.S.C. § 185 (2000).

12. Thomas J. Stipanowich, *Beyond Arbitration: Innovation and Evolution in the United States Construction Industry*, 31 WAKE FOREST L. REV. 15 (1996).

13. C. EDWARD FLETCHER, ARBITRATING SECURITIES DISPUTES (1990); Deborah Masucci, *Securities Arbitration—A Success Story: What Does the Future Hold?*, 31 WAKE FOREST L. REV. 183 (1996).

14. 9 U.S.C. § 1 *et. seq.* (2000).

15. *See* Timothy J. Heinsz, *The Revised Uniform Arbitration Act: Modernizing, Re-vising, and Clarifying Arbitration Law*, 2001 J. DISP. RESOL. 1.

16. *See* Charles N. Brower, *The Global Court: The Internationalization of Commercial Adjudication and Arbitration*, 26 U. BALT. L. REV. 9 (1997); W. Laurence Craig, *Some Trends and Developments in the Laws and Practice of International Commercial Arbitration*, 30 TEX. INT'L L.J. 1 (1995).

17. In labor arbitration, the parties typically discover the other side's evidence during the grievance procedure. In addition, arbitrators frequently possess *subpoena* power, and even when they do not, a request from an arbitrator for evidence is usually honored. *See* RUBEN, ELKOURI & ELKOURI, *supra* note 1, 355–62 (6th ed., 2003).

Binding arbitration offers several advantages when compared with court proceedings. It is generally speedier and more informal, and it usually avoids the series of motion hearings, extensive discovery and the protracted wait for a trial date that is now typical in civil litigation. At the same time, each disputant, such as a union member who believes that his rights have been violated under a collective bargaining agreement, retains his "day in court" and an opportunity to air his grievance. By avoiding litigation, parties often preserve their ongoing accommodative relationship. For example, in some areas such as labor or commercial grievances, arbitration is viewed as part of doing business, while initiating litigation is viewed as an extremely adversarial act.

Parties also may agree that unlike trials, arbitration proceedings are confidential. Confidentiality may be an important incentive for a party concerned about adverse publicity or the disclosure of trade secrets involved in a dispute. Other defendants find binding arbitration to be an attractive alternative in cases where they fear that an adverse precedent would be set if the case were litigated. It is precisely these factors that have led some critics to attack arbitration for its ability to hide from the public eye grievances that require societal attention and to avoid setting legal precedents protecting the rights of others who are similarly situated.[18]

Unlike the other processes discussed in this chapter, binding arbitration does not necessarily facilitate the negotiation process. In fact, a strong argument can be made that the availability of binding arbitration procedures—at least in areas other than labor grievances—reduces the incentives to reach a negotiated agreement.[19] In the absence of arbitration, one of the incentives to settle a dispute is to avoid the cost and delay involved in pursuing litigation. As those costs in money and time are reduced by substituting arbitration for litigation, more disputants probably seek adjudication by a third party instead of a negotiated agreement. Particularly with smaller claims, easy access to binding arbitration actually may reduce settlement rates.[20] However, the other advantages to having arbitration available as an alternative—particularly savings in time and expense at the same time the disputants retain their rights to a hearing—usually outweigh the importance of reduced settlement rates.

2. FINAL OFFER ARBITRATION

One variation of binding arbitration is designed specifically to facilitate the negotiation process and not to substitute for it. In *final offer*

---

18. *E.g.*, Edward Brunet, *Questioning the Quality of Alternative Dispute Resolution*, 62 Tulane L. Rev. 1, 15–31 (1987); Owen M. Fiss, *Against Settlement*, 93 Yale L.J. 1073, 1085 (1984).

19. In the labor field, a well-defined grievance procedure generally is available under the collective bargaining agreement. *See* Ruben, Elkouri & Elkouri, *supra* note 1,

at 198–276. Such grievance procedures facilitate a negotiated resolution. The combination of grievance and arbitration processes in labor grievances thus probably increases, rather than decreases, the rate of negotiated resolutions.

20. *See* Jane W. Adler, Deborah R. Hensler, Charles E. Nelson, Simple Justice: How Litigants Fare in the Pittsburgh Court Arbitration Program 95 (1983).

arbitration, the parties submit their last, best negotiating offers to the arbitrator prior to the hearing. After hearing the evidence, the arbitrator is restricted to choosing one or the other of the final proposals.

The most widely publicized use of final offer arbitration is in the collective bargaining provision governing salary disputes between major league baseball players and team owners.[21] Public employee bargaining statutes[22] also frequently provide for final offer arbitration, and sometimes it is used in other contracts to resolve disputes over compensation. When a baseball player and team owner cannot agree on a salary, each submits a last, best proposal. Casey Jones insists that his salary should be $9 million for next year, and the owners of the Mudville team insist that a fair salary for Casey is only $7 million. The arbitrator, after hearing testimony of Casey's exploits, perhaps in lyrical form, and evidence of the salaries paid to comparable players, must choose either the $9 million figure submitted by Casey or the $7 million figure submitted by the team owners. The arbitrator has no discretion to select a number between the two proposals or any other figure.

The effect of final offer arbitration is to encourage concessions during negotiation. The less that Casey demands, the more reasonable his demand looks to the arbitrator. Conversely, the greater the offer by the team owner, the more likely it is that the owner's proposal will be chosen. As each party strives to appear reasonable to the arbitrator, concessions are made on both sides, thus narrowing the differences between the parties. It is likely that they ultimately will reach agreement themselves in order to avoid the expense and the risk involved in a decision by a third party.

The available empirical evidence supports the assertion that final offer arbitration leads to more concessions and negotiated agreements than other forms of final arbitration.[23] Although the results of this process may be "reasonable" compromises, however, they are not necessarily "correct." For example, final offer arbitration would not be an appropriate system for resolving all personal injury or medical malpractice claims. It would entice the parties to negotiate seriously, thus reducing attorneys' fees and other litigation costs. However, an insurance company or uninsured defendant probably would be reluctant to refuse to make any payment whatsoever to a plaintiff, even if it believed the claim was utterly without merit. Even if the refusal to pay were correct, such a harsh stance might appear "unreasonable" to the arbitrators. Accordingly, the use of final offer arbitration in this context probably would lead to more payments in frivolous cases.

21. *See* Roger I. Abrahms, *Inside Baseball's Salary Arbitration Process*, 6 U. Chi. L. Sch. Roundtable 55 (1999).

22. These statutes often grant public employees the right to seek final arbitration when they are prohibited from striking. *See, e.g.*, Iowa Code Ann. §§ 20.12 and 20.22

(West 2001); Mich. Comp. Laws Ann. §§ 423.231–423.238 (West 1996); N.J. Stat. Ann. § 34:13A–16 (West 2000); Wis. Stat. Ann. § 111.77 (West 2002).

23. *See* Dean Pruitt, Negotiation Behavior 224 (1981).

C. EVALUATIVE, NON-BINDING DISPUTE RESOLUTION PROCESSES DESIGNED TO FACILITATE A NEGOTIATED RESOLUTION

This section describes several closely related alternative dispute resolution processes that involve a neutral party's evaluation of the parties' cases, but ones that are non-binding and designed only to facilitate negotiated resolutions.

1. NON–BINDING ARBITRATION

Binding arbitration produces a final resolution of the claim. Non-binding arbitration, on the other hand, promotes the negotiation process. The decision of the third-party arbitrator, although non-binding, assists the lawyers and their clients in realistically valuing the case, and thus provides a focal point for settlement discussions.

Non-binding arbitration typically is "court-annexed" arbitration, as contrasted with arbitration voluntarily agreed to by the parties. Statutes or local court rules authorize trial courts to require disputants in specified categories of cases, such as all cases in which the amount in controversy is less than $10,000 or all medical malpractice cases, to participate in non-binding arbitration prior to taking their cases to trial. The trial court administers the arbitration program. Hearings are informal and involve abbreviated presentations of cases by the litigants. If both parties accept the arbitrator's award, it is entered as the judgment of the court. If either party rejects the award, the case is set for a trial *de novo*. In most programs, the arbitration award is not admissible at trial. Sometimes, however, if the party rejecting the arbitrator's award fails to do better than the amount of that award at trial, it is forced to pay court costs, the other party's attorney's fees or some other specified penalty.[24]

As previously stated, court-annexed arbitration programs usually require that certain categories of cases be submitted to non-binding arbitration. If non-binding arbitration is elective as opposed to mandatory, however, what factors should suggest to the lawyer that a case should be submitted to non-binding arbitration? The most important factor to consider is unrealistic case evaluation by the other party. When the opposing attorney or his client is not evaluating the settlement value of a case realistically, non-binding arbitration may be useful because the results of such a process are likely to reduce the inflated expectations of the other party and her counsel. Conversely, non-binding arbitration also may be useful when an attorney believes that her own client has unrealistic expectations. Further, non-binding arbitration sometimes is helpful when the other attorney has not prepared the case fully enough to realistically evaluate it. The arbitration hearing requires the attorneys

---

24. *E.g.*, Cal. Civ. Proc. Code § 1141.21 (West 2002) (payment of court costs and experts' fees); Mich. Comp. Laws Ann. § 600.4921 (West 1996) (payment of court costs and reasonable attorney's fees).

to focus on the case, and that sometimes is all that is necessary for settlement.

The lawyer should recognize the risk, however, that some opposing attorneys using competitive tactics will view a request for arbitration, or the use of other alternative dispute resolution processes to value a case, as a sign that the lawyer is overly anxious to settle the case and to avoid litigation. In some instances, this may lead to even greater use of competitive tactics. Further, some attorneys use non-binding arbitration as a form of inexpensive discovery, without any intent to be influenced by the results.

How well has court-annexed arbitration succeeded in reducing the delays and costs involved in litigation? The empirical answers to this inquiry are, at this point, either mixed or inconclusive.[25] On one hand, court-annexed arbitration programs apparently have been successful in reducing case disposition time, and also are viewed favorably by the litigants and attorneys who participate in them. The evidence as to whether non-binding arbitration reduces either the aggregate costs of the dispute resolution system or the costs of the litigants, however, is inconclusive.

The question of whether court-annexed arbitration reduces the total costs of dispute resolution, including both court costs and attorneys' fees, requires a comparison of:

(1) the total system-wide costs of handling cases without court-annexed arbitration, which equals the sum of the costs of:

(a) cases which are settled; and

(b) cases which are litigated; with

(2) the total cost of a system with court-annexed arbitration. This cost equals the sum of the costs of:

(a) cases settled without arbitration;

(b) cases that are arbitrated and then settled; and

(c) cases in which the parties fail to settle following arbitration and proceed to trial.

The cost effectiveness of court-annexed arbitration thus depends upon two factors:

(1) How much is spent on unnecessary arbitrations? In other words, what is the total cost added by arbitration hearings in those cases that would have settled without arbitration? and

(2) How much is spent on unsuccessful arbitrations? In other words, how often will one of the parties reject the arbitrated award and

25. *See e.g.*, ADLER, HENSLER & NELSON, *supra* note 20, at 86–96; DEBORAH R. HENSLER, ALBERT J. LIPSON, ELIZABETH S. ROLPH, JUDICIAL ARBITRATION IN CALIFORNIA: THE FIRST YEAR 24–91 (1981); Stephen B. Goldberg & Jeanne M. Brett, *An Experiment in the Mediation of Grievances*, 106 MONTHLY LABOR REVIEW ONLINE 23, 23–29 (1983), *available at* http://www.bls.gov/opub/mlr/1983/03/art4 full.pdf (last visited May 10, 2007).

request a trial *de novo*, and how much expense is added by these unsuccessful arbitrations?

If court-annexed arbitration is to be cost effective, it must significantly reduce the number of litigants exercising their rights to trial. If a substantial number of litigants elect a trial *de novo*, a court-annexed arbitration system actually can be more expensive because of the cost added by the arbitration hearings. Again, at this point, the empirical evidence is inconclusive.

The issue of whether the litigants themselves realize significant cost savings from court-annexed arbitration also depends upon how attorneys' fees paid by the disputants are affected by arbitration proceedings. For example, it is not known whether plaintiffs' attorneys in personal injury cases, who typically use contingent fee arrangements, reduce their fees in cases resolved through arbitration instead of through litigation. Nor is it known if they increase their fees in cases involving arbitration that would have settled without arbitration.

The inconclusiveness of these answers regarding the system-wide impact of court-annexed arbitration should not discourage the lawyer from using this procedure in a particular case to facilitate the negotiation process to her client's benefit. If the local courts allow for the use of court-annexed, non-binding arbitration, it can be an important tool when the other lawyer or her client is not negotiating reasonably because he has not fully prepared his case or because he lacks a realistic opinion of its settlement value. In some cases, non-binding arbitration also assists the lawyer in the counseling process by resolving a discrepancy between the differing case evaluations of the lawyer and the client.

In recent years, the number of court-annexed arbitration programs in the federal courts has lessened, but a number of states still require court-annexed arbitration in various significant categories of cases.

2. EARLY NEUTRAL EVALUATION

Today a number of federal courts use a process somewhat similar to non-binding arbitration known as early neutral evaluation (or "ENE").[26] The ENE is scheduled prior to the beginning of significant discovery and therefore at a stage of the proceedings prior to when non-binding arbitration typically occurs. Before the ENE hearing itself, the parties submit to the neutral evaluator, usually an experienced attorney or retired judge, a statement of major disputed issues as well as the discovery that they believe will be necessary to prepare the case for trial. The hearing itself usually involves brief 15–minute opening statements by both parties and an opportunity for the neutral evaluator to ask questions. At the conclusion of the hearing, the evaluator typically identifies those issues upon which the parties are in apparent agreement,

26. *See* Rosenberg & Folberg, *supra* note 3, at 1487. *See also* Wayne D. Brazil, Michael A. Kahn, Jeffery P. Newman, Judith Z. Gold, *Early Neutral Evaluation: An Experimental Effort to Expedite Dispute* *Resolution*, 69 JUDICATURE 279 (1986); David I. Levine, *Northern District of California Adopts Early Neutral Evaluation to Expedite Dispute Resolution*, 72 JUDICATURE 235 (1989).

as well as the important issues that remain in dispute. The evaluator retires to another room to work on a written case evaluation. During this time, the parties may attempt to reach settlement. The evaluator then returns to the hearing room and asks whether the parties prefer that she announce her findings and evaluation or instead allow the parties to negotiate further. If the parties are interested in more settlement discussions, the early neutral evaluator facilitates these talks. Even if discussions held the same day as the hearing do not yield a settlement, the neutral evaluator helps the parties develop a case management plan. The entire processes generally takes no more than a morning or an afternoon. If the parties desire, they may hire the neutral evaluator to assist them in further settlement discussions at a later date.

The goals of early neutral evaluation are similar to those for court-annexed non-binding arbitration. The evaluation serves as a reality check for both the other party and perhaps for you or your client as well. Similarly, it forces busy attorneys to focus, at least a little, on this particular case, the facts of the case, and the controlling law. Because the ENE occurs *early* in the process, the litigants and counsel have not already consumed considerable time and money engaged in the discovery process. Further, ENE virtually forces the parties and their attorneys to at least explore the possibility of settlement following the hearing while the evaluator drafts his report. Often, settlement negotiations began at the ENE will reach fruition later, even if they do not at the ENE session itself.

A survey of attorneys participating in an ENE program has shown that approximately two-thirds of the attorneys were satisfied with the process, and that approximately half thought that it decreased the time necessary to achieve settlement.[27] The same survey showed that only about one-half of the participating attorneys thought that the process had saved money, but those who did report savings found the amount of the savings to be much greater than the expense involved in the hearing itself. Attorneys also reported that the ENE hearing served as an efficient and valuable way to become aware of facts that eventually led to a fairer settlement. The biggest concern expressed in the survey was about the uneven quality of the neutral evaluators.

3. SUMMARY JURY TRIAL

The *summary jury trial* is a third form of non-binding adjudication designed to assist the parties in the negotiation process.[28] The summary jury trial involves a brief summary presentation of evidence to a mock jury that issues an advisory opinion that becomes the focal point for further negotiation.

---

27. Rosenberg & Folberg, *supra* note 3, at 1506–09.

28. The use of the summary jury trial was pioneered by federal district court Judge Thomas Lambros. *See* Lambros, *Summary Jury Trial: A Flexible Settlement* *Alternative, in* ADR AND THE COURTS: A MANUAL FOR JUDGES AND LAWYERS 79–98 (Erika S. Fine, ed. 1987); Thomas Lambros, *The Summary Jury Trial—An Alternative Method of Resolving Disputes*, 69 JUDICATURE 286, 286–290 (1986).

Judges using the summary jury trial procedure generally carefully select the cases to be heard in this format. Although not limited to complex cases, the summary jury trial procedure usually takes a full day for the judge and the mock jury, so there is little benefit in using the procedure for a trial expected to last only a day or two. Typically, its use has been limited to those cases where the parties have been frustrated in achieving a negotiated agreement. Proponents of the summary jury trial process believe that its use should not be restricted to any particular category of cases, but identify four specific factors that suggest its potential application:

(1) there are substantial discrepancies between the opposing attorneys' evaluations of unliquidated damages such as "pain and suffering";

(2) the lawyers disagree sharply as to how the jury will apply the facts to nebulous legal concepts such as "reasonableness;"

(3) one of the parties lacks a realistic view of the value of the case; or

(4) one of the parties strongly desires to have his "day in court" or to have his case heard by an impartial jury.

Several of these factors demonstrate the desirability of having a jury involved in the process of obtaining a non-binding adjudication for settlement purposes, as opposed to other neutral legal professionals such as arbitrators.

A judge can adapt the precise format of the summary jury trial proceeding to meet the circumstances of a particular case. Generally, a mock jury is drawn from the regular venire. Counsel for each party delivers an abbreviated presentation, usually no more than one hour, of what she expects the evidence at trial to prove. Counsel is limited to facts drawn from discovery or from her good faith representations of what witnesses have told her. In addition to this oral presentation, each lawyer may present documents or tangible exhibits to the jury. The attorney's presentation is limited to representations based upon evidence that will be admissible at trial; evidentiary objections by opposing counsel are allowed but discouraged. A judge or a magistrate presides over the hearing and gives an abbreviated charge at the conclusion of the hearing. He then provides the mock jury with a jury form containing specific interrogatories, as well as general inquiries regarding liability and damages, so that each lawyer is given considerable feedback about how the jury views the case.

A summary jury trial can facilitate the negotiation process at a variety of different stages. An agreement sometimes is reached during the final pre-trial conference prior to the summary trial because the lawyers have prepared their own cases and evaluated the other side's case more carefully than before. Most judges require the parties themselves to attend the presentation of the case, and agreement may occur after the parties have heard the summaries of the evidence, even before the jury renders its advisory verdict. When the jury returns, both the judge and counsel for the parties are given the chance to question the jurors about how they perceived the evidence, thus contributing further to achieving a realistic settlement. However, most negotiated agreements do not occur until several weeks following the summary jury trial when the lawyers and their clients have had an adequate opportunity to assess the meaning of the mock jury's verdict and other feedback from the jurors.

Judges who regularly employ the summary jury trial report considerable success in facilitating negotiation in those "difficult to settle" cases which otherwise result in protracted trials.[29] This success appears attributable both to the careful selection of cases which are heard in summary jury trials and to the strength of the message regarding the value of a case when it comes directly from a jury. Although over half the federal courts have authorized the use of the summary jury trial, the actual number of cases handled in this manner appears to be very low.[30]

4. MINI–TRIAL

Mini-trials are voluntary and private proceedings in which both parties present evidence in order to assist them in reaching a negotiated agreement. The parties agree in advance about the rules and procedure for the conduct of the hearing. Generally, senior representatives of the disputing parties with settlement authority actively participate in the mini-trial. Mini-trials have been used primarily to resolve business disputes between parties with ongoing relationships.

The formats of mini-trials are extremely varied, reflecting whatever arrangements the disputing parties agree upon. Usually, the procedures resemble those of a summary jury trial with neither a jury nor a nonbinding decision from the neutral party. Each party presents a summary presentation of its facts. Usually a neutral advisor presides, but frequently she is joined "at the bench" by the senior representatives of the disputants. In other cases, the senior representatives preside without a neutral advisor. Placed in the role of listening to presentations of evidence, a senior representative often finds that he develops a more detached and neutral "judicial" view of the dispute that later aids negotiation.

After listening to the strengths and weaknesses of their respective cases, the senior representatives renew settlement negotiation. The neutral advisor does not issue a decision, but the senior representatives

29. In *Strandell v. Jackson County, Ill.*, 838 F.2d 884, 888 (7th Cir.1988), the Seventh Circuit Court of Appeals held that Rule 16 of the Federal Rules of Civil Procedure did not authorize a federal district court judge to *compel* litigants to participate in a summary jury trial against their will. *But see In re* Atlantic Pipe Corp., 304 F.3d 135, 144–45 (1st Cir. 2002) (rejecting the holding and reasoning of *Strandell* and finding that in some cases, particularly in complex cases, compelled summary jury trials are warranted).

30. ELIZABETH S. PLAPINGER & DONNA STIENSTRA, ADR AND SETTLEMENT IN THE FEDERAL DISTRICT COURTS: A SOURCEBOOK FOR JUDGES AND LAWYERS 5 (1996), *available at* http://

often ask her questions regarding her view of the case or about specific issues. Negotiation continues until either the parties agree, or they decide that they cannot agree.

Like non-binding arbitration, early neutral evaluations, and summary jury trials, mini-trials expose both the lawyers and the representatives of the parties possessing settlement authority to the strengths and the weaknesses of both sides of the case, and help show them how the dispute will look to a judge or jury. Mini-trials are probably most useful when there is a dispute of facts between the parties. The use of mini-trials has increased in recent decades, and participants claim that mini-trials have saved millions of dollars in legal fees by avoiding protracted litigation.[31]

D.   CONCLUSION

This book began at the *micro* level, introducing the negotiation process as a critical aspect of an individual lawyer's representation of her client. It has come full circle to a *macro* perspective—this last chapter addresses the legal culture's recent recognition that the negotiation process is an important form of dispute resolution and that institutional arrangements should be made to facilitate negotiation through mediation, early neutral evaluation and similar processes.

Ultimately, however, fulfillment of your client's interests depends heavily upon you, the lawyer. Your understanding of the negotiation process—as well as your knowledge of law, preparation, and character—contributes to solving problems, settling disputes, and creating opportunities for your clients.

www.jc.gov/public/pdf.nsf/lookup/adrs rcbk.pdf/$File/adrsrcbk.pdf.

31. *See e.g.,* Brian Panka, *Use of Neutral Fact–Finding to Preserve Exclusive Rights to Uphold the Disclosure Purpose of the Patent System,* 2003 J. Disp. Resol. 531, 536–41 (2003) (discussing benefits of ADR, including mini-trials, in patent litigation); "Modified Mini–Trial Bridges Communications Gap in $2.4 Million Case," Alternatives to the High Cost of Litigation, at 4, 6 & 14 (June 1986). When Sherwin–Williams sued a Chicago based corporation for non-payment under a contract for purchase of charcoal lighter cans, the purchaser counterclaimed for $2 million. After years of discovery and high legal fees, the parties used a mini-trial process to expedite settlement. Counsel for Sherwin–Williams reported saving "an incredible amount of money in legal fees." *Id.* at 14. Similarly, after using a hybrid mini-trial technique to settle a dispute between a publicly-traded company and one of its directors, a New York attorney reported that the total cost of the six week mini-trial was "a fraction—and I don't use the term loosely—of legal fees that would have been well in excess of $1 million." "The Hybrid Mini–Trial of a New York Lawyer," Alternatives to the High Cost of Litigation, at 1, 6 & 8 (June 1986).

*

Index

TIME
   See also Deadlines and Ultimatums;
      Stages of Negotiation
Pressures affecting power, 71–72, 82–83

TRANSACTIONAL NEGOTIATIONS
Defined, 41–42
Counseling, 195–96

TRIAL
Predicting outcomes, 54–56

ULTIMATUMS
See Deadlines and Ultimatums

VALUATION OF CLAIMS
General, 54–56

VALUE-CLAIMING
Defined, 14

VALUE-CREATING
Defined, 14

ZERO-SUM
See Distributive Bargaining Contexts

†